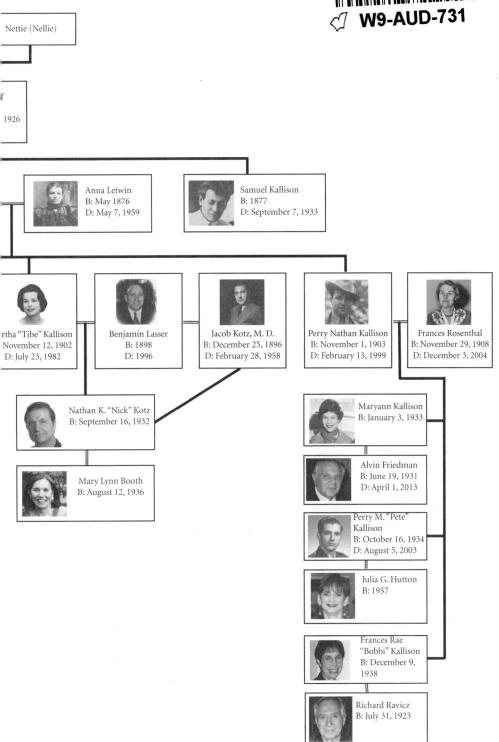

Nettie (Nellie)

1926

Anna Letwin
B: May 1876
D: May 7, 1959

Samuel Kallison
B: 1877
D: September 7, 1933

rtha "Tibe" Kallison
November 12, 1902
D: July 23, 1982

Benjamin Lasser
B: 1898
D: 1996

Jacob Kotz, M. D.
B: December 25, 1896
D: February 28, 1958

Perry Nathan Kallison
B: November 1, 1903
D: February 13, 1999

Frances Rosenthal
B: November 29, 1908
D: December 3, 2004

Nathan K. "Nick" Kotz
B: September 16, 1932

Maryann Kallison
B: January 3, 1933

Mary Lynn Booth
B: August 12, 1936

Alvin Friedman
B: June 19, 1931
D: April 1, 2013

Perry M. "Pete"
Kallison
B: October 16, 1934
D: August 5, 2003

Julia G. Hutton
B: 1957

Frances Rae
"Bobbi" Kallison
B: December 9,
1938

Richard Ravicz
B: July 31, 1923

The HARNESS

MAKER'S DREAM

Nathan Kallison and the

Rise of South Texas

Nick Kotz

To Bell and Jerry

Thanks for all you
have done to make
this a better world.

Nick

June 16, 2016

A joint project of the Center for

Texas Studies at TCU and TCU Press

Fort Worth, Texas

Library of Congress Cataloging-in-Publication Data

Kotz, Nick.
 The harness maker's dream : Nathan Kallison and the rise of South Texas /
Nick Kotz.
    p. cm.
"A Joint Project of the Center for Texas Studies at TCU and TCU Press"
 Includes bibliographical references and index.
 ISBN 978-0-87565-567-3 -- ISBN 0-87565-567-X
 1. Kallison, Nathan, 1873-1944. 2. Kallison family. 3. Businessmen--Texas--San
Antonio--Biography. 4. Ranchers--Texas--Bexar County--Biography. 5. Jews,
Russian--Texas--San Antonio--Biography. 6. San Antonio (Tex.)--Biography. I.
Title.
 F394.S2119 J5
 976.4'061092--dc23
 [B]
                            2013007143

TCU Press
TCU Box 298300
Fort Worth, Texas 76129
817.257.7822
www.prs.tcu.edu
To order books: 1.800.826.8911

Designed by Barbara Mathews Whitehead

CONTENTS

FOREWORD

T HE CENTER FOR TEXAS STUDIES at TCU was delighted when approached about partnering with the TCU Press to publish Pulitzer Prize-winning journalist Nick Kotz's outstanding story of an immigrant's move to and life in Texas in the early twentieth century. The Center's mission is to celebrate all that makes Texas distinctive. Nathan Kallison is among the distinguished individuals—from Native Americans to the "Old 800" and many others who followed—who have helped to form the culture of honor, entrepreneurship, courage, and resilience that characterize the state of Texas. They are at the heart of what we celebrate.

I wish to thank those many organizations and individuals who have contributed to the support of the Center for Texas Studies, in particular the Burnett Foundation, the Lowe Foundation, the Jane and John Justin Foundation, and the Summerlee Foundation. Without their sponsorship, worthy projects that celebrate Texas would not be possible.

—Mary L. Volcansek
Executive Director
The Center for Texas Studies at TCU

To my beloved wife and coauthor
Mary Lynn Booth Kotz

INTRODUCTION

I N THE DARK OF NIGHT, Nathan Kallison embraced his widowed mother and, for the last time, slipped away from their village in Czarist Russia. At the age of seventeen, he was heading out alone—first by foot, then oxcart, and finally on a train over thirteen hundred miles of hostile land—to board a ship in the German port of Bremen. That journey began in 1890. It would take him over an ocean and halfway across another continent to a future he never could have imagined, into a century where ideas and honest labor might grow fortunes and where dreams might become dynasties. He would found his family's own in Texas—almost a country within a country.

This is a story of twentieth-century America and the vast state of Texas, and a boy who fled the marauding Cossacks to build a new life there. In 1899, seeking a better future for their family, Nathan Kallison and his young wife Anna then moved from Chicago, their first home in the New World, to San Antonio, just as that Wild West city on the edge of Texas Hill Country was beginning to reinvent itself. Like San Antonio, the home he grew to love, Nathan, too, reinvented himself. The young immigrant became an innovative city retailer and a path-breaking pioneer rancher—the latter a rarity among Jews in America at the time.

His small and unlikely empire began with his skill as a harness maker, and then, propelled by his vision and hard work, developed into a dynamic and unusual dual enterprise: Kallison's store—which he built into the largest farm and ranch supply business in the Southwest—and Kallison Ranch, where he demonstrated to a suspicious and tradition-bound countryside the latest scientific methods in modern agriculture.

Nathan Kallison's path in his adopted country was shaped by bitter memories of the Russia he had escaped—a society where landless Jews and peasants were pitted against each other as each group struggled to survive under autocratic landowners and the iron thumb of the czar. In South Texas, this young immigrant saw an opportunity to create a different kind of society—one in which independent farmers and ranchers who had clashed bitterly over land use lived harmoniously with each other, as well as with those in the cities. Nathan believed that he and his neighbors could prosper together as they cooperatively planted their futures on the edge of an already shrinking western frontier—a prospect that offered great opportunities for those who were bold, hardworking, and wise enough to seize them. He saw, too, a progressive government to be embraced, not feared—one that could be a partner with private enterprise in developing the Southwest. It was a giant leap of faith. He was surrounded by many ready to "circle their wagons" against newcomers with new ideas, just as their pioneer ancestors had closed ranks against attackers.

Kallison and the wiser of his neighbors prospered as they embraced new ways to farm the land. In his store, he displayed the supplies and equipment with which they improved their livelihoods. With an uncanny sense of the future, Nathan took risks—always a step or two ahead of the fast-changing currents and trends in American commerce. More than fifty years before giant "box-store" discounters changed the retail landscape, he created a unique enterprise that offered, under one roof and at rock-bottom prices, a diverse inventory designed to meet all the needs of rural Texans—not only for their ranching and farming operations but for their homes and lives as well.

Building his family's future, Nathan never forgot his humble roots nor lost his moral compass. Embracing the ethical teachings of Judaism, he nevertheless abandoned the orthodox rituals he had practiced in his youth. Although he was freed from the virulent anti-Semitism of Czar Alexander III's Russia, in Texas he had to overcome a more subtle but just as deeply ingrained prejudice—not only against Jews, but also toward many other recent immigrants from Eastern Europe and Mexico.

Over the first two-thirds of the twentieth century, Kallison's family enterprises played significant roles in the rise of South Texas and its agribusiness economy, as well as in the civic, cultural, philanthropic, political, and religious affairs of their community and region. Nathan's two sons would carry his vision forward and expand on it: Morris, a crusader-developer for downtown commercial revival as well as a political kingmaker; and Perry, the relentless champion of the family farmer—a rancher, humanitarian, and dedicated conservationist whose early morning radio program won him praise as "the Voice of South Texas."

The Kallisons' saga is but a single thread woven into the fabric of a country that called itself "a nation of immigrants." Nathan was only one of twenty-three million men, women, and children—two million of them Jews from Russia and Eastern Europe—who surged into the United States from 1880 through 1920, adding muscle and brainpower to the nation's explosive growth during an industrial age that spawned burgeoning factories, steel mills, railroads, and unheard-of wealth. The story of the Kallisons' rise weaves its way into the warp and woof of the entire twentieth century—through wars and peacetime, flood and drought, boom and bust. The family's influence reached beyond San Antonio to impact all of South and Central Texas.

Nathan Kallison's dreams would be well realized and well rewarded over several generations. More than a century after the young harness maker from the Ukraine stepped off the ship, his story still resonates today as millions of new immigrants with dreams of bettering their own lives seek to become Americans.

Nick Kotz
June 1, 2013
Broad Run, Virginia

ONE

To Freedom

A T SEVENTEEN, Nathan Kallison faced stark choices as a Jew living in Imperial Russia. Forced conscription into the army would condemn him to years of privation and hard labor in Siberia. If he stayed in his small village of Ladyzhinka, he risked death in a wave of anti-Semitic violence sanctioned by Czar Alexander III and executed by his brutal Cossacks. Starting in 1881, a new wave of pogroms—the pillaging and burning of Jewish villages, the slaughtering of Jewish men, women, and children—swept across the country. If Nathan tried to flee Russia, he faced a long and perilous journey, fraught with danger—robbery, murder, or capture by Russian border guards. But for a young man determined to take fate into his own hands, the chance for a better life in America was worth the risk.

Even in Nathan's remote Ukrainian village, in 1890 word about America was spreading from home to home. In Ladyzhinka, near Uman, letters speeding back across the Atlantic on steamships or telegraph lines told of workers barely off the docks who were earning a living wage—enough to feed a family and even hope to buy a home. In the first year of what would be called the "Gay Nineties" in America, stories of opportunity and prosperity across the ocean grew from hyperbole to myth in the teeming cities of Europe.

As money from the faraway workers trickled back to help impoverished families in homelands from Dublin to Kiev, an exodus fever infected the young, even in nameless hamlets and country fields. The new continent, they said, would welcome and enrich immigrants. A mighty work force was required to build the railroads, forge the steel, run the factories. This dream offered adventure for some; for others, a means of survival. For Nathan Kallison, it meant survival. Driven by a relentless work ethic, an uncanny sense for opportunity, the courage to flee desperation and terror and then to forge a new life, he slipped out of Ladyzhinka one night in 1890 and never returned.

Officially, the Russian government did not authorize emigration. But Jews by the thousands were leaving anyway. With little money but a great deal of ingenuity and courage, many were making their way west illegally across the Russian border into Germany, then to the port cities of Hamburg and Bremen to seek passage to the United States. The hazardous journey to the ports was rife with robbers, muggers, unscrupulous guides, and ticket agents stealing the small savings the escapees carried with them. A sad fate was to be turned back by Russian or German border guards; a worse, to be denied entry to the United States at the port of arrival.

Nathan was but one of nearly two million Jews who, over a forty-year period, escaped from relentless deprivation within their small settlements, towns, and cities within the vast confines of the Pale of Russia, and poured into tenements in New York, Philadelphia, and shtetl-like ghetto communities in Chicago, where Nathan first found his way.[1] His hardscrabble life there gave way to adventure, however, and he took a road less traveled. Ladyzhinka, with its long and painful history, was forever left behind.

When he said goodbye to his mother that night in 1890, Nathan was leaving what had been his only home—and home to Kallisons (or Kalisons or Kolosons or Keilsons) either in Uman or the surrounding towns since the beginning of the eighteenth century.[2] Most had lived through similar times of terror and hardship. It was ever thus: since the first wandering *émigrés* made their way out of their desert homes during the Roman conquest of what is now called the Middle East, the rulers found ways to torture the stubborn monotheists who refused to give up their religion.

In Ladyzhinka, Nathan was born in 1873, the second of three

sons of Dina and Moshko (Moses) Kallison. Jacob was born in 1871, Samuel in 1875. Little is known about Moshko's life except that he died leaving a young widow with three very young children to raise and protect. Small in stature but gifted with courage and a strong will, Dina struggled to surmount poverty and to shield her sons from the cruelties Jews faced in Czarist Russia. From her own experience as a child, Dina understood the dangers—she had witnessed Jewish children of less than ten years being dragged away to certain death in the Russian army.

Nathan grew up in that shtetl, located in Uman province, halfway between Kiev on the north and Odessa on the south within the so-called Pale of Settlement where Jews were confined. Like other shtetls at that time, his was a jumble of wooden houses—frigid in winter, blistering hot in summer—built along narrow, twisted lanes that meandered out from a central marketplace. There, peasants from the rich agricultural lands surrounding his village brought livestock and wagonloads of grain, fruit, vegetables, fish, and hides in exchange for merchandise the town's Jews—who were prohibited from owning land—imported or produced: shoes, boots, hats, and clothing, furniture, lamps and oil, spades, tools, and other dry goods. Each shtetl at that time had its own synagogue and a religious school where young boys were taught to read Hebrew while learning the Torah and Talmud.[3]

Jewish families had lived in Ladyzhinka for at least a thousand years. They were not always despised. In the eighth and ninth centuries, Judaism as a religion attracted the Khazar rulers of the Caucasus, who became converts.[4] However, that influence faded in the tenth and eleventh centuries, when the Ukraine became the center of the first eastern Slavic state, Kyvian Rus. Late in the eighteenth century, this area, by then called Ukraine, was absorbed into the Russian Empire.[5]

Located sixty miles south of Kiev, Uman Province was an important economic and cultural center, home to a large Jewish community. Nathan's family had lived in Uman province at least since the late eighteenth century. Records show "Kalisons" as Uman town dwellers in the late 1700s and early 1800s.[6] By the mid-1800s, Kallisons lived in both Uman and Talnoye, a village northeast of Uman where Nathan's father Moshko, son of Duvid (David) Kallison, grew up with brothers Avrum (Abraham) and Yos (Joseph). All knew well the sad history of their ancestors in Russia.

Whether the land was under the control of Poles, Lithuanians, Ukrainians, or Russians, Jews had fared badly in the Ukraine, often as convenient whipping boys and scapegoats. Life was marked by grinding poverty, discrimination, and violence, all endured with little hope of escape or of achieving a better life. That history, told sadly through the generations, was seared into Nathan's consciousness. Down through the centuries, the czars of Russia would issue special edicts limiting the rights of Jewish citizens. The lowly peasants in the countryside also were kept in line by rulers who convinced them that they were at least superior to the Jews.[7] Even in relatively easier times, the Jews lived in a state of "permanent precariousness."[8] The degree of hardship and fear varied, depending on the ideas and practices of whichever czar was ruling the country.

For a time, Empress Catherine II had welcomed Jews as merchants and traders, believing they might help stimulate the economy. In her reign from 1772 to 1796, she earned the title "Catherine the Great" by expanding Russia's borders to include what had been Poland, Lithuania, Belarus, and the Ukraine, in the process adding several million more Jews to the population of greater Russia. However, the Empress's proclamation of tolerance did not last long.[9]

Czar Nicholas I, Catherine's grandson, who had declared "Zhids" (Jews) to be "the ruin of the peasants" and "full-fledged leeches sucking up (the) unfortunate provinces to the point of exhaustion," was particularly ruthless.[10] From 1825 to 1855, he issued six hundred edicts proscribing life for Jewish citizens, including a ruling that barred them from the villages where they had lived for centuries. Nicholas's motto—"Orthodoxy, Autocracy, and Nationality"—

meant that the elements for a strong Russian nation must be the Russian Orthodox Church, the unquestioned power of the czar, and the protection of Russian national purity. There was no room for people of different religions, faiths, or national origins. Nicholas I's objective was to destroy the Jewish community as a social and religious body. "The purpose of educating Jews," declared one secret edict, "is to bring about their gradual merging with the Christian nationalities and to uproot those superstitious and harmful prejudices which are instilled through the teachings of the Talmud." Nicholas then ordered the conscription of young Jewish boys into the Russian army for periods of up to twenty-five years.[11]

Memoirist Alexander Herzen described the fate of those boys as one of the most awful sights he had ever seen. ". . . pale, exhausted, with frightened faces, they stood in thick, clumsy soldier's overcoats, with standup collars, fixing helpless pitiful eyes on the garrison soldiers who were roughly getting them into ranks. . . . And these sick children, without care or kindness, exposed to the icy wind that blows uninterrupted from the Arctic Ocean, were going to their graves."[12]

That cruel fate befell at least two young Kallisons: Mordko Kalison, recruited in 1852 at age nine, and Avrum Kalison, first cousin to Nathan's father, wrenched from his home and family in 1839 before he turned six. Neither survived.[13] The cruel fates of Mordko and Avrum became family stories seared into the minds of future generations of Kallisons.

For the estimated five to six million Jews in the shtetls of Eastern Europe, one generation followed another without expectation of change. They lived in abject poverty, constantly fearing attack. They had little connection to the countryside immediately surrounding them or to the cities some distance away. Historian Irving Howe wrote:

Bound together by firm spiritual ties, by a common language, and by a sense of destiny that often meant a sharing of martyrdom, the Jews of Eastern Europe were a kind of nation without recognized nationhood. Theirs was both a community and a society: internally a community, a ragged kingdom of the spirit, and externally a society, impoverished and imperiled.[14]

What is astounding—and difficult for many to comprehend—was the passion, the determination, the conviction, the stubbornness of Russian and other Eastern European Jews. They remained steadfast in identifying with and practicing their ancient religion despite cruel laws and constant danger. Even at the risk of their lives, the vast majority refused to yield to the succession of czars demanding that they embrace the Russian Orthodox Church.

The Kallisons, like most Russian Jews, were heartened, therefore, when Czar Alexander II came to power in 1855. He reduced their military service requirement from twenty-five to five years. Businessmen and artisans were permitted to travel outside the Pale. Universities were even opened to some Jewish students. At the same time, he also freed forty million Russian serfs. His actions raised enough hope for some Jewish families to honor the czar by naming their sons Alexander.

But those hopes soon ended. On March 13, 1881, revolutionary terrorists on the streets of St. Petersburg tossed a bomb at Alexander II with reverberations that resounded throughout the Empire. The blast that killed the czar elevated his son Alexander III to power. Rumors spread across Russia falsely accusing Jews of the assassination.[15] Alexander III's edicts ushered in new waves of terror against Russian Jews. Cossacks swept across the countryside, robbing and destroying homes and businesses in Jewish villages, beating and killing the residents. This was the world that enfolded Nathan Kallison as a boy. When the Cossacks launched their reign of terror in 1881, Nathan was only eight years old; his brothers Jacob, ten, and Sam, six. Fearing for the very lives of her sons, Dina hid them at the first rumor of approaching danger. The young Kallison family and other Jews who survived this latest pogrom were subjected in 1882 to the new czar's more repressive laws, which again banned Jewish students from attending most schools, and even more narrowly dictated where adults could live and what few jobs they were permitted. Alexander III then announced his threefold "final solution" to the problem of "yids": one-third were to be killed, one-third driven out of Russia, and one-third converted to Christianity and impressed into the army.

In that moment many Jews within the Pale, particularly the strong and the young, decided to make a run for freedom. Their people had endured centuries of mistreatment; the young Jews refused to suffer any longer. With stories from across the Atlantic fanning their dreams, the mass exodus out of Russia began. Inspired by their faith in the idea that Jews were an "eternal people" imbued with the strength to start anew, a group of emboldened Jewish students started a movement they called Am-Oilam. They agitated for resettlement in America, a free country where they could begin new lives.[16]

The fervor of new thinking spread quickly from the cities to the shtetls in the rural areas. Hasidism, a movement of pietistic enthusiasm, brightened spiritual life. The *Haskala,* or Enlightenment, brought modern ideas to the middle classes. New political and cultural movements stirred social awareness among the masses. The colliding forces of the Enlightenment, the Industrial Revolution, and a new Yiddish culture of socialism and of Zionism combined to embolden Jews to embark on this mass departure.

Dina Kallison had done her best to prepare Jacob, Nathan, and Samuel to survive and to earn a living.[17] Because literacy was a religious mandate for Jewish boys, they would learn Hebrew and study the Torah, but secular education at a public school was not an option. Leatherwork, however, thought by most Russians to be undesirable, was one of the few crafts open to Jews. Dina apprenticed each of the three boys at an early age to a leathersmith to learn harness-making.

It was a useful occupation. Commerce depended on horse-drawn wagons to transport food from farms to villages and cities, and to bring manufactured goods back to the vast rural areas throughout Russia.

Ladyzhinka was surrounded by fertile farmland, much of it worked by subsistence farmers who produced enough vegetables and grains to sell and earn a small cash income. Because they were forbidden to own farm land, another of the few jobs permitted for Jews was as middlemen, going from town to town peddling small amounts of produce or a few small manufactured items. While working as apprentices to the local leathersmith, Jacob, Nathan, and Samuel Kallison each helped peddle their master's products, and young Nathan learned the rudiments of commerce.

But as the decade progressed, the already difficult life in Russia grew even more perilous for the Kallison boys. Young Jewish men were being slashed to death for what seemed blood sport. Yet somehow, that frightful wretchedness concealed the emergence of a heightened sense of hope. As the first Jews escaped to Western Europe, and as hundreds and later thousands were reaching America, their letters home revealed that life could become radically different—and for the better—in the country founded upon freedom of religion. *You can get out,* the immigrants reported home. *And you should come now.*

Among the first from Ladyzhinka and surrounding towns to reach the New World was Joseph Kallison, a cousin of Dina's late husband. Arriving in the United States in 1886, Joseph had made his way across the land to Chicago, where he found work as a tailor. Four years later, he'd saved enough money to send for his wife Ida and their two children, Samuel and Mamie.[18] His optimistic reports home greatly encouraged others in the Kallison family.

Bound by loyalty and their dedication to Orthodox Judaism, many older Jewish parents opposed their children's voyage to the New World. They chose to keep their families close. They feared for their safety on the journey. Most knew they would never see them again if they left. But Dina Kallison actively encouraged her sons to leave, to live in freedom—and to send for her when they could. "Go now, while you still can!" she implored them, knowing that she could no longer hide and protect her fast-growing teenagers, each now approaching manhood.

Striking out early in 1890, Jacob Kallison, Dina's eldest, finally made his way out of Russia. The ship's records reported his departure from Bremen, on the Baltic coast of Germany, paying sixty dollars (seventy-eight Russian rubles) for a berth on the SS *Werra*, a steamship of the Norddeutscher (North German) Lloyd line.

Before year's end, Nathan Kallison followed his older brother to America's shores traveling more than twelve hundred miles from Ladyzhinka to Bremen. At first he moved stealthily—traveling only at night—either walking or by hitching rides on wagons, as he cautiously tried to avoid detection and capture by the czar's soldiers. Finally, breathing a sigh of relief, he sneaked across the Austro-Hungarian border at Brody, and from there was able to board a train to complete his journey to the port of Bremen. With only a skill as his currency, the seventeen-year-old harness maker boarded a ship for America with a somber, frightened crowd of fleeing Jews. Although the ship would hold 125 passengers in its first-class compartments and 130 in second-class accommodations, Nathan was one of a thousand third-class passengers packed into overcrowded, foul-smelling, lice- and flea-infested steerage. He confessed no fear—only marveled that his escape, thus far, was a miracle. On the passage, he and his fellow third-class passengers lay on rough-boarded double bunks that lined the steerage from fore to aft. They tried to sleep on the straw mattresses with no blankets or bedclothes. The food they ate, served out of huge kettles, was miserable. Sanitation conditions were abysmal.[19] The trip took eleven and a half days.

Nathan's first glimpse of America was a chaotic one. Along with fellow émigrés, he walked down the gangplank from his ship and boarded a crowded barge that was towed across the North River (Hudson) to the Barge Office—a temporary immigrant processing center on the Battery in lower Manhattan that was used until Ellis Island opened in 1892.[20] A grey stone structure with an imposing tower and waves dashing against the seawall at its base, it "resemble(d) closely a baronial castle rather than a temporary home for the incoming strangers."[21] However, at times that year, "the Barge Office was not a comfortable place." Rain leaked through a roof in need of repair. "The moneychangers were obliged to place tarpaulins over the cages in which they transact business."[22]

"Steamer day" was one of "ceaseless activity and tireless energy at the Barge Office." Although "every particle of space was being utilized," for Nathan and his fellow *émigrés* emerging from cramped berths in steerage, its great rotunda offered breathing room.[23] Grouped and shuffled from one checkpoint to another, Nathan edged towards freedom; the fear of being turned away still his constant companion. A health officer examined him to see if he was sound of mind and body. Then an inspector fired a barrage of questions at him: "What is your name?" "How old are you?" "Are you married or single?" "Where were you born?" "Where are you going?" "Have you ever committed a crime in your country?" "How much money do you have?" Nathan spoke not a word of English. The translator had to be called in. There, Nathan learned that President Benjamin Harrison was head of his new country's government. After customs officials inspected his baggage and he exchanged his few rubles for dollars, Nathan walked through the portals of the Barge Office, breathed in the salt air, and entered what he hoped would be his promised land.[24]

The street outside the Barge Office bustled with activity: relatives and friends awaiting loved ones, horse-drawn wagons and cabs ready for hire, agents noisily offering their services in the new arrivals' native tongues—help in finding transportation, lodging, and jobs. The unscrupulous among them would steer *émigrés* to overpriced boarding houses that claimed to offer cheap housing and meals. If the new immigrants could not afford the inflated bills, the innkeepers would hold their baggage as collateral. Nathan did not fall prey to their offerings. His stopover in Manhattan was brief. With ticket and possessions in hand, he soon boarded a westbound train. He would join his brother Jacob and be welcomed in Chicago by their older cousin, Joseph Kallison.

When the Kallisons arrived in America, its western frontier was swiftly disappearing. Historian Frederick Jackson Turner declared "the frontier has gone, and with its going has closed the first period of American history." In July of 1890 Idaho and Wyoming entered the Union as the forty-fourth and forty-fifth states, and the vast Indian lands in Oklahoma became a territory of the United States. By year's end, a last vestige of the American Indians' ability to roam freely in the middle of the country would be snuffed out at Wounded Knee Creek in South Dakota, where blue-jacketed US Army cavalrymen massacred two hundred Sioux. Fewer than one thousand buffalo remained of the estimated twenty million that once roamed the Great Plains.[25] The next chapter of frontier history, however, was being written in the heartland. New waves of immigrants from Southern and Eastern Europe, filled with hopes for economic success and freedom, were just then starting to flood into America. For tens of thousands, including Nathan Kallison and his brothers, their pursuit carried them west to Chicago.

TWO

Chicago

W HEN NATHAN ARRIVED in Chicago in 1890, he saw young boys playing games in the street, riding bicycles, walking beside a mighty lakeshore with girls at their side. Steamy in summer, frigid in winter with fierce winds propelling pedestrians down snowy streets, the city had a pace, a quickening rhythm unlike any he had ever felt. How could he ever learn to understand their speech, he wondered, or to read the omnipresent newspapers hawked by screeching boys on the streets, boys as young as he was when he first learned to shape and soften the hide of an ox? The city was a mystery to be solved, an education in itself.

He found himself in the midst of a raw, turbulent, fast-growing metropolis that was leaping out of the Midwestern plains in an industrializing frenzy. No longer a sleepy town on the prairie, Chicago was smelting steel—its smokestacks belching fetid air; its nascent energy, palpable. Resurrected from the ashes of the Great Fire of 1871, Nathan's new city was virtually exploding in an unprecedented building boom, bursting into every available, empty, or restorable area. New office buildings, apartment houses, public buildings—courthouses and cultural halls—and lavish homes were rising from the ground in a crescendo as loud and fast as hammers could pound. The buildings that would signify Chicago's urban character and influence the nation were taking shape from designs by the nation's most innovative architects, among them Louis Sullivan, Henry Hobson Richardson, Daniel Burnham, William Holabird, Dankmar Adler, and a young Frank Lloyd Wright.

A mecca for capitalists, opportunity abounded in Chicago. Men such as Marshall Field, Philip Danforth Armour, and George Mortimer Pullman—dubbed "The Chicago Trinity" by the press—had amassed fortunes unimaginable to a poor peasant from Russia. Their success inspired him. In America anything was possible.

As many émigrés had when they first arrived, Nathan moved in with family. Where Jacob lived, 184 DeKoven Street, became Nathan's residence as well, just blocks from the alley where the devastating 1871 fire had started behind Patrick and Catherine O'Leary's home.[1] Ten years later, fires from pogroms halfway around the world were beginning to transform the O'Leary's Irish Catholic neighborhood.

Nathan Kallison's Chicago was a city of contrasts. The neighborhood where he moved in with his brother in 1890 was known as "the Near West Side," "the West Side Ghetto," "the poor Jews Quarter," or later, "the Maxwell Street neighborhood." It was the poorest, most densely populated area of the city—with more Eastern European émigrés arriving each day. In the shadow of its downtown grandeur—southwest of the Loop—thousands lived in squalor.[2] These Chicagoans subsisted in "brick tenement(s) of three or four stories, with insufficient light, bad drainage, (and) no bath, built to obtain the highest possible rent for the smallest possible cubic space."[3] Ramshackle one- and two-story wooden structures—some dating back to the 1850s and intended for a single family—were now occupied by several. They had been homesteads for Chicago's pioneer citizens before the prairie town had grown up around them.

Many of those West Side homes had "no water supply save the faucet in the backyard." An estimated nineteen thousand West Side residents depended on Lake Michigan and the Chicago River for bathing, an option not available in winter. More than 90 percent of Chicago West Side Jews had no ability to bathe at home (although those who could afford to pay a fee used one of the six community bathhouses). Most housing lacked heating as well, yielding a grim and filthy existence during the Windy City's frigid winters.[4] There were "no fire escapes, garbage and ashes (were) placed in wooden boxes . . . fastened to the street pavement." While some homes had been "built where they (stood), others were brought thither on rollers, because their previous sites had been taken by factories" which were powering Chicago's fast-growing economy.[5] Like that in the eastern cities, this vibrant economy was fueled by the long hours and diligence of immigrant workers flooding in to the new continent to build and become part of a vast capitalist enterprise.

In the center of the country, young Nathan Kallison became part of the third and mightiest wave of Jewish immigrants to settle in America. The first entrants, numbering only a few hundred, had arrived from Spain in the sixteenth century with Coronado's army, making their homes in what is now Mexico, California, and New Mexico; others landed in the Deep South and Florida with Hernando de Soto.

In 1654, twenty-three European Jews, most of Spanish and Portuguese descent, arrived in New Amsterdam (renamed New York when the English captured it in 1664) to found the first permanent Jewish settlement in North America. Escaping from the ongoing Inquisitions in Spain and Portugal, these Sephardic Jews first settled in Holland, then made their way to Brazil before coming to New Amsterdam.[6] Over the next one hundred fifty years other European Jews followed—including Ashkenazic Jews from Germany, Poland, and France—many settling first in New York, Newport, Philadelphia, Savannah, and Charleston. Those early Jewish immigrants chose to live in port cities where they could pursue careers in trade and commerce. By the time of the American Revolution in 1776, an estimated 1,350 Jews were living in cities along the East Coast, as well as in other cities that included New Haven, Connecticut, and Easton, Pennsylvania.[7] During the next fifty years, the Jewish population in the United States would increase very slowly, numbering only forty-five hundred in 1830.[8]

Starting in the 1830s, however, a growing second wave of Jewish settlers from the German states, which would form a united Germany in 1871, began arriving in America, settling primarily in East Coast cities, and spreading south and westward, many to Chicago.[9] Fleeing the spreading revolutions in Central Europe and seeking greater economic opportunity, these mostly German Jews had, by 1880, swelled the Jewish population in the United States to two hundred fifty thousand.[10]

The German immigrants quickly sank roots, and many of them rapidly grew to become successful, influential, and well-integrated into mainstream American life. Beginning as peddlers in the streets with packs on their backs, many of the first Chicago Jews from Germany later opened small stores. From those modest beginnings in Chicago grew some of America's outstanding retail companies, such as Sears, Roebuck & Company; Florsheim; Spiegel; and Mandel Brothers; as well as manufacturers Brunswick; Inland Steel; Kuppenheimer; and Hart Schaffner & Marx.[11]

In population, and eventually in influence, however, those Sephardic Jews from the Mediterranean and Ashkenazi Jews from Germany were soon vastly outnumbered by a huge migration from Russia and elsewhere in Eastern Europe: nearly two million souls desperate to escape tyranny and poverty landed in the United States between 1880 and 1920. This third wave of mass migration has been seen as "a momentous decision of a whole people," as fully one-third of the Jewish population fled from Russia and Eastern Europe.[12] As Jews combined their religious ideals with the demands of modern secularism, this exodus also spurred a late nineteenth-century cultural renewal. They sought a country in which their aspirations for freedom and achievement might thrive.[13] In the United States, they saw an ideal place to achieve their dreams.

These newest immigrants had settled first in New York, but then spread out to other major cities. Most of them wound up in Philadelphia and Chicago. No matter their land of origin in Eastern

Europe, the common tongue (Yiddish), and the ability of most to read in Hebrew created a bond between groups hitherto unknown to each other. And in their new circumstances, they were exposed to voices they'd never heard before. In close proximity to the teeming Jewish ghetto on Chicago's West Side were clusters of other recent immigrants from eighteen different nationalities and ethnic groups, bringing together Italians, Greeks, Bohemians, Irish, Swedes, Norwegians, and Danes—in far closer proximity than ever before.[14]

After 1837, Irish immigrants by the dozens had moved into wooden cottages west of the Chicago River. German, Czech, Bohemian, and French immigrants soon followed. Each sought to create a semblance of the culture they left behind in Europe. When Nathan arrived toward the end of the nineteenth century, Jews from Russia and Poland, along with Italians, had replaced the Irish and the Germans on the West Side. Italians settled between Polk and Taylor Streets, Jews southward to Sixteenth Street. A Greek settlement also claimed a small slice of this highly heterogeneous area. As these new Americans sought to make their way, many stuck closely together with their own countrymen—for mutual protection, economic support, and advancement. For several generations the proverbial melting pot did not melt, either smoothly or quickly.

Even as they sought to live in their own ethnic enclaves, the different ethnic groups could not avoid each other. Thrown together in close quarters, often competing for the same jobs and for limited urban space, the new immigrants traded slurs and insults, punctuating their arguments with name-calling, with Jews labeled as "yids," Italians as "guineas," and the Irish as "sheeny." Between the various immigrant groups, tensions often erupted into violence.

Nathan soon discovered, as did hundreds of other Russian Jews who were arriving weekly during the 1880s and 1890s, that he and his brother did not leave anti-Semitism and violence behind. At that time Chicago's West Side, according to Charles S. Bernheimer, PhD, " . . . was a place of filth, infested with the worst element any city could produce.

Crime was rampant. No one was safe."[15] One Lithuanian Jew, who arrived in Chicago ten years before Nathan came, said:

> Jews were treated on the streets in the most abhorrent and shameful manner, stones being thrown at them and their beards being pulled by street thugs. Most earned their living peddling from house to house. On their backs, they carried notions and light dry goods. . . . being out on the streets most of the time . . . and ignorant of the English language, they were subjected to ridicule, annoyance, and attacks of all kinds.[16]

Indeed, some new immigrants found life on Chicago's mean streets so hard and demoralizing that they actually returned to Russia. Not Nathan Kallison. Of medium height—five feet, eight inches—with muscles strengthened by the demands of his trade, Nathan was by nature a gentle, peaceful young man. However, when threatened, his deft fingers and strong hands became fists of iron. For the Kallisons, returning to the "Old Country" was unthinkable.

Much about Nathan's new home felt familiar. Like other immigrant groups before them, Russian and Polish Jews sought to create a semblance of the neighborhoods they left behind in Europe. In his neighborhood he heard Yiddish on the streets, in the kosher meat markets, live-chicken warehouses, and matzo factories.[17] Hebrew letters on signs identified dry goods stores, greengrocers, tailors like cousin Joseph, and seamstress shops.[18] Even "trades with which Jews (were) not usually associated—such as saloonkeeping, shaving and haircutting, and blacksmithing—(had) their representatives and Hebrew signs."[19] With its synagogues and public baths, the Kallisons' neighborhood came to resemble a transplanted European shtetl. Describing the West Side ghetto in 1891, a *Chicago Tribune* reporter wrote:

> [O]ne can walk the streets for blocks and see none but Semitic features and hear nothing but the Hebrew patois of

Russian Poland. In this restricted boundary, in narrow streets, ill-ventilated tenements, and rickety cottages, there is a population of from fifteen to sixteen thousand Russian Jews. . . . Every Jew in this quarter who can speak a word of English is engaged in business of some sort.[20]

A wide network of support groups had sprung up to meet the needs of the hordes of newcomers from Eastern Europe. Initially, aid for the new wave of Jewish émigrés came from their predecessors. The already-settled and successful German Jewish community organized the Society in Aid of Russian Refugees in 1891.[21] A similar multi-purpose networking effort evolved from the so-called *landsmanshaften* or *vereinen*, in which predominantly Yiddish-speaking immigrants from Russia and surrounding countries helped their fellow Jews.[22] Like his brother Jacob, Nathan took advantage of both organizations, depending on guidance from their older relative Joseph Kallison. From providing rail and ship tickets to finding jobs and places to live—and even to matchmaking—the "greenhorns" helped each other.[23]

As a greenhorn, Nathan Kallison would accept any employment. Having arrived during a harness makers' strike, he delivered milk in a horse-drawn wagon before he was able to find work to engage his own skills.[24] Had he remained in Russia, after a three-year apprenticeship, which typically began at age fourteen, he would have worked as a journeyman for several years to perfect his craft. In America Nathan would have to complete his training on his own, working for an established harness maker whenever and wherever he could—in a factory or small shop—full time, part-time, or paid by the piece. Fiercely independent and eager to make his own livelihood, Nathan's goal for himself was to open his own shop. As professor Charles S. Bernheimer observed about other Russian Jews, he would ". . . rather earn five dollars working for himself than ten dollars working for someone else."[25]

The 1870 US Census had listed the manufacture of harnesses and saddles as the thirty-fourth largest of the 258 industries tabulated in that report, and the industry was still growing. At that time, the census counted 7,607 harness and saddlery establishments giving employment to 23,557 workers.[26] In Chicago, harness making in 1890 was still a major industry—one that the new labor leaders sought to unionize. With the help of *landsmanshaften*, after the strike settled, Nathan finally found a job working in a small harness shop.

From the very first, Nathan believed that Americanization—in addition to hard work and saving money—was the key to success. Fluent in Yiddish, the vernacular of the Russian shtetl, and literate in Hebrew, the language of Torah, Nathan rushed to learn to speak, read, and write English. A serious, studious young man, he embraced every educational opportunity for immigrants in his neighborhood. Just blocks from Nathan's house, the Jewish Training School opened in 1890. It was founded and funded, for the most part, by Temple Sinai's German Jews, who believed it better "to have among their brethren more mechanics and fewer peddlers." Although Jews comprised the majority of its eleven to twelve hundred students, the school was nonsectarian, offering pupils ages four to fifteen a tuition-free, comprehensive course of study that included vocational training as well basic reading, writing, and arithmetic. For adults in the community, it offered evening classes in English and American history. Nathan studied and practiced at every opportunity.

Also within walking distance from where Nathan lived was the world-famous Hull House, renowned for its founder Jane Addams's prodigious efforts to help the impoverished immigrants. It became a progressive model for early settlement houses, as did the nearby Maxwell Street Settlement, founded in 1893 and built following Addams's prototype.

For Chicago's Jewish community, synagogues served as religious, social, and cultural centers. About forty synagogues served the Jews of the Near West Side Maxwell Street district.[27] Meeting in rickety wooden buildings, rented halls, rooms above stores, or in members' homes, most congregations were very small. Others, such as the

Romanian synagogue at Fourteenth and Union Street, worshiped in buildings that had once served as churches—reflecting the changing ethnic and religious makeup of the West Side ghetto. In Nathan's neighborhood, many walked to Anshe Kanesses Israel, the "Russische Shul," built in 1884 on Clinton and Judd Streets. As in Russia, synagogues also served as educational centers. Their members had a profound respect for learning, the advantages of which immigrant Jews were determined to acquire, if not for themselves, then for their children. Moreover, synagogues also provided "a variety of auxiliary services such as Hebrew schools, health funds, charitable aid, burial services, and loan funds."[28] And as conditions in Europe continued to deteriorate, the flood of immigrants—and their need for assistance—increased. All segments of the established Jewish community cooperated in helping the rush of newcomers. With a growing sense of urgency, Nathan and Jacob Kallison studied and worked as many hours as they could, saving every cent to bring their mother and younger brother Samuel from Russia. Jacob had also left behind his wife Ida, a bride of just a few months. By 1891, enough funds had been raised for Samuel's passage, and Jacob already had sent for Ida. Only their mother remained. Once reunited, Jacob and Ida wasted no time in starting a family. By the end of May 1892, they welcomed Nathan's nephew Perry P. Kallison into the world—their first-born American citizen.

That Nathan Kallison and his fellow Russian expatriates could so quickly gain a foothold in this country demonstrated the capacity of America to absorb endless streams of immigrants, offer them economic opportunity, and eventually absorb them into the larger society.

"Probably among no nationality does the economic condition change more rapidly than among the Russian Jewish people in the United States," concluded Charles S. Bernheimer in 1905, after studying the mass Jewish immigration of the 1880s and 1890s. "The transition period from the junk peddler to the iron yard owner, from the dry goods peddler to the retail or wholesale dry goods merchant, from the cloak maker to the cloak manufacturer, is comparatively short," he observed.[29]

With the help of the *landsmanshaften* network, Nathan and his brothers enrolled in a system of interest-free loans through which would-be entrepreneurs in Chicago and other cities were able to borrow money from their synagogues and from Jewish benevolent and self-help societies. For a small loan from the society, an applicant needed only a guarantor to vouch for his character and reliability. Usually for amounts of less than fifty dollars, the loans were repayable in equal weekly installments over ten to twenty weeks. The first free loan society for Chicago Jews, Chevrah G'Miluth Chassodim Mishno U'Gemoroh, was started in 1894, followed two years later by the Women's Free Loan Society, which proudly reported that in its long history it never had to take legal action against a single borrower.[30] Not dependent on banks, those small loans became even more critical during the depression of 1893-97.

Three years after Nathan arrived in America, the country was shaken by one of the worst economic depressions in its history. In the first nine months of 1893 alone, 396 banks and savings and loans failed, fifteen thousand businesses failed, railroads began closing down—156 of them before it was over. Mines were shut down, factories closed, and millions were left destitute and hungry. In Chicago alone, one hundred thousand men were sleeping on the streets. Yet in the midst of this human calamity, Nathan built up the courage and self-confidence to open his own harness-making shop. That same year, he was inspired by Chicago's celebration of the four hundredth anniversary of Columbus's arrival in America, the 1893 World's Columbian Exposition. The largest world's fair of its time, it drew twenty-seven million visitors and was considered the greatest demonstration of science, industry, culture, and entertainment mounted anywhere in the world during the nineteenth century. Electricity, then in its infancy, sprang into adolescence there. For the first time in the history of expositions, "all the lighting . . . decorative as well as service, and the operation of all machinery, was done by electricity."[31] For many, the fair replaced fear of electricity with fascination.[32]

Standing on Twelfth Street in the heart of the ghetto, looking up into the night sky, Nathan could marvel at the Exposition's searchlights. Steadfast in his determination to seek his own stars, the twenty-year-old harness maker couldn't help but wonder how he might progress to a brighter future. Inside the fairgrounds, Nathan could escape the present hard life and glimpse the possibilities—moving sidewalks, elevated trains, telephones, phonographs, moving pictures—inventions as grand as the Ferris Wheel and humble as the "clasp locker," a forerunner of the zipper. Standing transfixed in the Court of Honor, Nathan envisioned how he, too, might take advantage of the advances promised for the twentieth century.

Beyond the fairground gates, however, he and his brothers found themselves working to make harnesses and saddles in a city traumatized by brutal battles between owners of the burgeoning new industries and the fast-rising new labor union moment. Workers were torn between accepting pittance wages and draconian workplace conditions or risking their meager-paying jobs by joining unions. Chicago had become a center of the nascent union movement, which yielded both positive advances and bitter repercussions for the immigrants. For example, before Nathan's arrival, on the night of May 4, 1886, police had tried to break up a massive labor rally in Haymarket Square. A riot had ensued in which a bomb had exploded, killing several policemen. A year later, six men, all Jewish immigrants, were convicted on the thinnest of evidence and hanged for the bombing.

In 1894, ignoring pleas for restraint by Illinois Governor John P. Altgeld, President Grover Cleveland dispatched federal troops to Chicago to break a strike by workers at the Pullman railcar factory. In this strife-driven environment, the modern American labor union movement was forged, its ranks swelled by many of the new Russian Jewish immigrants to America who were swept up into the birth of radical social and political movements. Their ranks, however, were divided between workers who sought protection by joining, and others who were determined to save their meager incomes by working at any price, eventually aiming to become employers themselves. From that former group emerged some of America's great early labor leaders, including Samuel Gompers, Jacob Potofsky, and David Dubinsky. In the latter was the entrepreneurial Nathan Kallison, his American ideal of success only whetted by what he had seen at the World's Fair.

For four years, whenever he could, Nathan had set aside a small portion of his meager wages. He had worn second-hand clothing, eaten frugal meals. He had limited entertainment to visits with family and friends, or to walks downtown and alongside Lake Michigan. By 1894, he and his brothers had saved enough money from their leatherwork to bring their mother to America.[33] With Dina Kallison's arrival in Chicago, Moshko Kallison's family's exodus from Russia was complete.[34]

And so, confident in his own abilities, Nathan opened his own shop on Twelfth Street in the heart of the Near West Side ghetto in 1894. His Ladyzhinka-honed skills had become art; horse owners were asking specifically for his saddles and bridles. With those interest-free loans—coupled with his savings—he purchased one by one the tools of his trade: specially-shaped knives for cutting, splicing, and thinning leather; punches, hammers, and mallets; gauges and tools for setting out, marking, and ornamenting; awls and needles for perforating; clamps for gripping and holding work; and tools used in stuffing collars. Nathan also acquired a harness maker's bench (stitchinghorse), leather hides, threads, nails, and saddler's tacks of various sizes. He added bits, buckles, spurs, stirrups, and other harness furnishings. He loved his tools, he later told a grandson, and cared for them as though they were, in themselves, works of art.

Nathan's craft not only demanded the skills of an artisan, but also those of a chemist. He used bichromate of potash, logwood extract, vinegar, and copperas to make iron liquor for dyeing; pitch, resin, seal oil, lampblack, and linseed oil to make saddler's wax; guttapercha and bisulphate of carbon to make leather cement. These, along with alum, alcohol, gum arabic, and turpentine, could be found on the shelves in the space Nathan rented in a small wooden house at 163 West Twelfth Street between Clinton and Jefferson.[35] There he began crafting and repairing leather gear for the horses that pulled streetcars, beer wagons, and a wide variety of carts and carriages all over Chicago—and for those hitched to the ubiquitous fire department wagons always on guard to prevent another disastrous downtown fire.

A short walk from where he lived on Newbery Avenue, his shop stood among other similar unpainted buildings, many of which housed a store or handicraft workplace in front and crowded sleeping quarters in back. Along the street stood tobacco stands, saloons, scrap iron establishments, and squalid "fancy shops," with signs printed in German, Russian, and Bohemian. Twelfth Street boasted Gold's Restaurant, a popular destination for better-off Jews after they enjoyed the nearby Yiddish Theater. At the heart of the Jewish business community nearby was the open market on Jefferson Street, started about a decade earlier by Jewish peddlers with their two-wheeled pushcarts. A thriving bazaar—and a spot for Nathan to sell his wares outside his shop—it drew customers from all over Chicago.[36]

Encouragement and advice to small business owners like Nathan hoped to be were offered in 1891 by C. C. Martin of Chicago in his book *The Harness Maker's Complete Guide.* Against predictions that "small shops are going to be a thing of the past," Martin argued that "a shop worth even a hundred dollars need not depend on wholesale houses . . . [you] can show by your daily actions that you are full of grit and self-reliance—and can also make as good as you can buy."[37] Adhering to high standards of quality and customer service, Nathan's business thrived.

At twenty-one, Nathan was handsome, strong, and self-employed—a genial young man who had learned to greet the public with a smile and a handshake, who valued family above all. The matchmakers back in Ladyzhinka would have said he was "such a catch!" And indeed, the West Side matchmakers were eager to make the introductions. As it turned out, he needed none.

Every day except for the Sabbath, a petite, blonde, blue-eyed seventeen-year-old nanny and housekeeper, a basket on her arm, marched along the dusty street past the row of artisans and hardware merchants, on a mission to the kosher market and greengrocers her employer favored. Graceful and winsome, with an hourglass figure, she was aware of her own appearance—and kept her eyes downcast to avoid the leers and remarks of the street boys.

As she passed the harness maker's shop, however, a dark-eyed, dark-haired young man sat in the window demonstrating his skill. Passersby stopped to watch his deft hands shaping the leather straps, quickly punching holes, stamping an intricate design, carving a name or initials, adding heavy ribbons or silver bells. One day, with no one else around, she, too, stopped. He smiled, as did she. The next day he watched for her—as he confessed he had done for weeks—and hurried to the shop's door to speak. In English, he told her his name and asked for hers. "Anna," she replied, beginning a lifetime of conversation between Nathan Kallison and Anna Letwin.[38]

Anna had a mind of her own from the very beginning, according to her youngest brother Sam Letwin. She had arrived four years earlier, imported from a small town near Kiev, one hundred thirty miles north of Uman, to marry her widowed uncle, an accepted practice in those days. He had paid her passage across the Atlantic. Like Nathan, she desperately needed to escape, so she accepted his proposal.

Born into a family of eight children, Anna and her siblings from earliest childhood worked to help their parents earn a meager living as fruit and vegetable vendors—buying produce from peasants in the surrounding countryside and selling it in the town marketplace. But as the pogroms began and the crops shrank, Jewish peasants were squeezed out of income by equally poor gentile neighbors. Like those in Ladyzhinka, roaming bands of Cossacks terrorized the Jews in her village, and the Letwins suffered loss within their own family. Their mother died and their father remarried a widow with children of her own—more mouths to feed as pogroms choked the countryside with fear and hunger. The Letwins' much older uncles had already gone over to the New World, where distant relatives and landsmen could even hire village natives in a place called *Chi-cah-goh*. Anna's older sister Rivka was the first of her siblings to leave, her passage to Chicago paid by a man in need of a young wife. He was a brother of the widowed uncle who sent for Anna.

This story was told by Anna's youngest brother Samuel Letwin, the last of her generation to survive. In his nineties, by then a Texas oilman interviewed in 1982 at Fort Worth's Petroleum Club, he recalled Anna's stubbornness:

> She was just sixteen when she went. She got to Chicago and didn't like the man at all. He wanted a maid and somebody to raise his children. She said he was old and ugly to boot— and she just refused to marry him then and there. So she knew she had to find some way to pay for the ticket, and she got a job with the Greenblatts.[39]

With no place to live or a way repay him or support herself, she turned to a distant cousin, Lotte Cohen Greenblatt and her husband Leon. The young couple took Anna into their home as a "mother's helper" and housemaid. She would become almost a daughter.

Leon and Lotte, who arrived from Russia in 1885, were rapidly achieving success as manufacturers of woolen goods used to make fine men's suits. The Greenblatts soon began integrating themselves into mainstream middle-class society. It was not long before they had moved from the West Side ghetto to the Windermere, a fashionable apartment building on Michigan Avenue in the downtown Loop. Mrs. Greenblatt quickly discovered that her new nanny was intelligent and eager to learn. The girl was charming, imaginative, and fun. The three children adored her—especially Hannah. Their mother insisted that she learn English, which the little girls eagerly taught her. And from observing and imitating, Anna absorbed Mrs. Greenblatt's taste in dresses, table manners, fine china, and silver. She learned to serve when they entertained and to stay away from their imperious cook. With her new social skills, she adopted the urban behavior of Americans of rising means and expectations. Within this warm and generous family, Anna saw a life she wanted for herself.

When Nathan and Anna met, the attraction was instant and mutual. Unwilling to entrust her future to the whims of fate, Anna went out of her way to pass Nathan's shop on her daily errands for the Greenblatts. She would walk by, stop to chat, seizing every opportunity to capture the attention of the young man in the window. Nathan looked forward to these interruptions and made sure both he and his shop were presentable. He felt at ease with this high-spirited young girl. Like himself, she was smart and ambitious. Theirs was a mostly ambulatory courtship—Nathan did not yet own a horse. They exchanged talk of life in Russia, of their serious mutual hopes and dreams for the future, and then of their growing love for each other. They walked in the daytime through the neighborhood, and on rare afternoons off, along Lakeshore Drive, looking out at Lake Michigan. Soon Nathan asked the Greenblatts for Anna's hand in marriage—a proposal she accepted in the Greenblatt home with the hearty approval of her adopted family. On January 3, 1895, after a year's courtship, Nathan Kallison, age twenty-two, received a license at Cook County Courthouse to marry Anna Letwin.[40] By this time, with business expanding, Nathan had moved his shop to larger quarters at 159 West Twelfth Street. He and his bride lived in the small apartment behind the Kallison Harness Shop, and Anna became the primary salesclerk.[41]

In the following year the extended Kallison family of Chicago had much to celebrate. During a frigid winter, on January 15, 1896, Nathan and Anna's first child was born at home. They named him Morris—after "Moshko" (Moses) Kallison, a grandfather he would never know. In early spring, Samuel Kallison married Celia Goldberg, and in the autumn Jacob, Nathan, Samuel, and their father's cousin

Joseph all became naturalized citizens of the United States of America.

Citizenship requirements in the nineteenth century were lenient and casually administered. Immigrants could appear at any court of record to file their initial papers—the first step to becoming a naturalized citizen. The applicant had to be "a free white person" and to have been a resident of the United States for at least two years, including one year in the state to which they applied. After five years, one was eligible to become a fully naturalized citizen. Each had to swear an oath to uphold the US Constitution and renounce allegiance to any foreign sovereign.[42] Nathan Kallison eagerly took the oath of loyalty to his new country and was granted citizenship on October 12, 1896. A neighbor, F. Bakal from 155 West Twelfth Street, appeared as a witness to testify to his good character.[43]

In 1897, as the country gradually emerged from the four-year depression, Nathan's home-based shop, with Anna's help, increased production, remaining open every day and many nights. That year the Chief State Factory Inspector of Illinois in his annual report listed Nathan Kallison as operator of a harness and saddle making business at 159 West Twelfth Street with two employees, one a boy younger than sixteen years old. In the 1898 report, Kallison was listed with three employees, again including a boy less than sixteen. The 1899 report shows Nathan with three adult employees.[44]

As Nathan's business grew, so did his family. Although Michael Reese Hospital, built in 1881 to provide free care to indigent and newly arrived immigrant Jews, was just blocks away, Nathan and Anna's second child, Pauline, like their son, Morris, was born at home. After their daughter's birth, also in January in the midst of a fierce winter, Anna fell ill and developed a nasty, lingering cough. She was terrified of tuberculosis, then a serious scourge of urban life in Chicago. Her hope all along had been to leave the ghetto and move into an elegant apartment like the Greenblatts. Year after year, more and more immigrants were crowding into houses with poor lighting, insufficient drainage, no bathing facilities, crumbling outhouses, and unpaved alleys filled with trash. The nearby tenements reeked of broken sewer pipes, garbage, and filth. Incredibly, a survey showed that in the ghetto where Nathan and Anna lived, the population per square block was denser than that in Calcutta, India, a city infamous for its slums.[45]

Housing in the Kallisons' neighborhood was not just dilapidated; the structures could be deadly. Sweatshops serving Chicago's garment industry were crammed into already overcrowded rear tenements.[46] In those buildings, many families shared rooms or took in lodgers to help afford rents. The crush of people living in unsanitary conditions bred disease.[47] In Chicago in the early 1890s, ten to twelve thousand children under the age of five died every year, wracked by typhoid fever, bronchitis, pneumonia, and even cholera. One such innocent victim was six-month-old Frael Kallison—cousin Joseph and Ida's fifth child. Stricken with "cholera infantum," he died at eleven o'clock at night, Thursday, October 19, 1893, after eight days of uncontrollable vomiting and diarrhea. Nathan and Anna were frightened that the same fate could befall their children.[48] Not only did Chicago's dirt and grime, polluted air, and dangerous ghetto streets—now filled with rowdy thugs—take a toll on Anna's fragile health, but a new invention also posed a threat to the small self-owned business Nathan had built up over seven years. The first appearance of the "horseless carriage" in Chicago signaled to Nathan that change was coming and there would be fewer harnesses and saddles to sell. Where could they go? The Greenblatts, who had been to California and New Mexico, spoke about clean air and opportunity in the far West.

Investing in hope for a healthier climate and a market for their business, the Kallisons set out by train, first for Albuquerque.[49] Anna, whom Nathan thought was fearless, panicked: American Indians in native dress raced into town on horseback—some "rewarded" with alcohol for their wares. She had heard stories of scalping and kidnapping, stories not unlike the myths whipped up against the Jews. In Tucson, she was appalled by the "mud houses" in the Arizona

Territory, the absence of paved roads, and the clouds of dust that inflamed her cough. As they were preparing for a sad return to Chicago, the Kallisons met an older Jewish couple at their hotel. "You should come to South Texas," they urged. "San Antonio is much more 'civilized.' There's a synagogue, the weather is mild, and there are more horses than people." Encouraged, Nathan and Anna went home to learn more about Texas.[50]

THREE

Deep in the Heart

ATHAN AND ANNA, with two small children in their
arms, stepped off the KATY Flyer onto the wooden platform
of the San Antonio railroad depot; household belongings
and harness-making equipment would follow in a freight car. In
1899, their decision to move to Texas was a bold gamble: the culture
in which they would plant their future was far different from any they
had known in Russia or Chicago.

After that chance meeting with the Weiderman family in the
Arizona Territory, Nathan had studied about San Antonio. His new
friends had sent information about the climate, the business community, and the areas in which they could live and work. Now, in the fading light of a Texas sunset, he and Anna took their first steps into
another new world, a new home. Stories of the city that lay beyond
the station had captured the Kallisons' imaginations. In the not-too-
distant past, its sunbaked streets had hosted Indian raids, cattle
drives, and Wild West shoot-outs. When Nathan and Anna arrived,
though, San Antonio was a city-in-transition. Mesquite blocks, which
were hexagon-shaped wooden pavers, kept the dust down on many of
its major downtown thoroughfares. At the end of the nineteenth century, electric lights—not dim gas fixtures—illuminated downtown
plazas, and electricity-powered streetcars had replaced those pulled
by mules. Telephone service, available in homes for a dollar a month
and in businesses for twenty-five cents more, had begun to link people together in ways unimagined before. Most important—for a man

whose livelihood depended on crafting leather harnesses and saddles—the horse was still king in San Antonio.

Just blocks from where the storied Alamo lay in ruin (used only as a warehouse at the time), Nathan and Anna soon rented a small one-story wooden building at 124 South Flores Street that would double as Nathan's harness and saddlery shop and their residence. Nearby, they could hear the bells of the historic San Fernando Cathedral ring in the cathedral's soaring Gothic bell tower. They filled the front two rooms with their most vital possessions: special knives, forms, cutting gauges, leather punches, and other tools of Nathan's trade, as well as samples of his wares—collars, halters, and saddles. While he set up his shop, Anna made a home for the family in the two back rooms. Unlike many apartments in their Chicago ghetto, their new home had "modern" amenities. Their landlord, veteran wool buyer Colonel Theodore H. Zanderson, installed sewer and water lines at his Flores Street property for the first time in November, 1899—an improvement Nathan and especially Anna welcomed.[1] And their home had refrigeration—a wooden icebox lined with tin and insulated with sawdust.[2] Emptying the water pan underneath was a daily chore for Anna. To request a delivery, she displayed a sign that read "Ice Today."

Although Anna's icebox extended the shelf life of perishable foods, she still had to shop frequently for bread, chicken, potatoes, and fish. At C. E. Lane's Grocery on East Houston Street, a store that catered to a diverse clientele, she could buy sauerkraut and imported *Frankforterworst*, as well as kosher beef and *schmaltz* (kosher chicken fat). In season, local farmers sold fresh fruits and vegetables from their wagons at Military Plaza. The summer the Kallisons arrived in San Antonio, Anna was able to find beets for borscht for five cents a bunch, onions for twenty-five cents per peck, and squash for ten cents per dozen. Due to a lack of rain, though, availability was limited.[3]

Even during San Antonio's modernization, vestiges of the frontier remained. In the heat of summer, the unpaved street in front of Nathan's shop was dry and dusty; when the ever-needed rains came, it became a muddy track. Because of the city's location between a semi-arid area to the west and a wetter, more humid area to the east, monthly and yearly precipitation varied widely. In 1899, the year Nathan and Anna arrived, floods ravaged Central Texas in late June and early July, with rains continuing unabated, damaging crops and paralyzing railroad traffic.[4] Then in August, not one drop of rain fell on the parched earth of Flores Street.[5] Farmers despaired as plants wilted in the fields. The *Daily Express* reported that nearby, the cotton crop in Hondo ". . . was burning up and that if it did not get rain in a very short time that very little cotton would be made in that vicinity."[6]

Looking forward only to the sunshine and milder winters, Nathan and Anna were not prepared for the vagaries of South Central Texas weather and the impact it would have on business. Nathan's leather-crafting shop depended on the farmers and ranchers who surrounded the city. When his customers suffered, so did he and other suppliers. But Nathan reminded his despairing wife that he had opened his shop in Chicago in the midst of a deep depression, and he had done well, nevertheless. They would learn to survive and thrive here, despite Mother Nature.

South Flores Street meandered northward to the Plaza de Armas (Military Plaza) near Main Plaza, the heart of the business community. On Saturdays during the open air market, the plaza bustled with tradesmen and their customers—city dwellers as well as farmers and ranchers from the surrounding countryside. In addition to dry goods, the open air markets sold every kind of food. The odors of *cabrito* (barbecued goat) mingled with the smell of spicy chili that arose from boiling cauldrons tended by Mexican women. From piles of manure in the street, swarms of flies buzzed to land on freshly slaughtered sides of beef.[7] The vivid colors, pungent aromas, music, laughter, and languages seemed exotic to Anna as she wended her way through the Plaza, basket on her arm.

Kallison's shop was also just around the corner from the old Southern Hotel, where rooms, in 1899, cost two dollars a day. It was the unofficial club for cattlemen in town to buy and sell livestock, shop for supplies, swap stories, and more. San Antonio was a wide-open town for entertainment that ranged from the opera and stage shows to houses of prostitution in the downtown areas where dozens of bars were located. For those who lived far out in the country, a trip into town in the 1890s was not easy. A farmer from Poteet, for example, would ride his wagon for a day to the Medina River, camp overnight, and arrive in San Antonio the next afternoon, parking his rig in the wagon yard that bordered Kallison's store on South Flores Street.[8]

The unmistakable aroma of polished leather from Nathan's shop offered familiar comfort to the cowboys and ranchers who came into town on Saturdays to outfit their horses and wagons. In his crowded workspace, Nathan cut the rolls of leather he purchased on credit, then shaped them into saddles, harnesses, and horse and mule collars. And he learned to craft new items—western-style saddles suited for the work of cowboys rounding up, roping, and tying cows and calves. Although western saddles required new forms and patterns, the challenge for a leather crafter remained the same—arranging pattern pieces on a hide to maximize the hide's yield. Nathan's talent for fitting disparate parts together like a puzzle and his ability to minimize waste were skills that carried over to other aspects of his life. So were his precision and his attention to detail. Kallison's front shop was crowded, but it was always tidy. Everything had its place. His tools were well cared for—his knives always honed. Nathan knew the only thing more dangerous than a sharp knife was a dull one, which was much harder to control.[9]

From the very first, those who came to admire him and his work observed that his wit and his business instincts were as sharp as his knives. Nathan Kallison already fit the mold of Texas manhood. Not exactly the picture of a tall, strong, silent cowboy, he nevertheless lived the essential values that produced that stereotype. Nathan was slow to anger, but he would not be cheated. Early on, he had picked up a shoplifter and thrown him out the front door. A man of medium height, unusually strong and agile, Nathan spoke softly and directly, with polite charm. But he was tough physically and mentally, and quickly became known as a man of his word—an admirable western trait. Deals with Nathan Kallison could be closed with a handshake.

In those early days, Anna was a full partner with Nathan in the business. No-nonsense Anna—under five feet tall and stylish with her tiny cinched waist and upswept blonde hair—matched her husband in intelligence, perseverance, and strength of spirit. She knew what she wanted, and she was not to be trifled with. Her smiles of approval were infrequent and had to be earned. At times, however, her unyielding work ethic, proprietary nature, and iron will would set her at odds with family—especially Nathan's family.

The friendliness of their first Texas customers surprised and heartened the Kallisons. They had worried about being able to assimilate into a culture so different from the one they had left behind. Their West Side Chicago ghetto teemed with Jews from the "Old Country." It seemed as though there were synagogues on every block. In San Antonio, the pealing cathedral bells, joined by those of other churches throughout the city, had given Nathan and Anna an initial shock. In their Russian villages and nearby cities, the bells had signaled the czar's edict: convert, flee, or be killed. Would they be accepted in this community, they wondered? As newcomers, Nathan and Anna feared isolation in their new home, a city which had drawn pious Christians for centuries.

Even though the Wiedermans had assured them that they would be welcome, they soon learned that San Antonio's Spanish heritage, so evident in its architecture, was centered in its history of Catholic missions. The first priest to hold mass in Texas, Juan de Padilla, had accompanied Coronado's conquering army in 1541. A block north of Nathan's store on Flores rose the San Fernando Cathedral, around which the Spanish conquerors and Catholic settlers had centered the new colonial settlement in 1730, and for which the Spanish viceroy of Mexico issued the formal order to design the community as the villa of San Fernando de Bexar. It was built across the San Antonio River and west of the original late seventeenth-century mission, which the Spanish had named San Antonio de Valero, later called the Alamo.[10]

Jews who practiced their religion openly could not live in Texas (for that matter, neither could Protestant Christians) until 1821, when Mexico won independence from Spain and absorbed the colony of Texas. Until then, only Catholics could legally take up residence in San Antonio or other settlements in the Spanish territory. In the 1830s and 1840s, after Spanish rule ended, several thousand Protestant and Catholic Germans immigrated to South Texas and San Antonio. The first Presbyterian church in San Antonio was built in 1847, followed by the Trinity Mission of the Episcopal Church in 1850, a Methodist church in 1852, an Evangelical Lutheran church in 1857, and the first Baptist church in 1861.[11]

At the turn of the twentieth century, the Jewish community in San Antonio was very small. The more established German Jews—whose families had lived in San Antonio for at least a generation—were a close-knit group, among them several of the city's most successful merchants. Not all of them warmly welcomed the Russian émigrés, whom they considered less educated and cultured, into their social circles. Anna, however, was determined to weave her family into their midst.

Working side by side, the Kallisons made a strong team. Nathan appeared to be easygoing, earning a reputation for kindness and generosity. He struck a hard bargain—but gently. Diminutive Anna turned out to be a shrewd businesswoman who charmed the customers while keeping an eye out for shoplifters. She handled the family's finances and enforced a strict family budget. Although she was still unable to read and write in English at that time (evidenced by the use of an "X" as her signature on a legal document), she had no problem counting money or keeping records of expenses and income.

From the moment Nathan opened his store with a three-hundred-dollar investment, his skills and wits were tested by competition from more than a dozen harness and saddle dealers already in downtown San Antonio.[12] Kallison's customers could compare his crafts-manship and prices merely by walking up and down the street. Within a block of Nathan's shop, a rancher could buy a horse at Morin's, get it saddled at Lone Star Saddlery, Theodore Steubing's, or Charles H. Dean and Company, and take it to be shod at Vollrath's blacksmith shop. The city's buggy and carriage builders and dealers also sold a complete line of harnesses. Sam H. Woodward Buggy Company, three blocks north of Kallison's on Dolorosa Street, advertised that it had "the right goods, and at prices as low as the lowest . . . for any want in the vehicle or harness line at any time." And the US Army itself at one time employed twenty-six civilians to craft harnesses and saddles at its armory on South Flores.[13]

Writing in a harness maker's trade journal, C. C. Martin cautioned manufacturers and dealers that "consumers now want the best of leather and first-class work, as they well know that this grade of harness is the cheapest in the end and that a good set of harness is worth a half dozen inferior ones." Nathan's stock in trade was the highest quality hides and his own meticulous workmanship.

Kallison's customers entered a crowded showplace with barely room to maneuver from one side of the shop to the other. Discerning patrons, however, quickly recognized excellence: the fine leather and array of hardware Nathan used to craft his saddles and harnesses and the level of skill shown by his small, even-running stitches recessed into the harness straps to reduce wear on waxed threads and prevent them from rubbing against the horse, irritating the animal's skin. Impressive too were the intricate hand-tooled details on his custom-made saddles. As in Chicago, Nathan offered quality merchandise at a fair price, and his business blossomed. Before long, he had five full-time employees crafting leather.[14]

Cattle still drove the San Antonio economy at the turn of the twentieth century. Kallison's soon became a place where farmers and ranchers, as well as city dwellers, liked to congregate. Nathan was not shy about approaching people—bankers for a loan or cowboys for a saddle sale. A "straight-talker," he laughed with the farmers and quickly adopted the vocabulary of the cowboys and ranchers, listening carefully and talking to strangers as though he'd known them for years. Many customers spoke German, a language Nathan Kallison, with his knowledge of Yiddish, had easily acquired. The rudiments of Spanish—and the slang of "Tex Mex"—also soon flowed from the tongue of the young man whose leatherworking skills and language facility had drawn customers from all of the region's ethnic backgrounds. Immaculately dressed for work in a three-piece suit, white shirt, and necktie, Nathan appeared serious and formal, a staid businessman who inspired confidence. Yet it was the twinkle in his eye as he peered through the small round lenses of his glasses, coupled with an easy smile, which drew repeat customers to his store.

Nathan's patrons were not limited to ranchers and farmers. Pioneer Flour Mills and the city's breweries used his gear for their horse-drawn delivery wagons.[15] The crowd of German immigrants who had poured into South Texas earlier in the nineteenth century enjoyed drinking good beer, and with their talent for making it, they had established the young city as a center for the beer industry. Beer wagons for San Antonio Brewing Association and Lone Star Brewery crisscrossed San Antonio.[16] They were pulled by teams of horses wearing strong collars and harnesses decorated with logos, slogans, bells, or leather-stenciled or stitched messages.

As he had in Chicago, Nathan vied with other saddleries to outfit the fire department's horse-driven wagons. In the Alamo city he also competed to service the revered and venerable US Cavalry. Early in San Antonio's history, the federal government had established a military presence to protect the trade routes that passed through the city. Thereafter, the US Army continued to expand its presence in San Antonio and became the city's largest employer. In 1898, Lieutenant Colonel Theodore "Teddy" Roosevelt brought national attention to the city as he recruited and trained the First Volunteer Cavalry, known as the Rough Riders. That famous story was even known to Nathan back in Chicago, and added to the appeal of San Antonio. A majority of the ten thousand Rough Riders came from Texas, including cowboys and ranch hands who brought along their own saddles and harnesses. By day, the horsemen trained in Riverside Park (later renamed for Theodore Roosevelt) near the Lone Star Brewery, rehearsing the tactics they would employ as they charged up San Juan Hill in Cuba to defeat the Spanish in 1899. At night, the cavalry— Texas cowboys, New York bankers, and Boston bluebloods—mingled and drank whiskey at the bar in the Menger Hotel, in lesser saloons, and in those houses of prostitution throughout the city.[17]

Although the Spanish-American War was over before the Kallisons moved to South Texas, they went out to see President Theodore Roosevelt when he returned to San Antonio in 1905 for a reunion of the Rough Riders, commemorating their victory over the Spanish in Cuba. Roosevelt's parade route took him from the Fair Grounds on the outskirts of town to Military Plaza by way of South Flores Street, passing by the Kallisons' shop. A visit by the nation's highest elected official was cause for great celebration, and the Kallisons joined the jubilation. In stark contrast, Anna recalled a visit through her Russian village by the "exalted" czar that caused a far different reaction from the family. Her younger brother Sam, fearing for his life when word spread that "bloody" Nicholas II's entourage was nearing the town, had run to hide in a pickle barrel. Peering out, he saw the czar, preceded by soldiers, enter the village in an elegant coach and step out to be helped onto a white horse, which he rode through the single street. Then the czar dismounted, re-entered the carriage, and continued on his way.

During that first year in Texas, Nathan worked long hours in the Flores Street shop, building a customer base. Morris, almost five years old, and Pauline, at three, were often underfoot. The hum of Papa's sewing machine, the clatter of his clamps and pressers, the warmth of his smiles and jokes drew them to his side. Ever vigilant, an anxious Anna kept constant watch over their children around the sharp knives and tools. She wanted a home separate from the shop. In 1900, only a year after the business opened, Nathan was doing well enough to move his family into a small rented house on Matagorda Street, about one mile from the shop. There was room for Morris and Pauline to play outside in their own yard or next door with Leo and Amelia, children of Jacob and Rachel Haskell, immigrants from Polish Russia whose jewelry store was not far from Nathan's shop. Like Nathan and Anna, Jacob and Rachel had first landed in Chicago, but they came to San Antonio by way of Montana.

Shortly after Nathan and Anna settled in their new home, Nathan's younger brother Samuel moved down from Chicago to work with him in the harness shop. The sign above the storefront now read: "Kallison Bros." Sam, his wife Celia, and their three children moved into a house on Victoria Street, about four blocks from Nathan and Anna's home on Matagorda. For several years, the brothers worked together, but Sam Kallison was hot-tempered, and it was whispered in family circles that he had a problem with alcohol. In 1904, most likely after a falling out with Nathan and Anna, Sam went into business for himself, opening The Racket Store, a dry goods shop at 132 South Flores Street—a rental property also owned by T. H. Zanderson. On January 26, 1905, Sam got into a scuffle with a police officer. A *San Antonio Gazette* columnist wrote about the incident: Officer Gold "tried to put the bracelets on him for obstructing the sidewalk." Gold said Sam had "saws and everything scattered along the wall," but Sam said he just had a few frying pans hung up for sale. "By all accounts three gray coats were used to get Kal (Sam) in." The article ended with a curious line: "Kal used $5 this morning to get in the Ju Club."[18] Anna, not one to mince words, was outraged. Whether tensions with his brother's family or the police incident with its anti-Semitic undertones—or both—prompted Sam Kallison to leave, he and Celia moved back to Chicago by year's end and remained there for the rest of their lives.[19]

As his clientele grew in numbers, Nathan provided jobs for a succession of other relatives—including his older brother Jacob, who had also moved to San Antonio briefly and whose sixth son was born there in 1908. Several nephews also worked briefly in Kallison's. They did not stay long. Some missed the urban life and pace of Chicago.

For others, Nathan's unbending work ethic—long hours, six days a week—was too demanding. The pay was poor, and Anna did not extend herself to make relatives feel wanted. Nathan welcomed his kinfolk, but Anna resisted sharing their little business with others. Even her own younger brother Sam Letwin didn't stay long. Sam made his escape to America in 1906 at age eighteen. He came to Texas to work at Kallison's after living for a while with relatives in Chicago. Seeing a lack of opportunity for advancement and feeling that Anna looked down on his wife Goldie, who still spoke Yiddish and was less accomplished at assimilating into the broader society, he headed for the oil boom towns of West Texas—and wound up with a gusher.[20]

Nathan and Anna's stay at the house on Matagorda Street was brief. With another child on the way, they wanted more space. They rented a larger house on Dashiell Street in 1902 and that November, Morris and Pauline had a new baby sister, Bertha. Bertha was nick-named "Bertie," then "Birdie," but came to be known as "Tybe," or "Tibe," a Yiddish word meaning "little bird."[21] Shortly afterwards, Anna became pregnant again. Now with three children crowded into their home on Dashiell Street—and another on the way—they searched for an even larger house. Anna insisted it must be in a neighborhood with good schools, with good students from "good" American families.

The home they found, at 125 Mission Street, met all of Anna's criteria. It had four bedrooms and was within walking distance of Bonham School, which had a reputation as one of the finest elementary schools in the city. Also important to Anna, they were only two blocks away from the prestigious King William neighborhood, where the city's most affluent German American merchants and tradesmen lived. Half a century earlier, these solid, stolid, and conservative burghers began to build the first planned development in San Antonio, naming it King William after Wilhelm I, King of Prussia, who later became German emperor. Families named Altgelt, Steves, and Groos, followed by others, spent freely, building their brick and stone mansions in the nineteenth century Early Victorian architectural style.[22] More significant for the Kallisons, however, Nathan, who was forbidden to own land in the country of his birth, could for the first time purchase a home of his own. On January 19, 1903, he paid $1,775 to Mina Beversdorff for the house—$1,275 in cash, securing the balance with a $500 loan from the D. & A. Oppenheimer Unincorporated Bankers.[23] Funds for the down payment came from the Kallisons' personal savings as well as a $350 profit earned from the quick purchase and sale of a vacant city lot—their first foray into real estate investment.[24] With uncanny vision, Nathan took advantage of San Antonio's rapid growth in the early twentieth century. He would buy, then quickly sell, more than a dozen investment properties, each time realizing a profit.

On November 1, 1903, in the bedroom of their new home, Anna gave birth to their second son, Perry Nathan Kallison—named for his Grandmother Dina's late father, Perry Elloff. The following year, Anna could for the first time afford to hire a full time maid, a German American girl from the countryside, to care for her children. In the absence of his brother Sam, Anna again was needed in the store—and she wanted to be there. She found being a businesswoman exciting, and she was good at it.

People of means in early twentieth-century San Antonio still lived next door to workers of modest income in the neighborhoods bordering the downtown business district. On Mission Street, the Kallisons and their four children made friends easily with a wide range of middle- and working-class families. The neighborhood appeared to be an idealized version of a successful American melting pot, with its mixture of second- and third-generation German Americans, Anglo-Americans, mostly from the Deep South, and a few immigrant Jews. It was a picture-book example of American democracy. Among the Kallisons' immediate neighbors were the families of two successful attorneys, Elijah F. Matheny and August Altgelt; bartender Eugene Gulley, who worked at the Sunny South Bar; Sam Wenner, a cigar manufacturer; Henry Goertz, cashier at Henry Boerner's Saloon; Otto Hegeman, operator of a photo shop;

August Zuercher, a butcher on Avenue D; R. L. Weibling, bookkeeper at the Southern Ice & Cold Storage Company; John F. Rips, operator of a paint and seed store; C. B. Conrad, a machinist; R. S. Coomes, a contractor; and Frank Huck, a saddler with Ben Varga Company.

As they settled into their new home, the Kallisons made friends and began to enjoy a social life with people from the neighborhood as well as from San Antonio's small Jewish community. On December 11, 1904, Anna and Nathan attended a festive party with their new friends. *Chanukah*—the eight-day "Festival of Lights"—had ended the night before and set the stage for a continuing celebration. They all were invited to a surprise party for a Mrs. Evans of St. Louis, "a venerable old lady who had attained the ripe old age of seventy-nine and (was) as young . . . as many a woman of fifty, being in possession of all her faculties."[25] Mrs. Evans was visiting her daughter and son-in-law, "Old Reliable Smith"—a prominent photographer in San Antonio with a first-floor studio.

Arrangements were made for guests to meet at the Smith photographic studio on East Houston Street, and then board trolley cars to travel to the Smiths' home on Cooper Street in the South Heights neighborhood. There the diverse partygoers dined and danced and sang. The two dozen or so guests included Sophie and John Pfeiffer, the local "chemist"; John Udalle, a twenty-seven-year-old fireman for the railroad, and many other Russian Jewish expatriates: Lana and Isaac Raffee, a forty-three-year-old police department patrolman; Dr. Alex Brown, a young physician born in Elizabethgrad; and the Dubinskis, who later would become relatives of the Kallisons by marriage.[26]

The warmth that suffused the Smiths' soiree lingered on, especially for Anna. The following week, details of the December 11 party for Mrs. Evans were reported in the *San Antonio Sunday Light*. Listed among the guests in a two-column story under "The Realm of Society" were Mr. and Mrs. N. Kallison. It seemed a miracle of sorts. Only fifteen years from the poverty and violence of their youths and safe from the bloodshed of the impending Russian revolution,

Nathan and Anna Letwin Kallison stepped onto San Antonio's social stage. It would not be their last mention in the city's society pages—Anna would see to that. While Nathan expanded their business, she cultivated their social life. Anna had lofty goals for her family, especially for her four children. She wanted them to have opportunities and earn an education that had been denied her. Schooled by the Greenblatts' Chicago way of life, she understood the synergy between social connections and business success. Charming and warm when she wanted to be, Anna became a catalyst for those King William area relationships.

Nathan, also ambitious, realized quickly that he needed to expand his range of merchandise. In 1905 Nathan's block on Flores, between Dolorosa and Nueva Streets, hummed with activity. Thirty-one businesses operated out of the sturdy one- and two-story wooden buildings that lined both sides of the street. Just north of Nathan's harness shop, the entire neighborhood resonated with the sounds—and odors—from the Murin Stockyard's pens of cattle, sheep, and goats. Across the street on Flores, Kansas City Fruit and Vegetable Company displayed its produce in large open bins placed outside. At night, Nathan's entire block bustled with revelers from Joe's Saloon and the Black Elephant Saloon, and with traveling salesmen staying at the Commercial House hotel on the corner. Only one storefront on the entire block stood vacant that year.[27]

Despite the apparent prosperity, Nathan realized that his business would have to change. He was acutely aware that drays, beer wagons, and buggies were headed for the past. Just a few years after the first gasoline powered automobile—a Haynes-Apperson—had rumbled onto the streets of San Antonio in 1901, there was enough activity for a concerned city government to pass ordinances restricting the speed of autos and bicycles to six miles per hour in the downtown, and shortly thereafter, another requiring automobiles to be numbered.[28] The massive discovery of oil in 1901 in the Spindletop well outside Beaumont, Texas, ensured that liquid fuels would be plentiful and that Texas would prosper by supplying the nation.

Indeed, the entire country was changing as new modes of transportation—automobiles, trucks, and airplanes—transformed America. Nathan prepared for the change.

As the first Model Ts were rolling off Henry Ford's production line in Detroit, Nathan sold his harness and saddle-making business. With a healthy loan in 1908, he then converted the rented space on South Flores Street to a general merchandise and ranching supply store.[29] During the next few years, Nathan continued to lease more and more space, which allowed him to expand his merchandise. If a customer should want an item and the store didn't stock it, Nathan would rush out to satisfy his customers' needs and buy the item elsewhere.

Studying the shopping habits of his leatherwork customers, Nathan had conceived an original idea: he saw that farmers and ranchers and their families, after traveling long distances to San Antonio—at first by wagon, then by car and truck—would rush all over the city to buy their agricultural products. And they had many options. There were a dozen shops alone, including Kallison's, where they could buy their harnesses and saddles. At other stores, they could buy feed, seed, windmills, and other farm equipment. While husbands searched for farm and ranch supplies, their wives and children would visit other stores to buy clothing, furniture, and other items for their homes. At day's end, or the following morning, they would head for their often distant homes, their wagons and trucks bulging with their purchases.

How could his business grow? How could he expand to meet as many needs as possible for his farm and ranch customers? Nathan began by adding a wide range of other farm and ranch supplies to his inventory of saddles and harnesses. Then he ordered hardware, lumber, and later, clothing and furniture. Downtown department stores were booming, with Joske's the leader in San Antonio. Studying their success, Nathan started to build his own department store—one targeting a farm and ranch family's wide range of needs. Even for South Texas, his store was unique.

Another key to the enterprise was the relationship that Nathan built with his customers. They grew to rely on his friendship, his integrity, and his determination not to be outsold by his competitors. Kallison's was still remembered as a harness and saddle shop even after the horse had passed from the urban scene except for parades, rodeos, and equestrian competitions. Their new downtown store sold everything from windmills to cattle chutes, however, along with branding irons, cattle dehorners, barbed wire, fence posts, veterinary medicine, fertilizer, feed, seed, baby chickens, cowboy hats, boots, and other farm work clothes, later popularized as "western wear." In addition, Kallison's began to sell such traditional hardware as tools and nails. Gradually, Nathan expanded his store space on South Flores and purchased the property he originally had rented.

In 1909, San Antonio was faring well—and the Kallisons along with it. The city had grown rapidly in the first ten years after Nathan opened his shop, with a population increase from 53,321 citizens in 1900 to 69,614 in 1910, sparking a boom in both commercial and residential building. During Nathan's early years there, San Antonio became the commercial locus for a wide region of Southwest Texas and was fostering a growing trade with Mexico. Businesses and cultural activities were flourishing. The National Bank of Commerce was chartered in 1903, and seven years later, the city's ambitious businessmen created the Chamber of Commerce. The downtown was particularly prosperous. There, the St. Anthony Hotel opened in 1910, providing a second deluxe establishment to compete with the historic Menger. That year the Grand Opera House featured a matinee lecture by Madam Yale on "Beauty Culture" and evening performances of Francis Wilson in "When Knights Were Bold." The Kallisons and their children enjoyed walking to the Royal, Empire, and Happy Hour Theaters, which featured the new silent movies and live entertainment.[30] For the hardworking Kallison family, life in this "boomtown" was swift and sweet. Although he had come far in the twenty years since he first crafted saddles in Chicago, Nathan did not take good fortune for granted. Despite the store's success, he never repainted the ceiling over the space occupied by his original harness shop. That small patch of peeling plaster, he said, reminded him of his humble beginnings.

In 1910, Nathan Kallison embarked on a new venture, one that had been on his mind since he came to San Antonio. At the time, the open ranges west of San Antonio were still being settled. From the very beginning, Nathan was enchanted by the expansiveness and independent spirit of Texas, and longed to be a landowner, too. Always chafed by the strict laws against owning land in czarist Russia, this one grateful immigrant was determined to own a ranch of his own and had been putting aside the money to do it. But more importantly in his life as a Texan, he envisioned how a ranch could help build the business of his San Antonio store.

FOUR

The Land

ROM HIS FIRST DAYS in San Antonio, Nathan was curious to see the countryside surrounding the city, the land on which his customers lived and worked. Cowboys wearing dusty broad-brimmed hats, boots, and spurs rode into town to hitch their horses in front of his shop. He learned the rhythms of their strange accents—so different from Chicago English—and he asked them how far they had ridden with a broken harness for him to mend or an old, worn saddle to trade in. He would ask the same of the ranch owners, whose hats of fine felt were less dusty as they dressed for an evening in the city. They came to inspect the quality of his saddles and compare prices with other leather crafters. He imagined how his store and a ranch could work in tandem to help his customers and grow his business. Whenever he could, Nathan would ride out on the roads around San Antonio, some of them just trails. A bespectacled man on a tall horse, he'd venture outside the city on a Sunday to watch cattle graze on the wide pastures. There were big ranches as well as many small, fenced-in farms with a cow or two and chickens in the yard, and a barn sturdier than the house appeared to be.

Later, after Nathan's shop became a store and he had bought his first automobile, he drove further. He saw farms and ranches with cattle, sheep, goats, crops of vegetables, corn, hay, and cotton. Past the flat ranch and farm land, he drove north and west to what was sometimes called the "Hill Country," exploring the rising terrain—hillsides of live oak trees and craggy boulders—and stopping to look at deer and jackrabbits.

In these South Texas lands, he saw hardworking people making a life for themselves. He wanted to learn how they lived and worked—and what they needed that he could supply.

Foremost in his mind and his imagination was the fact that in America, in Southwest Texas, even people of little means could own farm and ranch land. Nathan Kallison, formerly of Ladyzhinka, Ukraine, was determined to own a ranch.

In Russia, the thousands of acres of fertile farmland surrounding his village had been dominated for centuries by feudal landlords. They had been empowered by the czars to rule over both the land and the serfs who toiled there. Even after Alexander II freed the serfs from bondage and permitted them to own land in 1861, Jews still were denied that right. It was not just the romance of becoming a rancher that drove Nathan's vision, however.

In Chicago and the eastern cities where most of the nineteenth- and early twentieth-century immigrants had clustered, Jews, for the most part, aspired to become merchants or bankers, scholars and professional men (lawyers or doctors), with some eventually becoming wealthy philanthropists. Ranching, with its cowboy life, did not enter the picture. But in Texas, Nathan became entranced by the stories of successful Jewish ranchers.

Although the mythology of the early West contains few stories about Jewish cowboys or ranchers, they played significant roles in the history of Texas ranching. Charles Weil, born in Alsace, France, arrived in Corpus Christi in 1867 and founded the Cross Six Ranch, which stretched over forty thousand acres in South Texas.[1] Another pioneer, A. Levytanksy, a Lithuanian, came as a jeweler to Luling in Southwest Texas and developed ranches that sprawled over parts of Dimmitt and LaSalle Counties. And the Halff brothers—San Antonio merchants and founders of the Alamo National Bank, who immigrated to Texas from Alsace in the 1850s—built a Texas ranching empire encompassing more than six million acres. Although linking a livelihood to the land was risky, Nathan believed what Mayer Halff famously declared more than a quarter-century before—that success could come to any person in San Antonio who "believed in the 'gospel of work' and whose soul is in the struggle."[2] And as Nathan searched for ranch property for sale, he couldn't help but recall his mother's words: "Buy land and hold on to it. Someday it will feed your family." His instincts told him in 1910 that the time had come to buy land.

Nathan Kallison had worked hard and lived frugally, always saving and planning for a future in which he would own a ranch. Toward that end, he had made a few shrewd investments in real estate—among them, his 1907 purchase of 284 acres south of San Antonio along Leon Creek. That year, a financial panic had swept the nation and the price of ranch land had plummeted.[3] Nathan saw opportunity and seized it. He paid $5,050, or $18 per acre, for the land and sold it the following year for a profit of $2,613, a sum that would have taken him—as an employed harness maker—more than four years to earn.[4] Taking such risks paid Nathan huge dividends. With the profit from that quick sale, he had money to make the down payment on a ranch of his own.

After several years of searching, Nathan finally found land that seemed perfect—property offered for sale by the Hoffmann family, out on Culebra Road just eighteen miles west of the city. At first sight, Nathan was awed by its majestic beauty. Arriving at the entrance, one could see a succession of flat fields with abundant crops of hay, cotton, and corn. Farther north in the foothills of the Hill Country, he watched cows and goats grazing on prairie grass. In spring, the ranch boasted a profusion of bluebonnets, mountain laurel, juniper, black cherry, chinaberry, mesquite, and live oak trees. Wild turkey, rabbits, boar, armadillos, and herds of white-tailed deer roamed free, while eagles soared overhead and bobcats hid in rocky outcroppings. Lurking in the brush were rattlers and copperheads—a prime reason to wear cowboy boots.

Nathan had listened carefully to his farm and ranch customers and learned what to look for in a ranch property. This spread of land seemed to fill the requirements. Not only were the wide fields good for growing crops and the grassy slopes well-suited for grazing live-stock, but in the Hill Country (a part of the Edwards Plateau) water was plentiful. A farmer could drill a well, construct a windmill, and tap into the deep pools of the Edwards Aquifer far below to provide drinking water for his family and animals. In drought-prone Texas, water was liquid gold. Years later, R. G. Jordan, farm editor of the *San Antonio Express,* would confirm Nathan's appraisal. "One would be forced to search at length before he could find a farm and ranch more ideally located and where the topography of the land lends itself to agricultural pursuits."[5]

The history of the land that became the Kallison Ranch—and that of the Hoffmann family from whom he bought it—is woven into the intricate fabric of the story of Southwest Texas.[6] Even in 1910, the northwestern end of Bexar County was sparsely settled, its land still mostly owned by first-generation pioneer ranchers and their descendants. Although battles with Native Americans had finally ended, the land still bore traces of a recent past when nomadic tribes of Apache and Comanche roamed freely on open range stretching endlessly westward, and terrorized any white families who dared to settle there. At the remains of Indian camp sites, Nathan—and later his children and grandchildren—would find hundreds of arrowheads, shards of clay pots, and still-sharp stone heads of hatchets and tomahawks.

Not until 1849 did the US Army dispatch Lieutenant Colonel Albert Sidney Johnston to explore and carve out routes west of San Antonio toward El Paso and beyond to California in order to build and supply frontier military posts, which would protect the scattered settlements of the Southwest. One of those westward trails out of San Antonio cut through range land that became part of the Kallison Ranch.

Ranching settlements west of San Antonio finally came in the mid-1840s with the arrival of the thousands of German immigrants (about two thousand of whom were brought to Texas by the empre-sario Henri Castro, a Frenchman descended from Portuguese Jews who founded the town of Castroville on his land grant twenty-five miles west of San Antonio in Medina County. Among the families who came from Germany with Henri Castro were Franz and Suzanne Hoffmann and their five children, who soon prospered and multiplied in this corner of Southwest Texas. Few were more successful than Franz Hoffmann's son Jacob, who was only eight years old when his family arrived in Galveston from Prussia in 1845.

Ambitious and hungry for daring adventure, young Jacob Hoffmann struck out on his own when he was barely a teenager, first working for other farmers, then carrying wagonloads of supplies westward and serving as a guide for the army. In 1852, at age fifteen, Hoffmann earned his reputation as an "Indian fighter" when he shot and killed two Comanche warriors shortly after the Comanches murdered his older brother, who was at work building a home on the Medina River.[7]

In 1862, Jacob and his bride Caroline Bauer Ernst, the daughter of another Castroville immigrant, began to buy ranch land west of San Antonio, outside the previous safe "settlers' line" that extended from East Texas only as far west as Fort Worth, Austin, New Braunfels, and San Antonio. When Jacob Hoffmann died in 1903, his nearly thirteen thousand-acre ranch was the largest in Bexar County. Family circumstances forced a gradual breakup of Hoffmann's estate, though, which in 1910 gave Nathan Kallison his opportunity to become a rancher.[8]

The Kallisons paid Jacob Hoffmann's son Frank and his wife Jamie $4,840, or $3.76 an acre, for 1,280 acres of the former Hoffmann Ranch. At the same time, Nathan purchased an adjoining 403 acres, which included the rustic Hoffmann ranch headquarters building, from Frank Hoffmann's brother Charles, for $12,118.50.[9] Paying a portion in gold coin and borrowing the remainder from bankers Daniel and Anton Oppenheimer, Nathan became what easterners considered an anomaly—a Jewish rancher.[10]

With the same intensity and determination with which he had learned to craft leather and to master English, Nathan thrust himself into ranching. Driven to acquire the knowledge he needed to succeed at this new venture, he educated himself about the best farming and ranching practices from seeds to cattle breeds. Much information was available to him through the US Department of Agriculture, what he read in the agricultural and local presses, and the teachings of Texas A&M College—the first public institution of higher learning in the state. A land-grant college owing its origins to the Morrill Act approved by the US Congress in 1862, it was established officially as the Agricultural and Mechanical College of Texas by the state legislature on April 17, 1871, and instruction began on its campus near Bryan, Texas, in 1876. The college established the Texas Agriculture Experiment Station in 1886, and soon after began sponsoring instructional institutes for farmers throughout the state. Texas A&M's pioneering work contributed to the creation in 1914 of the US Agriculture Extension Service, in which Texas A&M and other colleges worked together to help farmers and ranchers.[11]

Nathan studied and applied the knowledge he learned from the scientists. Even as a neophyte, he embraced innovative agricultural practices and carefully heeded the advice of agronomists who repeatedly warned that Texas agriculture was vulnerable to severe economic loss in bad times because of a heavy dependence on two sources of income—cattle and cotton. Texas cattlemen were stubbornly resisting recommendations to move away from their cattle "monoculture" and to diversify their use of land by growing a variety of grain crops for sale. But Nathan listened. He wanted to make his own ranch more productive.

Although he was very comfortable on horseback, Nathan never saw himself as a Texas cowboy. Pictured on the ranch wearing a sweater, shirt, and tie with leggings (leather protectors from knees to shoes) over his trousers, the clothing he wore to his ranch reflected the melding of Nathan's two worlds. He was a businessman; the ranch, a careful investment. From the very beginning, however, it was far more than just a monetary pursuit. He envisioned his rural enterprise as a living laboratory, a goal echoed by the sign he posted at the entrance to Kallison Ranch: "Established in 1910 for development of better farming and ranching."[12] He saw potential beyond the hoped-for profits from raising and selling livestock and crops. Owning a ranch would help him better assimilate into the cattle culture that still dominated Southwest Texas. It would bring him closer to his store's farm and ranch customers and, since he would share the challenges they faced, help him understand their needs firsthand.

More importantly, with the rise of the scientific movement in agriculture, he hoped his example—in establishing and running a progressive operation that profited from the latest research and used the most modern equipment and advanced technology—would benefit his neighbors, many of whom were reluctant to embrace change. As an editor of the *Experiment Station Record* noted: "There has been no more significant development in agriculture in time than the acceptance during the past quarter of a century of the truth that scientific experiment and research are the most effective means for determining methods of improving and safeguarding agricultural production." Yet the editor was concerned that ". . . the antagonism between science and what is designated as 'common sense' still finds expression."[13] Against this background of skepticism, Nathan saw how he could combine science and practicality in ways that would advance his business. At the same time, Nathan eagerly made plans to demonstrate to his customers how they might earn a better living from farming. And of course, in those demonstrations, he would promote the products sold at Kallison's store. With those joint aims, Nathan became one of the first farmers in Southwest Texas to plant Abyssinian Durham wheat, a species that proved hardy enough to grow in the volatile climate. For sixteen years he experimented with seeds, fertilizer, and cattle breeds—following the lead of Texas A&M College and the US Department of Agriculture's Extension Service as though he were an agriculture student. He saw that Texas cotton farmers were in desperate trouble after having put eighteen million acres into cotton, and watched prices tumble in 1926 to just twelve cents a pound.[14] At the time, locals had argued that wheat, a cold weather crop, could not be grown in Bexar County. Nathan Kallison proved that it could. In 1927, with the largest wheat field in Bexar County, the Kallison Ranch produced twenty-five bushels to the acre. "Why help flood the market with cotton when we can raise wheat?" his son Morris Kallison declared. A newspaper story featured photographs of both Nathan and Morris astride a threshing machine, sacking wheat.

Placing an advertisement in the *San Antonio Light* on June 5, 1927, Nathan invited the public to come to the Kallison Ranch to see the record wheat crop being worked by a new Harvester Thresher which came from the Krueger Implement Company, the first of its kind in Bexar County. "It was great looking," recalled Morris's eldest son, Jimmy, describing fields of golden wheat swaying in the breeze.[15] In a similar experiment, Kallison Ranch became the first in South Texas to grow flax.[16]

The successful flax and wheat-growing programs not only demonstrated to local farmers and ranchers the advantages of diversification, they exemplified the economic synergy between Kallison Ranch and Kallison's store, which sold the wheat and flax seeds. And it helped Krueger's Implement Company, another local business on South Flores Street not far from Kallison's store. By 1932, however, fewer companies were making linen from flax, and the price of wheat had dropped so low that Nathan decided his land could be used much more profitably to grow feed crops for the Kallison cattle herd.

The herd was at the heart of his ranching venture. At the same time that industrial developments were continuing to transform cities in America in the 1920s, ranching in Texas had changed dramatically —and the Kallison Ranch had become a leader in promoting that change. Instead of just raising cattle and sending them to a wildly fluctuating beef marketplace—as Halff and others had done in bygone days, driving the ready-for-market cattle up the Chisholm Trail— Kallison and other progressive Texas ranchers developed "cow-calf" operations. They maintained herds of breeding cows to produce steers for the beef market, while keeping the best heifers (young females) to build up the herd. And they dedicated part of their land to raising feed for the cattle. The Kallison herd grew in quality as well as in quantity. But the change that Texas A&M scientists advocated, and the Kallisons promoted, did not come easily or quickly.

Old traditions die hard, and in the cowboy culture, cattle ranchers did not raise crops—that's what farmers did. But Nathan, later followed by his son Perry, persisted in practicing and advocating modern science that would help farmers and ranchers earn a better living. He embraced the idea of diversified agriculture, and called the lower crop-producing half of his property "the farm," where he raised feed crops like oats or Johnson grass that dried into hay. The upper half was "the ranch," where he assembled a small herd of commercial cattle, white-faced, red-hide Hereford cows, to breed and produce calves for market.[17] Inviting other ranchers to visit his operation, he convinced many that they too should employ modern practices. Because Nathan Kallison was one of the earliest Texas ranchers to embrace new concepts of scientific farming and ranching, his success in the field led the *San Antonio Light* to dub him a "pioneer" agriculturalist.[18]

When Nathan Kallison began operating his ranch, he did not fully realize just how much the cruel, fickle weather in South Texas could assail farmers and ranchers. In the Hill Country and surrounding area of South Texas, coping with drought and marginal soils was a continual struggle. Both as businessmen and as ranchers themselves, the Kallisons were in the thick of the fight. The mild climate that had drawn Nathan and Anna to Texas had seemed ideal for farming. But rain—mainly the lack thereof—would become a constant preoccupation for three generations of Kallison ranchers. Periodic droughts sometimes lasted for years. And the farmers and ranchers from Nathan's time onward paid dearly for the earlier, profligate abuse of the land when cattle roamed freely, and natural grass cover was badly compromised by overgrazing.

The Kallisons could do nothing about the vagaries of Mother Nature or the inevitable ups and downs in the agricultural market. But they had a "safety net"—their thriving store in the heart of the city. Diversification was as beneficial in financial investments as it was in growing crops and raising livestock. Because the Kallisons did not depend solely on income from ranching and farming, they could afford to take risks as they investigated ways to improve agricultural practices. Thus, the family enterprise prevailed and grew during hard times, when ranching and farming in Texas tested the determination of most men and women just to hold on to their land.

FIVE

Tradition!

O N SATURDAY MORNINGS in the early years, Anna Kallison would walk out of her Mission Street home to shop or run errands, often with her young children at her heels. She would visit the small neighborhood grocers and dry goods stores or head to Market Square where fruit and vegetable vendors from farms around the city sold their produce from horse-drawn wagons. On occasion, she would pass men wearing black hats or small skull caps called *yarmulkes*, walking to Agudas Achim, the Orthodox synagogue at the corner of Aubrey and Guilbeau Avenues—about six blocks from the Kallisons' home.[1] They knew Anna and they frowned, observing that she was ignoring the Jewish prohibition against work on the Sabbath. Their families rented or owned residences within walking distance of their synagogues. For these men, many of whom were recent Russian émigrés, piety on the Sabbath was a rule not to be broken. For Anna and Nathan, however, as well as many others Jews in San Antonio, living in a new land meant embracing new rules of observance.

In Texas, the ancient Old World customs and rituals of Orthodox Judaism felt to Anna like a wool dress in summer, chafing her under its weight. When they were confined to the shtetls of Russia, and then the West Side ghetto in Chicago, Nathan and Anna both had followed the rigorous religious customs and strictures. Beginning their new life in the Southwest, they remained committed to their religion— but equally determined to take part in the wider secular life and freedom available to them in San Antonio. They were eager to assimilate.

Moreover, Anna saw that their more affluent Jewish neighbors, many of whom were of German descent, were identified as Reform Jews. Ever alert to opportunities to achieve the higher social status of the Chicago couple who had "adopted" her, Anna saw that Reform Jews had discarded many rigid traditions and observances of the Old World.[2]

Nathan and Anna soon decided that their young family would modify old customs and traditions. Nathan especially wanted to adjust his life to blend in with what he saw as the realities and practicalities of life in America. The men who frowned at Anna shopping on the Sabbath—and at Nathan working in his harness shop—tried to practice Judaism as they did in Russia and Europe, with services all in Hebrew, men and women seated separately, strict kosher dietary laws, and no work from sundown Friday to sundown Saturday.[3] If they were to join Agudas Achim, the Orthodox synagogue founded in San Antonio in 1889 by Eastern European Jews, Nathan could not violate the Sabbath by selling harnesses, or by traveling on horseback or in a carriage or wagon, and Anna would not be able to cook their meals.

Instead, they chose the liberal traditions of Reform Judaism. Soon after they arrived in San Antonio with toddler Morris holding his father's hand and baby Pauline in Anna's arms, the young couple walked from their Flores Street shop and home to Temple Beth-El, a Reform congregation founded in 1874 by German Jews, many of whom had arrived twenty to thirty years earlier.[4] There they were warmly greeted by Rabbi Samuel Marks. The rabbi, intent on raising funds to build a new sanctuary, saw the energetic, ambitious Kallisons as good additions to his congregation. He explained the requirements of membership and helped Nathan apply to the board in writing. Once approved, they would purchase or rent a pew in the temple.[5] They joined a membership that in 1899 numbered more than eighty other families.

At Temple Beth-El, they soon met the brothers Daniel and Anton Oppenheimer, founders and pillars of the congregation. The Oppenheimer banking connection almost immediately provided a vital ingredient to Kallison's early business success. D. & A. Oppenheimer Bank loaned Nathan and Anna money to help them buy their first home on Mission Street as well as funds to expand their store, and later, money to buy their ranch. (At the time, it was unlikely that the city's other banks would have loaned money to an unknown immigrant Jewish newcomer.) As matters turned out, the Kallisons' relationship with the Oppenheimers and their bank lasted through the entire history of Kallison's store.

In joining Temple Beth-El, Nathan and Anna were choosing what they thought would be the best avenue for their children to become successful participants in mainstream American culture, lifestyle, and social structure. At the same time, they also wanted their children to embrace the family's Jewish heritage and values—a belief in one God, the obligation to love one's neighbor, and to care for the less fortunate. Anna wanted the children to develop friendships with children from respectable families and find "good" husbands and wives. In Temple Beth-El both Kallisons saw a religious community that would foster those aspirations. They hoped the congregation would be supportive of their family and their business.

San Antonio's early business community grew alongside the story of Temple Beth-El. After Texas became the twenty-eighth state of the Union in 1845, then again after the Civil War ended, Texas was part of the United States. In the new Southwest, those first German Jews who began migrating in the 1840s and 1850s to San Antonio and other cities throughout Texas found acceptance more rapidly than they had in the East. They prospered because as merchants or tradesmen they filled vital roles in the commercial development of their communities. Their Anglo-American neighbors, who soon filled Texas with its majority population, had come primarily as small farmers from throughout the South. Lacking craft or commercial skills, most only sought better opportunities to farm their own land; this in turn created opportunities for the German immigrants, including the Jewish settlers, who brought skills in commerce and banking.

A pattern developed in San Antonio and in virtually every Texas city or town: Jewish immigrants, former peddlers and street vendors, soon opened stores. For example, Julian Joske's first store, J. Joske, located on Main Plaza in San Antonio, opened in 1867 and grew to be the city's dominant department store.[6]

From the time they arrived in San Antonio, the first few Jewish families were intent on preserving their religious identity. In 1855, Seigmund Feinberg, Elanora Lorch, Louis Zork, and the Moke brothers purchased land for a Jewish cemetery. The Hebrew Benevolent Society was organized in 1858 to provide "a decent burial for indigents, to care for the sick in poor circumstances, and especially for needy people without relatives."[7] Beginning around 1870, Jews in San Antonio held simple religious services in private homes. Lacking a rabbi, laymen led the services on Saturday mornings. A year later, families began meeting for Sabbath services in the old Ruellmann Hall opposite Joske's store on East Commerce Street. By 1870, there were enough Jewish women in San Antonio to form a Ladies Hebrew Benevolent Society, which met the first Saturday of each month "to relieve families of Jewish faith in distress" and to assist in burying the women who had died.[8]

Then, after a series of planning and organizational meetings that had begun two months earlier, forty-four men met on July 5, 1874 in Odd Fellows Hall to found a congregation "for the purpose of perpetuating the cause of Judaism in all its essential purity and promote its great and fundamental principle—the rock upon which our undying faith is founded—the belief in, and the worship of one God. . . . "[9] The name they selected—Beth-El, Hebrew for "House of God"—embodied that concept. Of the forty-four charter members, only two had been born in the United States. Five had emigrated from Alsace, France; eleven from Bavaria; and seven from Prussia. Most of the other nineteen had come from other German states. Some founding members had been active in the beginnings of liberal Judaism in their native countries.[10] Among them were San Antonio's most prominent Jewish businessmen of the day: Daniel Oppenheimer, A. B. Frank, M. Halff, Samuel Mayer, L. Zork, and M. Goldfrank.[11]

Aside from their common religious heritage, Temple Beth-El's early members were a diverse lot, quite a few of whom had already achieved economic success. Dry goods merchants Mayer and Solomon Halff also owned vast cattle ranches in different parts of Texas. Daniel and Anton Oppenheimer, natives of Bavaria, had begun as merchants in Rust, Texas, moved to San Antonio, and then formed the D. & A. Oppenheimer Bank, on which Nathan would come to depend. Abraham Frank and Max Goldfrank owned Goldfrank, Frank & Company, which sold wholesale dry goods, boots, shoes, and hats. In the raw frontier town, the new Jews were not marginalized, but quickly woven into the fabric of a larger business community.

That some had gained early acceptance by the larger Christian population was illustrated by the remarkable public career of Louis Zork, who emigrated from Prussia to San Antonio in the 1840s, one of the first Jews to settle permanently in the city. His business ventures included real estate and a store at the southwest corner of Main Plaza for which he advertised "an extensive assortment of staple and fancy groceries and cutlery at prices twenty percent cheaper than any other store in the city." Zork was even included in exclusive gatherings of well-heeled German Catholics at Dosche and Riche's Buckhorn Bar.[12] When Louis Zork died in 1885, his forty-year career had seen his election to a variety of public offices, including service as a city alderman and as treasurer of Bexar County.[13]

The Zork story was a motivating tale for Nathan and Anna. Adding to the lore were stories of Temple Beth-El founders who had lived through the violent, often lawless, "Wild West" era of Southwest Texas. Some even added to the era's reputation. Settling a bitter dispute over a dog in 1857, Benedict Schwarz, a pawnbroker, was said to have murdered Seigmund Feinberg, another Jewish merchant. Never charged with a crime, Schwarz became a Temple Beth-El board member and a pillar of the Jewish community, until he too was murdered, by a thief in his pawn shop in 1882.[14] Surprising to later immigrants, at least a few of the early Jewish settlers also had profited from the slave trade. An 1859 edition of the *San Antonio Daily Herald* featured an advertisement for the firm of Moke and Brother, offering: "Lands for sale, two Negro boys, two American work horses, a buggy, and an ambulance." The Moke Brothers were charter members of Temple Beth-El. When war erupted in 1861, some San Antonio Jews, including the brothers Daniel and Anton Oppenheimer, served as volunteers in the Confederate Army. Others joined the Union Army, among them Samuel Wolfson, a survivor of the First Battle of Manassas.[15] A majority of the German Americans in San Antonio, Jewish and Christian alike, had little sympathy for the Confederacy, however. They had come to America seeking freedom and prosperity, not to see their new country torn apart by a ruinous Civil War.

By 1874, Jewish veterans from both sides had united as a congregation, and had raised $12,300 in gold coin to build Temple Beth-El at the corner of Travis and Jefferson Streets. The Reform dedication ceremony on December 10, 1875 turned out to be a citywide event: Jews, Protestants, and Catholics came together to celebrate the new synagogue, and the *San Antonio Daily Herald* reported that "the beautiful edifice was filled by the most cultivated audience of ladies and gentlemen we have ever seen in San Antonio. There seemed to be present representatives of every nationality and religious belief."[16]

In 1899, Temple Beth-El had much to offer the Kallisons. In addition to the "regular divine services" held Friday evenings and Saturday mornings and the annual holiday and festival celebrations, there was weekly religious school for the children on Sundays at 10:00 a.m.; Hebrew "sessions" and history classes on Mondays and Thursdays, Bible circle on Tuesdays, and confirmation classes at Rabbi Marks's home on Wednesdays after school at 4:00 p.m. There were social and cultural events, too: the Temple's Literary and Chautauqua Club that met at members' homes, Sunday school picnics in Southwestern Park, as well as parties, plays, and concerts for children and adults at the Harmony Club—the "social arm" of the Temple.[17]

Temple Beth-El opened its services to the community, announcing in the San Antonio newspapers Rabbi Samuel Marks's "discourses," which included "The Labor Question and the Church," "The Types of Human Character," and "Nature's and Humanity's Gifts"—noting as they did during the "Feast of Sukkos, originally the harvest festival . . ." that "(t)he public generally is cordially invited to attend the service."[18]

As a Reform temple, Beth-El's services also included a "greatly augmented and excellently trained choir," consisting of both Jews and non-Jews. (In Orthodox synagogues, music is forbidden in the services except for prayers or songs chanted in Hebrew by the rabbi or the cantor.)

Embracing modernity was well-suited to the Kallisons in San Antonio, where Jews were such a small minority they seemed less of a "threat" to anti-Semites. In Temple Beth-El, they worshipped like their Christian neighbors, with men and women sitting together, and music and prayers were recited primarily in English. The Kallisons wanted a community based around a modern religion, freed from the old rules for prayer, dress, holiday, and kosher food. (Beth-El's board had even voted in 1874 to forbid men—with the exception of the rabbi—from wearing the traditional yarmulke head-covering in the synagogue.)[19] The bar mitzvah, for centuries marking the coming of age of Jewish boys at thirteen, soon gave way to classes for both boys and girls, with graduation or "confirmation" at fifteen.[20] The children's classes became "Sunday school" and, for a time, the rabbis were addressed as "reverend" rather than "rabbi."

A proud moment for Nathan and Anna as new Americans came on May 4, 1901, when President William McKinley visited San Antonio. Beth-El's Rabbi Samuel Marks stood with him on the VIP reviewing stand in Alamo Plaza. The rabbi presented *The Book of Gold* to the president for his signature, and the president scrawled

"With Kindest Regards, William McKinley" across its first page.[21] (Rabbi Marks had created *The Book of Gold* as a fundraising incentive. It would bear the names of those who contributed to the fund to build a new temple.)[22] Four months later, President McKinley was assassinated by an anarchist, Leon Czolgosz, in Buffalo, New York.[23] Vice President Theodore Roosevelt, of the San Antonio-trained Rough Riders, assumed office. The Kallisons were horrified—and fearing repercussions, hoped that the assassin was not a Jew.

In joining Beth-El at the beginning of the twentieth century, the Kallisons were committed to maintaining their Jewish identity—but they were equally determined to become part of mainstream American life and to appeal to their children who, as Texans, had little knowledge of the ancient ways of a faraway continent. The new Temple was as "mainstream" as any church in town.

As a new congregant, Anna quickly and eagerly began developing her own friendships with other members of Temple Beth-El. The Kallisons now immersed themselves in religious services and social activities. Even though it was no longer a mandatory ritual in the Reform movement, Nathan Kallison still wanted his first son to experience the same coming-of-age ceremony that he himself had celebrated in Russia. And so Morris, at age thirteen, became a bar mitzvah at Temple Beth-El in 1909, along with seven other Jewish boys who either joined him or were, instead, confirmed that same year.[24] Nathan's younger son Perry did not follow Morris to become bar mitzvah. He and his sisters Pauline and Tibe regularly attended Temple Beth-El's religious school, though, and at age fifteen, each would be confirmed in the Reform temple ceremony that had replaced the traditional coming-of-age ritual.

There were two sets of children for Anna to raise: Chicago-born Morris and Pauline, and—as they liked to call themselves—"born and bred Texans" Tibe and Perry. Morris worshipped his father and tolerated Perry, who was seven years his junior. Pauline, almost five years older than Tibe, became a second mother to her baby sister. Even with the demands of trying to build a small business, Anna was deeply involved not only in the academic performance of her children, but also in actively promoting their participation in a wide range of cultural and social pursuits. The Kallisons' own hard work was motivated in large part by their determination that their children would have opportunities denied their parents. Her own formal education was very limited, although she eventually learned to read and write English with difficulty, but Anna Kallison pushed her children into all kinds of social and cultural activities, and was a fixture herself at the events in which they participated.

All four of Nathan and Anna's children had learned at an early age that their parents set high standards for them. They were expected not only to excel in school and with their religious studies but also to help out at home and in the family's business. The Kallisons had no tolerance for idleness. Work, they believed, built character and fostered independence—traits they instilled in all their children by example.

At seven years of age, Morris, the eldest, asked for a job: he diligently picked up leather scraps and swept the floor in the harness shop. "I was practically born in the store," he would joke. Determined to earn his own spending money, Morris also washed buggies in the San Antonio River, hawked newspapers on street corners, and shined shoes. "I never asked my dad for anything," Morris said proudly.[25] The boy was both enterprising and gregarious, strong and competitive. In boxing bouts in Beethoven Hall, the local Golden Gloves arena, he fought as a teenager under the name "Kid Morris." ("Some thought he could have been a professional," recalled Morris's son Jimmy.)

In 1910, after completing the ninth grade, Morris Kallison dropped out of school to work in the expanded Kallison's store. "I liked working far better than a textbook," he told his sons. Whether he was encouraged by his father to help in the store or whether his mother needed time to furnish her new home and trusted Morris to fill in is unknown. After all, Morris reasoned, Nathan had learned a trade at an early age, why couldn't he? Nevertheless, he later took night classes at the Alamo City Business College.

From an early age, Morris Kallison was highly motivated to excel, especially in business. He brimmed with self-confidence, proud of his hard-muscled body and handsome features, which were set off by an abundant crop of black hair, its dark waves always carefully brushed and pomaded. As a teenager, Morris captured the attention of young women as he strode down the San Antonio streets. They sought him out as a dance partner at social gatherings. A newspaper story in 1917 reported Morris at "a formal ball in 1917 staged by a group of Jewish girls, at West End Lake."[26]

From early childhood, the Kallison boys were schooled in commerce. Nathan presented the mechanics of buying and selling in near-romantic terms: profit was earned by long hours and hard work, a clean and attractive work place, attention to and respect for customers, and a close eye on the cash register. "Profit comes from your reputation in business," Nathan instructed. "You earn that reputation by honesty, no matter what. The bank and the customers must know that your word is as good as gold—that Kallisons cheat no one."

The family business would become an exciting challenge for Morris and Perry—for Morris, an adventure far more interesting than school, and for Perry, a stage from which he could reach a friendly audience. The store itself was an education for them. Commerce as a life goal became an almost noble calling. "Build a good reputation in business," said Nathan, "and you'll soon be known as leaders in the whole community."

Morris's work at the store allowed Anna to spend more time with the three younger children. Pauline, easygoing and charming, loved school. She made friends easily, and very early blossomed into a winsome young woman. Anna did not want her daughters to work like Morris, but to learn how to manage a home and acquire gracious manners and excellent taste—like Hannah, Rose, and Lily Greenblatt, the girls she had tutored. Anna insisted that her girls would be educated. Piano lessons, educational trips, vacations in and outside Texas were meant to broaden their vision of the world. Pauline was fun-loving, and like Morris, full of self-confidence. She convinced her father that she could be a good employee—and once Anna had taught her the rudiments of running the cash register, she worked during school vacations.[27] And she loved it. Popular, uncommonly attractive, and gregarious, the older daughter drew her friends in as customers, and they in turn brought their parents. There were new people to meet, new conversations to open. But penny-wise Anna kept reminding Pauline of the reason she was working in the store—to earn her own spending money.

As children, Tibe and Perry, who were raised like twins, also helped their working mother at home by running errands in their Mission Street neighborhood. Pulling their little wagon, with their dog "Tippy" at their heels, Tibe and Perry would walk to the nearby markets to fetch the family's groceries. In the Kallison home, even the dog had a job. Tippy amused neighbors, carrying the empty basket to the store with his teeth, then neatly toting the newspaper home the same way while the children balanced the full basket between them. As a teenager, Perry also assisted his parents and Morris in the store, working after school and during summer vacations and holidays. Perry took pride in his most important after-school assignment: riding his bicycle from Kallison's store to deliver its daily receipts to the D. & A. Oppenheimer Bank. Entrusted with large sums of money from a cash-intensive business that in the present day would be serviced by an armored car company, the youngest of the Kallison children justified the faith his parents placed in him. Not one of the cash deposits was ever lost or stolen.

Although Anna expected to work in the store—and it was important to her—she was more interested in mentoring her daughters. She wanted them to acquire the education and develop the social graces that would make them upwardly mobile and lead to marriage to successful young men. Toward that end, Anna immersed herself in activities at the children's schools, first at Bonham Elementary School, which was an impressive three-story brick building built in

1889 and named after James Bonham, a martyred hero at the Alamo. To Anna's delight, her daughters' names graced the society page of local newspapers on many occasions. One story picked up by the *Galveston Daily News* on Sunday, March 17, 1907, noted Pauline as an invited party guest "in honor of a birthday anniversary" for one of her friends. She was nine years old. At Bonham, then considered one of San Antonio's best elementary schools, Morris and Pauline, followed by Tibe and Perry, not only learned their writing and arithmetic, but performed in a rich extracurricular program that included school plays and musicals with students accompanied by a teacher playing a pedal-type reed organ. Given the city's rapid growth, however, overcrowding had become a problem. Anna Kallison joined others in the parents' organization at Morris's school in 1905 to complain about classes packed with as many as fifty children.[28]

Later, Anna served as a member of the Mother's and Teacher's Club at their middle school, Stephen F. Austin School on West Marshall Street. Even though she was a working mother, she did everything she could to enhance her children's educational experiences. No task was too small. When the school held its outdoor lawn fete in May of 1914, for example, Anna—a member of the refreshments committee—took time off from the store to serve ice cream at the gathering.[29]

That same year, Anna proudly applauded from the audience as eleven-year-old Tibe played a piano solo at a Saturday afternoon gathering of the B Minor Musical Club, which met at the San Antonio Woman's Club. Already in the eighth grade, Tibe was academically precocious. Petite like her mother, Tibe had an alabaster complexion and rosy cheeks. Serious and shy, with her close-cropped hair she often was taken for a tomboy.

In contrast, her older sister Pauline—tall, willowy, and vivacious—was a jolly girl, happy-go-lucky, fond of a good time. She often clashed with her headstrong, dominating mother, who scrutinized each beau most harshly. At the age of fifteen Pauline had already settled on Chicago, and the loving company of wealthy

Hannah Greenblatt-Sigmund, whom she called "Aunt Hannah," as her ultimate destination. "That's where my life will be," Pauline told her young sister.

Tibe was a different case entirely. By all accounts, she was a prodigy. She was serious and not content to have "housewife" as her principal duty. At an early age she had determined that she would become a professional someday.

Anna had a different vision for her daughters. She wanted Pauline and Tibe to grow up in a comfortable home, in comfortable surroundings. She taught by example. Under her tutelage, the girls were brought up in the customs forged by early twentieth-century Jewish women. "You will learn how to handle money," Anna told them. "You must know how much it is worth—and how to save it—for the time you will be managing your own home and family, because women rule their homes." They would master the social graces of entertaining, of appearing stylish but not ostentatious. Preferably assisted by a maid, they would keep their tastefully decorated homes neat at all times—homes that would be near their parents' home.

With all this grooming for a life of wifery, however, the Kallison sisters were also taught of their obligation to give volunteer service to the disadvantaged of the community. The practice of *Tzedakah*—giving of self to needy others—was deeply engrained in the Kallisons, not simply a matter of *noblesse oblige* because of their economic status, but as a religious and moral imperative.

In 1914, the family left Mission Street for an imposing three-story white frame Victorian home at 701 San Pedro Avenue, in an area known as "the fashionable quarter of San Antonio."[30] The Kallisons' new home featured elaborate "gingerbread" woodwork, wide wraparound porches, and a rooftop turret overlooking an expansive front lawn flanked by tall palm trees and Anna's azaleas and other garden flowers. As she studied the homes and wardrobes of her neighbors in this wealthier area, Anna also refined her tastes in décor and style. The Kallisons bought new furniture—the massive dark wood then in vogue, soon to be called "traditional." Anna carefully chose china and silverware for her new home—something she could not afford to do as a young bride. She dressed her children handsomely and indulged herself as well. She ordered clothing from Chicago's fine stores or purchased it on her trips north by train to visit the Greenblatts as well as Nathan's mother and brothers and their families. As they advanced financially and socially, Nathan bought jewelry for Anna to wear—a luxury she had only dared to dream about.

Although social interactions between them were limited, San Antonio was an easygoing city in which the various ethnic groups tolerated each other. Its long multicultural history of settlement had first brought the Spanish, then the French, followed by Germans, and then by Anglo-Saxon southerners. The Mexican Americans, some of whom were descended from the original Spanish settlers, worked at menial labor and lived primarily on the west side, most in grinding poverty. The Germans clung together in their own social and cultural organizations, with their intellectuals organizing the German-English School on South Alamo, and the well-to-do businessmen making the Casino Club their exclusive preserve. Successful Anglo-Saxons of various backgrounds banded together in 1881 to form their own private San Antonio Club. What brought the various groups together were the necessities of commerce.

Describing San Antonio as a city "with many concentric but very separate circles," Texas historian T. R. Fehrenbach wrote:

> The leading men of the growing town did business with each other daily, and they had to organize an effective politics and local government out of disparate groups. The story of San Antonio was that no group ever completely assimilated the others—although an Americanization process went on—they were all forced into a peculiar mutual tolerance. This, indeed, created a wonderfully tolerant town . . . They might

not adopt each other's ways, however subtly influenced by them—but they got along.[31]

Nathan and Anna "got along." Little more than ten years removed from the shtetls, the Kallisons had mastered English quickly and adapted to life in South Texas. Although Anna still read a Yiddish newspaper and spoke English with a slight accent, Yiddish was seldom spoken at home. Their younger children never heard it, except for certain descriptive phrases that stuck: a *gonnuf* was a thief, a cheater to be scorned. A piece of clothing of inferior quality was still a *schmatta*. And the Kallisons remained conscious that as Jews, they were different; privately they sometimes referred to certain Christians as *goyim* (a sometimes derogatory term for gentiles). Jews were *yahudim*, a description later politely Americanized by the next generation into M.O.T.—as in "member of our tribe." Nevertheless, Kallison children were raised to feel at home with friends of all faiths and backgrounds. Within the Reform community and among those totally non-religious Jews in San Antonio, the "two-ness"—as Jews and as Texans—was easier on Nathan and Anna's children than it would have been in more segregated eastern cities such as Baltimore and Philadelphia. Nathan, Anna, and their children as they grew up integrated far more comfortably into San Antonio life, including its cultural and civic activities, than did their eastern counterparts.

Unlike the Kallisons, though, not all newly-arrived Jews in Texas wished to conform to modern American life and culture. Alexander Gurwitz, for example, came to San Antonio from Russia in 1910 with other goals in mind. Trained as a Hebrew scholar, Alexander Gurwitz's principal motive in coming to America was the same purpose first stated by those pilgrims who sailed from England on the Mayflower—to practice his religion freely. He knew he had to escape from Nicholas II and his henchmen to find that religious freedom.

Gurwitz was a beneficiary of the "Galveston Experiment," in which New York philanthropist Jacob Schiff helped Eastern European Jews reach America through the port of Galveston, Texas, from 1907 through 1914. The Galveston Experiment brought only ten thousand Jews to America, but it resulted in many of them achieving success in the small towns and cities of the Midwest and West. Schiff believed that the recent immigrants would find better economic opportunities in the emerging Midwest and West than in the crowded cities of the East, but he also wanted to steer them away from New York, worried that these poor, non-English-speaking immigrants might somehow heighten prejudice and endanger the acceptance already won by the established German Jews.[32] In Texas, Alexander Gurwitz wished only to worship as he had done earlier in Russia, in spite of persecution.

Gurwitz chose to learn only very limited English. He supported his family by teaching Hebrew and working as a *shochet*, a religious man who slaughters animals humanely for food, in accordance with Jewish law. He devoted himself to Hebraic studies and, like a missionary, taught a younger generation. His Hebrew students came from the several hundred Orthodox families who belonged to synagogues Agudas Achim and Rodfei Sholom.[33]

In his autobiography, *Memories of the Generations*, written in Yiddish, Gurwitz contrasted differences between the lives of the German Jews in San Antonio and those newly arrived immigrants from Russia who came to San Antonio in the first part of the twentieth century:

> . . . The Jews were divided into two categories: German *yahudim* (East European derogatory term for German Jews, implying assimilationist snobbery) and Orthodox. The *yahudim* were the affluent Jews in town. The largest commercial enterprises were theirs, and there were about a hundred families of them. Among them were some very wealthy men. They had an imposing Temple with a Rabbi spiritual leader as the Reform way of life dictates. They had little to do with the Orthodox. It is unnecessary to add that there was no social contact between them. The Reform Jews made *Shabbos* (Sabbath) for themselves.

There were several hundred Orthodox Jewish families. Among them there were also—but fewer—affluent men with large businesses. But the majority were of a poorer class, small shopkeepers and peddlers. But abjectly poor there were none. When a *greener* (new immigrant) came to settle, he took at once to peddling. If he had a bit of money, he bought a horse and wagon, secured some merchandise, and took his "itinerant store" into the Mexican neighborhoods. They paid him on the installment plan, and since the risk was very high, so were his prices.[34]

Alexander Gurwitz ridiculed his fellow Russian Jews in San Antonio, "who having made a little money, want to . . . be among the German social climbers . . . and want to go up in the world and join the Reform temple" (Beth-El).[35] He also criticized Orthodox Eastern European men who, like the Reform Jews, did not celebrate the traditional Jewish Sabbath by maintaining a day of rest and prayer. "The store owners," he wrote, "of course could not bear to leave their places of business and come to the synagogue, for the best business day was Saturday." As a result, Gurwitz complained, he and other observant Orthodox Jews constantly had "to go up and down 'Jerusalem Street' to round up a *minyan*, a gathering of the ten Jewish men needed to hold a religious service."[36]

"Jerusalem Street" or "Little Jerusalem" was a four-block stretch on East Commerce Street, west of City Hall, where immigrants—most members of the two Orthodox synagogues—operated small stores. The name "Jerusalem Street"—first passed around in ironic humor by one of the merchants there—soon found its way into the city's vocabulary like a "Chinatown" or "Little Italy," because so many immigrant shopkeepers who began as peddlers had found a street where rents were cheap enough for small stores. Yiddish was spoken. Merchants sold yards of cloth or "affordable" ready-made apparel for children and adults, known as "dry goods." Many of the stores had Spanish names, in an effort to appeal to the poor Mexican Americans who were the stores' principal customers. On West Commerce, Morris Spector and his son Jake owned La Estrella, which offered men's suits and general clothing. In the tradition of immigrants helping each other, the Spectors also supplied still newer Jewish arrivals with inexpensive merchandise—including cheap chenille robes—to sell from pushcarts in the city's poorer neighborhoods. On Commerce, the Sinkin family sold their dry goods in a store named La Nacional; Lewis Eastman, down the street, called his La Feria. The three Penner brothers, Sam, Ben, and Max, and their heirs eventually expanded their Commerce Street shop into Penner's, a department store still in business in 2013 and advertising "the World's Largest Supply of Authentic Mexican Guayaberas!" (Mexican wedding shirts).[37]

In the 1800s and early 1900s, the Jews of San Antonio, as in other communities in the South and Southwest, encountered relatively little overt discrimination and anti-Semitism, perhaps because they constituted only a tiny percentage of the population. Absent was the strife found in large eastern cities, where hordes of immigrants from different countries frequently were perceived as a threat by others with longer histories as Americans. Yet there was always discrimination in San Antonio—most overtly against African Americans—its intensity often dependent on national events and public attitudes.

In his book *The Chosen Folks: Jews on the Frontiers of Texas*, Bryan Edward Stone writes about the status of Jews in Texas:

Though sympathetic to the racial minorities in their communities and treating them with somewhat more respect than did other whites, Texas Jews as a group did not identify with them or define themselves as a persecuted minority despite the occasional slights they received from individual gentiles. On the contrary, Jews . . . stood firmly within white business and social circles in positions of civic leadership. The [rise of the Ku Klux Klan], however, and its support

Top: According to the 1895 Russian census, Kallison relatives lived with another Ladyzhinka family in a straw-roofed clay house similar to this one in a Ukrainian shtetl. *Yad Vashem Archives.*
Above: Liberty Street in the Jewish District, Chicago's West Side Ghetto, c.1900. *American Journal of Sociology, vol. XVII, July 1911.*

Above: Chicago's West Side Maxwell Street Market (Jefferson Street), c. 1890-1910. *Chicago History Museum (ICHi-14059).*

Left: Alley view, Jewish district, Chicago's West Side Ghetto, c.1900. *Metropolitan Planning Council records, MPC 0000 0000 0117, University of Illinois at Chicago Library, Special Collections.*

Above: Nathan Kallison (center) and brothers Jacob (right) and Samuel (left), harness makers in Chicago, 1896.

Right: Anna Letwin in Chicago, employed by a distant cousin to care for her children, 1892.

Above: The Kallison family in Chicago, 1899. Standing: Nathan and Anna. Dina Kallison, the family matriarch, is seated with granddaughter Pauline in her lap. Young Morris stands at his grandmother's side.

Opposite, top: Chili stand in the open-air market on Military Plaza, San Antonio, late 1880s. *General Photograph Collection, MS 354: 102-0637, University of Texas at San Antonio Libraries Special Collections from the Institute of Texan Cultures.*

Opposite, bottom: Ruiz House commercial building in the Military Plaza market area, c.1880s. *General Photograph Collection, MS 362: 098-1250, University of Texas at San Antonio Libraries Special Collections from the Institute of Texan Cultures.*

Top: Military Plaza Vegetable Stands, 1886. *General Photograph Collection, MS 362: 101-0050, University of Texas at San Antonio Libraries Special Collections from the Institute of Texan Cultures.*

Above: Temple Beth-El, a Reform Jewish congregation at the corner of Travis and Jefferson Streets in San Antonio. Photograph c.1877. *General Photograph Collection, MS 362: 093-0384, University of Texas at San Antonio Libraries Special Collections from the Institute of Texan Cultures.*

Top: Pioneer Flour Mills, an enduring San Antonio business founded in 1851 by German immigrant Carl Hilmar Guenther, who established this mill along the banks of the San Antonio River in 1859 one mile south of the city. Photograph 1891. *General Photograph Collection, MS 362: 082-0642, University of Texas at San Antonio Libraries Special Collections from the Institute of Texan Cultures.*

Above: Laying a cornerstone for the new Bexar County Courthouse in San Antonio, May 17, 1892. *General Photograph Collection, MS 362: 073-0203, University of Texas at San Antonio Libraries Special Collections from the Institute of Texan Cultures.*

Opposite, top: Streetcar Tramway Sprinkler No. 6, working to keep the dust down on the unpaved city streets, 1897. *General Photograph Collection, MS 362: 075-0856, University of Texas at San Antonio Libraries Special Collections from the Institute of Texan Cultures.*

Opposite, bottom: Bexar County Courthouse, 1900. *General Photograph Collection, MS 362: 101-0083, University of Texas at San Antonio Libraries Special Collections from the Institute of Texan Cultures.*

Above: Electric light arches on Commerce Street in downtown San Antonio, 1899. *General Photograph Collection, MS 362: 101-0102, University of Texas at San Antonio Libraries Special Collections from the Institute of Texan Cultures.*

Above: Nathan and Anna Kallison in their harness and saddlery shop
at 124 South Flores Street, San Antonio, Texas, c.1906.

Above: President McKinley addresses a crowd at Alamo Plaza in front of San Antonio's Grand Opera House, May 4, 1901. *General Photograph Collection, MS 362: 075-0199, University of Texas at San Antonio Libraries Special Collections from the Institute of Texan Cultures.*

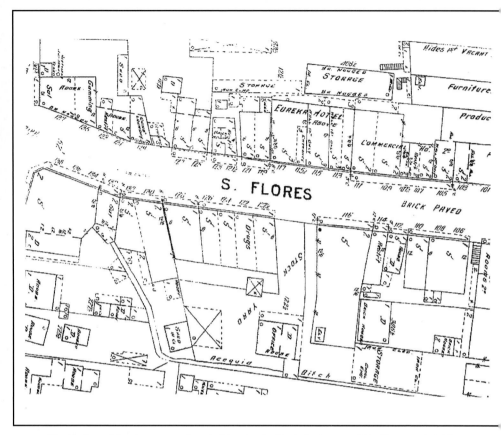

The Sanborn Map Company, founded in 1866 by D. A. Sanborn, originally created richly detailed maps to help insurers estimate fire insurance liabilities. Noting street names and addresses; building footprints, construction materials, and usage; property boundaries; and natural features, these maps have become a valuable historical record. The above 1904 Sanborn map shows that Nathan Kallison's harness and saddle shop at 124 South Flores—then a brick-paved street—conveniently adjoined a stockyard (Murin Stockyard) where his ranch and farm customers bought and sold livestock.

Above: President Theodore Roosevelt in San Antonio for a reunion with the Rough Riders, April 1905. *LOC 3b43780u.*

Right: Tibe and Perry Kallison with their dog Tippy going to the market, 1909.

Above: Morris Kallison's bar mitzvah portrait, 1909.

Opposite, top: The Southern Hotel where cattlemen, at the turn of the twentieth century, stayed for $2 a night when they came to San Antonio, 1912. *DRTL Aniol Collection 23-5.*

Opposite, bottom: Horse-drawn carriages still shared the streets with automobiles on Main Plaza in 1914 near the Frost National Bank and the San Fernando Cathedral. *General Photograph Collection, MS 362: 069-8765, University of Texas at San Antonio Libraries Special Collections from the Institute of Texan Cultures.*

Top: Boys washing buggies in San Antonio River c.1917, a job young Morris Kallison held to earn money. *General Photograph Collection, MS 362: 074-0141, University of Texas at San Antonio Libraries Special Collections from the Institute of Texan Cultures.*

Above left: Perry, Pauline, and Tibe Kallison (left to right) the day before Pauline left for college, 1916.

Above right: Nathan Kallison, c. 1915.

from business, civic, and political leaders challenged that arrangement and forced Jews to reevaluate the degree to which they were really welcome.[38]

The early twentieth-century wave of migration to the United States of nearly two million Eastern European Jews and other ethnic Europeans provoked a nativist backlash in America, leading to 1921 and 1924 laws limiting immigration. In the forefront was a resurgent Ku Klux Klan, which unleashed verbal attacks against Jews and Catholics almost as hateful as their physical, often murderous attacks against African Americans.

Fear of the Klan and its influence spread rapidly after the case of Leo Frank in Atlanta, in which a young Jewish businessman was accused, convicted, and lynched in 1915 for allegedly having raped and murdered his thirteen-year-old employee, Mary Phelan. The Frank affair became a national cause célèbre. Although evidence strongly indicated Frank's innocence, passions were aroused against him and the wider Jewish community. He was torn from his cell by a mob, beaten, and hanged from a tree for public viewing. The case received sensational national publicity, spurred in San Antonio by a *San Antonio Light* story in which the mayor of Atlanta declared that "the lynching of Frank was justifiable."[39] San Antonio's Jewish population held its collective breath.

Known as "Knights of the Invisible Empire," the Ku Klux Klan gatherings could be quite spectacular. In September 1923, San Antonio Klan No. 31, together with other South Texas chapters, staged an initiation at the San Antonio Speedway that sent shivers down the spines of many residents. After the formal "naturalization rites," held before a burning cross and altar, an airplane with an electric cross attached to its underside streaked across the night sky, circling and diving above the city.[40]

The most obvious anti-Semitism involved epithets and ridicule publicly aimed at Jews. Bernard Rapoport, whose Russian immigrant family started out as peddlers in the Little Jerusalem neighborhood on West Commerce Street, recalled years later how his father and others were treated: "When I was a child . . . people were much more obvious with their bigotry and prejudice. In the 1920s many people in Texas were quite suspicious of 'foreign elements' in the country. I can remember how people in San Antonio laughed at my father and his friends because of their thick accents. Those Jewish Russians sounded strange to native Texans, many of whom would make fun of them in a rude and disrespectful manner. Our family was so unmistakably Jewish that we were frequently the object of anti-Semitic remarks and jokes." As a boy, he endured the taunts of kids yelling "Jew Boy" at him.[41]

Rapoport, who became a founder of the American Income Life Insurance Company and also well known nationally as a major supporter of liberal causes, recounted that anti-Semitism was overt, with Jews, Catholics, and blacks serving as the favorite targets for San Antonio's sizeable chapter of the Ku Klux Klan. The Rapoports represented still a fourth group of Jews in San Antonio. In addition to those who became members of Temple Beth-El, Agudas Achim, and Rodfei Sholom, a small number were bound together by their idealistic and radical beliefs in an inevitable world revolution that would produce a utopian socialist or communist society—one in which all people would be treated equally. For these Jews, socialism became their secular religion.

As an immigrant from Dvinsk, Latvia in 1913, Bernard's father David Rapoport started out in San Antonio as a street peddler, selling cheap blankets and cheap clothes—ten cents down and ten cents a week in payments—to Mexican Americans on the dusty streets of the West Side. Later, he sold insurance door-to-door, but the senior Rapoport's passion and energy were committed to the Socialist Party of America. He led its small group of followers in San Antonio. The younger Rapoport, who died at age ninety-four in 2012, remembered his father standing on a soap box in Milam Square, across from Santa Rosa Hospital, "speaking fervently (with a Russian accent!) about the coming socialist utopia, waving his fist at the small groups of curious people who would gather around him." (David Rapoport and his circle became disillusioned with Soviet Communism as practiced by Joseph Stalin, but they would later join with liberals in the 1930s Depression to support strikes by workers and the candidacy of progressives such as then congressman and later mayor Maury Maverick.)[42]

Rabbi Samuel Marks, who served Temple Beth-El from 1897 to 1923, worked tirelessly to combat allegations by the Klan and other anti-Semitic groups. Jews could not be loyal American citizens, those groups charged, if they were dedicated to the Zionist goal of establishing Israel as a homeland for all Jews. The accusations disturbed Rabbi Marks's San Antonio congregation and those in the Orthodox community. American Jews, including those in San Antonio, were sharply divided about Zionism. Some even worried that support for Israel would endanger their own standing as Americans. In his 1906 Temple Beth-El sermon, reprinted in the *San Antonio Gazette*, Rabbi Marks stressed that American Jews did *not* want a homeland for themselves. "We sympathize with persecuted Jews in Russia and other countries, who always found hope in the biblical prediction . . . of an ancestral homeland in Palestine."[43]

Rabbi Marks's lectures about how Jews should seek to fit comfortably into American society addressed a question that early immigrants had faced from the moment they arrived in America. For Jewish immigrants from Germany in the mid-nineteenth century and those from Eastern Europe in the late nineteenth and early twentieth centuries, the quest was to honor fully their religious and ethnic heritage, while at the same time becoming fully integrated into and accepted in American society. On important religious, community, and national issues, Rabbi Marks constantly emphasized the unity and common purpose of Jews and Christians. When President Woodrow Wilson proclaimed Jewish Relief Day in 1916 to provide assistance to Jewish victims of European battles preceding America's entrance into World War I, Marks emphasized that "(t)he happy rela-

tions between Jews and non-Jews in San Antonio is a noticeable char-
acteristic of this city and cooperation from all creeds in the movement to relieve suffering humanity is expected."[44]

For those early Jews who came to Texas, the added goal was to be
accepted as "real" Texans—products of that state's unique culture. "In
newly settled diaspora regions (such as Texas) acculturation—blending in without being absorbed—became the key to survival and
Jewish continuity," explained Hollace Weiner, in *Lone Stars of David:
The Jews of Texas*.[45] "In fact, the primary job of Reform rabbis of that
day was to be the Jewish ambassador[s] to the gentile world," noted
Samuel Stahl, Rabbi Emeritus of San Antonio's Temple Beth-El.[46]

Yet Rabbi Marks was one of many Jewish leaders who also were
warning about a growing xenophobia and anti-Semitism that had
begun to arise in the United States after the turn-of-the-century wave
of immigrants flooded into the country. Demagogues and hatemon-
gers were raising fears that the newcomers were radicals or revolutionaries, that they would take jobs from established American citizens, or
simply that they were "foreign and strange," speaking different languages and bringing with them practices perceived as antithetical to
American culture. The rise of the second Klan in the 1920s fanned
those flames of intolerance. Without expressing it publicly, Nathan
and Anna were nervous.[47]

Fearing repercussions, many San Antonio Jews remained publicly
silent about the Ku Klux Klan and its activities. However, Temple
Beth-El member Rubin Jorrie, who owned a large downtown furniture store, lashed out against the Klan. Years later his son, Sam, also
condemned the Klan's institutionalized bigotry and their vicious
attacks against African Americans, Catholics, and Jews. Wearing
white, hooded robes, the Texas Klan responded by burning a cross in
front of Jorrie's store.[48] The flames that scorched the grass and lit the
night sky seared terror into the hearts and minds of the Jorrie children, forging memories that would haunt them for years.

Concern about the growing anti-Semitism in the 1920s led to
defensive lectures about how Jews should behave to avoid unfavor-

able stereotyping. A 1924 editorial in the *San Antonio Jewish Record*, aimed at its Reform audience, urged that Jews guard against "being loud in their speech" or "ostentatious in their dress." The editorial cautioned that Jews "not do things on Sunday that are contrary to the spirit of our Christian neighbors' Sabbath," and warned that it would be the "failings of the few [Jews] that the others have to suffer." Later, after a Jewish man was charged with a crime, an article in the *Texas Jewish Press*, the only Jewish community newspaper in San Antonio, warned that the "entire Jewish community is condemned by the unlawful actions of a single Jew. Therefore every one of us should be a living example of good Jews."[49]

The Kallisons learned that although the social mobility and acceptance of Jews like themselves seemed much broader in the Southwest than in the East or Chicago, social equality was by no means complete. Some private schools boasted quotas limiting the number of Jewish students. Premier social clubs, such as the San Antonio Club, generally did not admit Jews as members—nor did the Casino Club, the gathering place of German businessmen. Other San Antonio clubs and fraternal organizations were more welcoming. Rabbi Marks, for example, served for twenty-five years as the chaplain of San Antonio's Elks Lodge, where others of his congregation were members. Nathan Moses Washer, a Temple Beth-El president and an owner of Washer Brothers men and boys' clothing store, rose to the Masonic post of Most Worshipful Grand Master for the state of Texas.

Even within their own community, however, American Jews still discriminated against each other. Temple Beth-El's mostly German members, whose families had come to San Antonio a generation or two earlier, did not easily embrace Eastern European immigrants, new to American customs and struggling to earn a living. This prejudice also emerged within social organizations, including the fashionable downtown Harmony Club, a social extension of Temple Beth-El. Excluded from the prestigious social clubs of the city's affluent white Protestants, Jews of the Harmony Club held their own soirees. But the young women to be presented at their debutante balls came from the leading German—not Russian—Jewish families.[50] Similarly, Jews unable to join the San Antonio Country Club formed their own Hillcrest and North View Country Clubs for dining, tennis, and swimming. But those clubs were also informally "restricted" as well, with most of their members secular Jews or Reform Jews from Temple Beth-El, and only a few from the strictly Orthodox synagogues.

As Anna and Nathan Kallison sank roots more deeply into the community, with Anna's social skills they managed to straddle the cultural divide between the German Jewish pioneers and Russian newcomers, many of whom soon climbed the economic ladder to equal or surpass the first German arrivals. Despite the intra- and inter-faith discrimination and social snobbery in the community, Nathan was relatively indifferent to the social layers of class and origin that surrounded him. He had demonstrated the competence and confidence to deal not only with German Jews, but also with Texans from every walk of life, from the city's business leaders to the farmers and ranchers and cowboys who became his customers and friends. A pioneer individualist himself, he judged people on their merits. He had no personal aspirations for a life in "high society"—and he divorced himself from Temple politics. Instead, he focused on business, tending his growing empire with a firm hand. Anna, ever conscious of "status" and its benefits, emulated the dress, décor, and mores of her German neighbors, studying her surroundings carefully and moving accordingly.

The cross-pollination Nathan had envisioned between Kallison's store and Kallison Ranch also was bearing fruit. His rural enterprises thrived under his keen attention and adaptability to the needs of his customers and neighbors. As the scratchy notes of Al Jolson's "Swanee" poured out of Victrolas across the land, Kallison's businesses entered a decade of prosperity and expansion that marked the "Roaring Twenties" throughout America.

SIX

War, Peace, and Prosperity

IN 1914 NATHAN, ANNA, and their fellow Eastern European immigrants learned that the Old World could never be left behind. When Archduke Franz Ferdinand of the Austro-Hungarian Empire was assassinated on June 28, World War I ignited in Europe. The Kallisons' concerns were about Jewish victims left behind and caught in the crossfire, and the ever-present fear that murderous anti-Semitic scapegoating would follow another royal assassination. The following year, the war came closer to home: a German submarine sank the British ocean liner *Lusitania* on May 7, 1915, killing 128 American passengers. The United States prepared for war.

With the military buildup, the economy of San Antonio boomed. The US Army vastly expanded its presence in the city, with seventy thousand soldiers crowding into Fort Sam Houston and others streaming in for pilot training programs at newly-opened Kelly and Brooks Fields.[1]

Morris was torn: at twenty years old, he was the energetic, ambitious sales manager for his father's store, and he enjoyed a host of friends. But as he served the soldiers who came into Kallison's to buy supplies, he was swept up by their eagerness to get into the war, to serve their country. Anna, however, was terrified. What good did it do to leave European oppression for America, only to send her beloved firstborn back into mortal danger?[2]

After the United States declared war on Germany on April 6, 1917, however, Anna had no say in the matter. Morris Kallison was drafted into the United States Army. Assigned to the Fourth Field Artillery at Fort Sam Houston, he quickly rose to the rank of first sergeant. Always driven to work hard to achieve success, Morris took pride that he served in the artillery rather than in the supply corps, a non-combat role at the base. He learned how to handle heavy weapons and to teach others to use them—which bolstered his self-confidence and ambition. And he learned he could compete successfully with men from all backgrounds and regions of the country, with easterners and westerners, and with men who had the college degrees Morris lacked.

He never saw battle in the trenches of Europe, never fired the one hundred fifty-millimeter Howitzers and six-inch mortars of his expertise; he saw "combat" in the fort's mess hall. Assimilated as a teenager into San Antonio's diverse community, Morris was stung by the anti-Semitism he encountered in the army. Seared into his memory was one incident that would shape the way he dealt with bigotry and prejudice for the rest of his life. During a meal that left a bitter taste in his mouth forever, Morris asked a fellow soldier to pass the sugar across the table. The man repeatedly ignored Morris's polite requests, finally responding with a vicious, anti-Semitic epithet. Explosive when his own fuse was lit, Morris invited the soldier to step outside. With the strength and the skills he had honed while boxing as "Kid Morris," Kallison pummeled the bigot.[3]

Years later, Morris told his sons that the mess hall incident strengthened his resolve never to endure prejudice passively, as he had perceived his father had done. On the office wall behind his desk at Kallison's store, Morris had mounted a large stuffed American bald eagle that for him held symbolic importance. "When I was a kid and was sweeping out the store," Morris explained, "I used to see how those establishment folks were mean to my father. One day I saw an eagle up in the sky and I vowed that if I ever got rich, I was going to fly around over those people just like that eagle." The interviewer who quoted him only alluded to the action Morris said "the eagle might take while aloft."[4]

Forty-three-year-old Nathan Kallison was too old to serve in the military during the war, but he and Anna participated when the small Jewish community of San Antonio quickly organized itself to support the troops. Working with the Jewish Welfare Board, a national federation of local agencies and organizations, volunteers opened centers at Kelly Field in south San Antonio and in the basement of the Gunter office building downtown "for the purpose of providing recreation and entertainment for the soldiers irrespective of creed or race."[5] Local Jewish organizations also sponsored weekend dances for soldiers at Harmony Club Hall in downtown San Antonio.[6] Feeling empathy for young men separated from their families, the Kallisons welcomed soldiers to their home on San Pedro Avenue and to their ranch—especially during holidays. Many of the young troops, enchanted by nineteen-year-old Pauline, came under Anna's scrutinizing eye.

In 1918, Anna also served on the "committee on religious observance," as the three Jewish congregations mounted an ambitious and highly coordinated program to ensure that every Jewish soldier stationed at a base in San Antonio would be welcomed to a place of worship for the High Holy Days and afterwards to break the traditional fast at a private home at the conclusion of Yom Kippur—the most sacred of Jewish holidays.[7] The joy of the Jewish New Year 5679 was dampened almost immediately, however, as the worldwide influenza epidemic reached San Antonio. The first case of "Spanish flu" in Texas was reported on September 23 1918—just one week after Yom Kippur. On October 2, a military edict quarantined area bases. Shortly afterwards, the epidemic swept through the city. The mayor, assisted by the military leaders, "decreed that all churches, schools, theaters and public places of amusement be forthwith closed and the people requested to become recluses until danger had passed." Military bases were particularly hard hit, and scores of young men were sent to the hospital gravely ill. Anna worried about her children—especially Morris, who was living in close quarters with other soldiers at Fort Sam Houston.[8] When the pandemic ended the following year, fifty million people had perished worldwide—more than five times the number (nine million) who would be killed in World War I. The city-wide ban was lifted just before the Christmas holiday. Although the Kallisons escaped the flu, about twenty-five million Americans contracted the disease and an estimated 550,000 died as a result.[9]

For the most part, San Antonians of all faiths joined in efforts to support the war: they bought war bonds and War Savings Stamps, supported the Red Cross, conserved food by planting war gardens and limiting the use of fat and sugar, foregoing wheat products on Mondays and Wednesdays, beef on Tuesdays, and pork on Thursdays and Saturdays.[10] An exception to the city's patriotic unity during the war was its shameful treatment of San Antonio's citizens of German heritage, stirred by government propaganda portraying German soldiers as barbarous Huns. Anna and Nathan Kallison, who themselves had known humiliating discrimination, were appalled as the war stirred a frenzy of xenophobia and anti-German prejudice. Some of the vitriol was directed at their longtime customers and friends, the San Antonio area's proud and successful German American ranchers, farmers, and businessmen whose generations-long patriotism and loyalty were beyond question. Businesses owned by German Americans were boycotted; slurs were aimed at adults and children alike. King William Street, home of the most successful families of German heritage, was called "Sauerkraut Bend." During the war, even the street's name was changed from King William (the name of the German Kaiser) to Pershing Street, after US General of the Army George Pershing.[11]

After four years of bloody trench warfare in Europe, the "Great War" came to a close on the morning of November 11, 1918, as the Allies signed an armistice with Germany.[12] Nathan, Anna, and fifteen-year-old Perry witnessed the city's jubilation, its celebrations spilling out into the streets. Pauline, a junior at the University of Chicago, joined Tibe, a precocious University of Texas freshman who would turn sixteen the next day, as they congregated with hundreds of fellow students in a huge outdoor gathering at the center of their Austin campus to celebrate the Allied victory.

At that time only about 7 percent of women in America attended college. Many parents scorned education for their daughters, believing that a woman's first priority should be as homemaker for husband and children. But Nathan and Anna thought Pauline and Tibe were especially bright and talented and deserving of a college education. The sisters, four years apart, were best friends, yet they were a study in contrasts. As an adult Pauline was tall, glamorous, and fashionable. After World War I, her modest ankle-length skirts gave way to the short skirts and high heels of the twenties. On one of her frequent trips to Chicago, Pauline bobbed her hair, drawing attention and comments at the dance parties when she returned to San Antonio. She was lighthearted, carefree, always eager for an adventure. She loved athletics, with an aptitude and appetite for golf and other sports. With her many friends, Pauline went on outings to watch—and wager on—horse races, and made long trips to gambling casinos. Drawn by the excitement of the big city and her mother's fondness for the Greenblatt family, Pauline attended the University of Chicago upon her graduation from Main Avenue High School in 1916. After her freshman year, however, she transferred to the University of Texas at Austin where she studied for two years, dropping out in 1919 before earning a degree.

Tibe, a serious student, decided from an early age that she would go to college and learn the skills to become a professional social worker. Like her mother Anna, Tibe was steel-willed and determined to get her way, and was already creating a formidable presence locally and at the university. Just as her name Bertha became "Bertie," then "Birdie," and then "Tibe," this bright child of Nathan and Anna's would transform her own personality more than once, adopting different personae as new challenges and opportunities arose in her life.

Tibe Kallison also embraced the challenges of being one of the youngest students on the Austin campus.[13] Academically advanced but socially shy, she found that the university exposed her to a wider world, especially through her roommates, two outgoing, self-reliant girls from rural Texas, who became her best friends. Both of them towered over the petite sixteen-year-old. The girls took her on visits to their ranch homes and introduced the San Antonio native to life beyond her sheltered upbringing under Anna's strict and watchful eye. Reminiscing later about her new friends, Tibe said: "I got to know girls in my dorms—country girls who were tall and robust. They had worked all their lives and had lots of energy. Their backgrounds were so different from mine. They were ambitious, serious students. They wanted to make something of their own lives. I had never known women like that before. I admired them."[14] When American women finally won the right to vote in 1920, both Kallison sisters cheered on the long-fought victory for women's rights.[15]

After receiving her bachelor of arts degree in 1922 at nineteen, Tibe headed to graduate school at the University of Chicago, where she continued to gain experience and expand her social views. She interned at Jane Addams's Hull House, and her thesis included research on nutrition for expectant mothers. Renowned for its work in helping poor immigrants become successful citizens in America, Hull House was on the West Side of Chicago, in the same Jewish ghetto where, thirty years earlier, her father Nathan had arrived as a seventeen-year-old immigrant.

With his older sisters away at college, Perry enjoyed his parents' attention at home.[16] Like his father, he cherished the family's ranch, which became his favorite retreat. He explored the fields and woods on horseback with his father and camped out with friends on the Hill Country land. On Sunday mornings, as soon as he was able to drive, Perry would drive Nathan to the ranch, a ritual for the two and a bond between them that would last for decades and would strengthen their love for cattle and the land. Like Pauline, Perry was outgoing and witty. In the 1920 Main Avenue High School yearbook, he is pictured sitting cross-legged in a small washtub, fully dressed, wearing a shirt and necktie. He holds a garden hose above his head, as if about to take a shower. His list of "favorites" printed below the picture:

"Scenery: With somebody fifty miles from nowhere with a blowout song. Song: 'Minnie Shimmy for Me.' Book: Telephone Book. Pastime: Joy Riding. Trait in man: Ambition. Trait in woman: Common sense."

After graduating from Main Avenue High School in 1920, Perry followed his sister Tibe to the University of Texas.[17] A "C" student as a business major, he left the university a year later and returned home, deciding that he would rather work with his father and brother in the store—and on the Kallison Ranch, where he rode horses and could get involved with the ranch's new experiments in modern agriculture. His interest in economics was practical, spurred by the postwar business boom in San Antonio.

In the years bounded by the end of the Great War and the onset of the Great Depression, America was experiencing astounding growth and prosperity. After a brief recession while the country retooled from war, construction boomed. Demand for automobiles and other consumer goods soared. Marked by individualism, materialism, and experimentation in fashion, literature, music, and the arts, the Roaring Twenties saw new freedoms and new strictures: women got the right to vote, and prohibition against alcohol became the law of the land. Jazz, dance marathons, bathtub gin, "talking" pictures, and gangland crime characterized an era that saw a human life expectancy of about fifty-four years, average annual earnings of $1,236, and paved roads totaling 387,000 miles country-wide.[18]

As the decade wore on, the continued dynamic growth of the military, tourism, and a surging construction industry fueled the San Antonio economy, providing dazzling new opportunities for businessmen bold enough to seize them. Nathan still specialized in farm and ranch supplies, but urged by Morris and Perry, he expanded to meet the wider needs of city dwellers as well. After adding new lines of merchandise in the 1920s, Nathan ambitiously renamed his business "Kallison's Department Store."[19]

Calling his business a "department store" was more than just an affectation. After the war, Nathan Kallison recognized that the nation and state were changing rapidly in ways that shrewd businessmen would have to accommodate. His sense of future trends again held true. They would keep up with the times to be successful. Morris and Perry, young men of the times, were his scouts. Nathan knew that the Roaring Twenties represented far more than just the stereotypical high life, patrons sipping bootleg whiskey in speakeasies, "flappers" dancing the Charleston. Nathan enjoyed watching his daughters dancing the new dances in their stylish dresses, but he sensed a more fundamental change in America—a possibly precarious shift in values. With the country on a joyful roll, celebrating life and driving the stock market to dizzying heights, he figured that the Kallison role was to balance new ideas with the practicalities of Texas farm and ranch existence.

Burnishing their new department store image to entice middle and upper-class city dwellers whose postwar preoccupation with graceful living had swept the nation, Nathan added new items of merchandise. Now he sought to compete also with the city's finest hardware stores, Toepperwein Hardware and Sterling Hardware. Nathan stocked the fancy new Silent Rich lawnmower. A 1922 advertisement, with Kallison's as a cosponsor, touted how this new push-mower would help produce lawns as magnificent as those gracing the fanciest English estates. According to the ad, the Silent Rich mower was "durably constructed of the finest materials (no cast iron), scientifically designed to cut lawns three to four times faster, to cut closer without missing a blade of grass, and to operate well-nigh noiselessly." And the eighteen-inch model for average-size lawns could be purchased for just $23—a bargain for a mower that cut "keen as a razor."[20]

Nathan agreed with President Calvin Coolidge's famous 1925 exclamation that "the business of America is business." Understanding Coolidge's message as one of praise for a hardworking American society, Nathan and his sons embraced the challenge. As the store expanded, its appearance reflected its balancing act between old and new. Kallison's still looked more like a big old country store than the increasingly popular, sleekly organized modern department stores. New product lines were squeezed into whatever vacant spaces could be found, often next to very different kinds of merchandise. In the men's work clothes section, for example, customers could hear the nearby peeps and smell the baby chicks. The result was by no means tidy, but in that unique atmosphere, Nathan made his country customers feel at home—and city neighbors stopped by for bargains, smiling at the store's folksy eccentricity.

Again urged by Morris, Nathan began advertising in the local newspapers, to highlight his wider range of goods. In the *San Antonio Light* on August 8, 1925, Kallison's promoted a sale on "barb wire, corrugated iron, and fencing," and ran a separate announcement for "bathtubs, toilets, and sinks at one-third discounts."[21]

Aiming for profit from the booming construction business, Kallison's also offered "Two Carloads" of 23-gauge corrugated iron priced "for quick sale" at $4.95 per square.[22] His newspaper promotion for "Old Lumber" was headlined "Must be Removed at Once."[23]

After his discharge from the army, Morris resumed work at Kallison's Department Store as a manager, now assuming more responsibilities. Nathan approved of his son's love of merchandising and his nose for profit. At twenty-four, Morris was eager, self-confident, and ready to start a family of his own. On January 21, 1920, after a brief engagement, Morris "made a good marriage," which pleased Anna to no end. His bride was the strikingly attractive Ruth Dubinski, the nineteen-year-old daughter of Benjamin and Leah Dubinski, who had emigrated from Russia to St. Louis before settling in San Antonio. Ruth's father Ben, a masterful storyteller, was also an ingenious inventor whose electrical innovations included a coin-operated phonograph and an electric clock. After he developed what he called the reliable battery, Ben Dubinski manufactured and sold batteries from his Standard Electric Company on San Pedro Avenue. Ruth Dubinski Kallison, a lovely young woman with a soft manner and a thirst for knowledge, later would recollect her happy, carefree days growing up in San Antonio in the early years of the twentieth century: "Walking from Marshall Street School to San Pedro Springs for picnics by the lake and drinking the fresh spring water; riding the trolley with its five-cent fare to Brackenridge Park to see the deer; the special treat of trips to Harnisch and Baer ice cream parlor; the taste of luscious melted-cheese sandwiches at Schultze's outdoor beer garden on Alamo Street . . . "[24] Ruth and her friends also enjoyed walking to Electric Park to watch its live vaudeville acts and practice their rifle skills at the shooting galleries. Her favorite sport was basketball, she said, which the girls (wearing bloomers) played fiercely in the school gym. And the boys she most admired were the debaters, rather than football players. The boys admired Ruth, too, not only for her beauty but for her intelligence and the kindnesses she offered to her classmates.

The Dubinskis were also members of Temple Beth-El, where Ruth had been confirmed in 1915. Rabbi Marks, who officiated at the ceremony, implored the young graduates "to be a blessing to your faith, a blessing to your country, and a blessing to humanity . . . " and to "carry the message of the modern Jew: one truth, one God, one brotherhood. . . . Be true to every American ideal. Be loyal to every American cause."

The formal Dubinski-Kallison wedding was held on January 21, 1920, in the venerable downtown Menger Hotel. Filled with the drive to succeed in business, Morris promised his bride that someday he would be a millionaire. The young couple honeymooned in St. Louis and returned to set up housekeeping in the Laurel Apartments, 520 East Laurel Street. After their first child, James Morris Kallison (always known as Jimmy), was born in 1922, Nathan bought the young couple a small wood-frame home at 600 Poplar Street, around the corner from his and Anna's big home on San Pedro Avenue.

Just as Kallison's store was launching a major expansion, the infamous 1921 flash flood struck the city after midnight on September 7, 1921, with torrential rains overflowing the San Antonio River, rushing through residential neighborhoods to the north, then flooding the entire central business district. San Antonio was devastated by the worst flood in its history. Tragically, fifty-one Mexican Americans, including infants and the elderly, were drowned on the west side as the torrents of water swept through their crowded low-lying neighborhoods.[25] Millions of dollars of merchandise were ruined or lost as waters nine feet deep swirled through Houston and Commerce Streets, Main Avenue, and other business arteries. The floodwater virtually destroyed the new downtown synagogue that the Orthodox Agudas Achim had just erected at the corner of Main and Quincy, forcing the congregation to start anew, meeting in temporary quarters.[26]

Although the Kallisons also suffered significant losses, they cleared the debris quickly and reopened the store. Nathan remained optimistic about growth. In 1924, with his sons at his side, he bought the building adjoining the store on South Flores, and constructed a $10,000 addition.[27] Watching real estate developers transform downtown San Antonio around him, Nathan decided that he too wanted to make a significant contribution to growth and revival in the construction boom that was sweeping through San Antonio. With careful planning, he first purchased most of the west side of the 100 block of South Flores across the street from Kallison's store, tore down the ramshackle nineteenth-century buildings on the site—including the famed Black Swan Saloon—and commissioned architect Harvey Smith to design a commercial building for him. "Make it work for me," he instructed. "And make it beautiful, too."

The result was called "the Kallison Block," an extraordinary two-story brick structure with a unique artistic design that featured elements of historic Spanish architecture, including an elaborately decorated "mission style window" modeled after those in the seventeenth-century Spanish missions built by the first settlers in San Antonio. *American Builder* magazine, in its March 1926 issue, praised the building as the first commercial structure in San Antonio to incorporate historic Spanish architecture in its design. "Probably no building has created so much comment in building circles throughout the Southwest as has the new Kallison Block," the magazine declared.[28] Now with the new building and its twenty-six tenants, Nathan Kallison became a landlord.[29] And with the wide publicity attending the construction of a prominent urban building, Nathan and his family joined the process by which America was becoming a more cosmopolitan society.

The Roaring Twenties brought about more than just economic good times. Women were liberated, exposing their knees and earning voting rights. Silent movies and vaudeville acts were new additions to popular entertainment. And in cigarette smoke-filled "jazz clubs," where brown paper bags concealed bottles of bootleg or homemade liquor, a fierce battle over Prohibition dominated Texas politics for more than a decade. It was part of a larger clash between the urbanization of America and the old values of a rural white Protestant society, which felt threatened by change and sought to enforce its own moral standards. Spearheaded by Carrie Nation and the Women's Christian Temperance Union, the 1919 law favored morality and forbade the manufacture, sale, or transportation of alcoholic beverages. At the same time his achievements were soaring, Nathan felt caught in the middle—between his "dry" rural customers and those in the city who vehemently opposed Prohibition. Drinking alcoholic beverages in moderation didn't violate his own moral standards. Personally, he said, "for its medicinal value," he drank one shot of whiskey to relax before dinner. The last thing Nathan wanted was to become involved in the controversy over Prohibition.

To his great surprise and mortification, on March 26, 1927, federal alcohol agents raided the Bottlers Supply Company— a tenant in the new Kallison Block—seizing merchandise which they claimed could be used to make beer and alcohol. Nathan, his son Morris, and Bottlers Supply merchant H. L. Worman were charged with violating the Volstead Act, the federal law that also forbade the advertisement of alcohol or the manufacture or advertisement of equipment used to make and distribute it. The federal indictment charged that the three men had "in their possession, sold and advertised for sale utensils designed to make intoxicating liquor . . . to wit: five copper stills, four crates of empty bottles, large can of seals and corks, one carton of caps and sealing machine, two ounces of flavoring extract." A second count alleged that they had sold one still, twenty-five feet of copper pipe, two ounces of flavoring extract, a fifteen-gallon whiskey keg, thirty-six one-gallon bottles, a one-gallon copper measure, and one funnel. A third count charged that they had openly advertised these items for sale by displaying them in a store window. The Kallisons and Worman as defendants testified that the equipment was not offered for the manufacture of liquor, but for "legitimate use." A federal jury thought otherwise. Morris Kallison was found guilty of one count of possession, and Worman was sent to jail for six months after he was unable to pay a $750 fine. Nathan Kallison, with his stellar reputation of honesty and rectitude, was found innocent of all charges.[30]

When the verdict was reported on the front page of the *San Antonio Light* under a six-column headline: "Fine San Antonio Merchants on Rum Count: Charge Sale of Illegal Utensils," Nathan was furious at his elder son for joining in the widespread practice of local merchants who were flouting the unpopular law.[31] Citing the Kallison case as a warning, US Attorney John Hartman signaled a crackdown against San Antonio businesses violating the Volstead Act. "If they do not desist immediately," Hartman declared, "merchants who sell equipment that can be used in the manufacture of liquor, including home brew, are due for prosecution in the US Federal Court." The crackdown drew jeers from other downtown merchants, who argued that the government could not prove that the equipment was not being sold to make root beer and soda water, rather than home brew or "moonshine" whiskey and beer.[32] Critics of the Prohibition law questioned why the federal government had focused on merchants helping local residents make a little "home brew," rather than going after major bootleggers who were importing thousands of cases of whiskey from overseas, including shiploads arriving in ports along the Gulf of Mexico such as Galveston and Corpus Christi, as well as truckloads moving over the Texas border from Mexico.

In one notorious incident, Federal Agent Charles A. Wood and his partner Agent Stafford Bennet were gunned down in 1921 as they confronted a bootlegging gang at the Sherman Ranch in El Paso, near the Mexican border. Working from an office in San Antonio, Agent Wood had headed federal enforcement efforts in sixty-two Texas counties. A native of Abilene, he was known as "Honest Arch" Wood, a reference to his integrity in a federal force that was riddled with agents who had been corrupted by the mobs.

From its inception in 1919 until its repeal in 1933, the country was bitterly divided over Prohibition. Hundreds of ministers from fundamentalist churches advocated and supported the Women's Christian Temperance Union and the law, as did the Ku Klux Klan. Appealing to fundamentalist congregants who supported Prohibition (a recruiting target for the Klan), the Klan charged that intoxicating beverages would stimulate more crime by Negroes against whites, particularly attacks on white women. The Klan's hateful appeal to racial prejudice was effective enough in the early 1920s to give Klan members and their endorsed candidates control of the Texas state legislature as well as of many local governments.[33]

Opposing the Prohibition laws, Temple Beth-El Rabbi Marks wrote an article titled "The Jews Objections," published in the *San Antonio Light*, in which he called Prohibition "unjust, unwise, and morally pernicious." In his list of reasons he cited: "Prohibition caus-es and programs are usually of a religious character and are led by Christian clergymen. They are 'given the atmosphere of a revival campaign' beginning and ending in prayer," which he saw as an abuse. "[A]nd the abuse of religion and prayer are worse than the abuse of liquor. The movement is often a cloak for intemperance in argument and invective, and can array citizens in bitter conflict." Marks's article, especially the way he appeared to speak for all Jews, infuriated many in Beth-El's congregation—including those who may have shared his views. The Temple leadership chastised Marks for "his publication of the anti-Prohibition article . . . without first having obtained approval of the president and board of trustees," believing that this act was "hurtful to the welfare and advancement of Congregation Beth-El."[34] They wanted their rabbi to philosophize about religion—and to stay out of divisive politics and social issues.

In San Antonio, the strongest protests against Prohibition came from the large Mexican American and German American communities—the Germans not only loved to drink beer, but were heralded as brew masters who had founded many of the country's leading breweries, including Anheuser Busch, Blatz, Pabst, Schlitz, Spoetz, and Heileman. San Antonio's earliest and most prominent breweries, which included the popular Pearl and Lone Star brands, were founded by German Americans.

By 1927, when the Kallisons were arrested for selling utensils for making home brew, the political steam had gone out of the Prohibition Movement. William Randolph Hearst, owner of the country's largest newspaper chain and an early proponent of the law, had changed his mind. Along with a majority of other Americans, Hearst decided that Prohibition was not only extremely unpopular, but actually promoted lawlessness and the rise of criminal syndicates that dominated bootlegging, including the infamous Chicago mob headed by Alphonse "Scarface" Capone. Hearst's *San Antonio Light* newspaper began running editorials opposing Prohibition, calling it a stimulus to violent crime and other illegal activities. Within minutes of the end of Prohibition in Texas at midnight on September 15, 1933, it was reported that one hundred trucks and twenty-five railroad cars loaded with beer rolled out of the grounds of the Pearl Brewery.[35]

As the Kallison children grew into young adults in the 1920s, the entire family engaged itself in Jewish community affairs, driven by the concept of *tikkun olam*—the obligation to "repair the world."[36]

Anna Kallison was involved with the San Antonio chapter of the National Council of Jewish Women (NCJW), serving a term as president. Founded in Chicago in 1893 by Hannah G. Solomon, NCJW dedicated itself from the very beginning to meeting the needs of women, children, and families. Pioneers in the settlement house movement, members worked with Jane Addams's Hull House in Chicago.

In the decades that followed, NCJW members committed time and resources to social justice causes throughout the United States. They advocated for children in court proceedings, sponsored adult study groups to foster learning and leadership, established penny lunch programs in public schools, and developed school health programs and free health dispensaries. Among many other accomplishments, NCJW also worked to bring health care to rural communities through the Farm & Rural Work Program.[37]

With "a faith in the future and a belief in action," Anna encouraged Tibe, Pauline, and Morris's wife Ruth to join the organization whose causes she believed in.[38] At their annual meeting in 1924, Tibe Kallison, who had returned home after her stint in graduate school at the University of Chicago, delivered the membership report, announcing growth of the San Antonio chapter to three hundred fifty members, and the national organization to fifty thousand.[39]

Nathan Kallison contributed to Temple Beth-El's effort to build a landmark new synagogue, and while Perry was a student at the University of Texas, he had contributed to University Menorah Society, a nationwide campus organization promoting Jewish values.

The most profound religious influence on the Kallison children had been the arrival in San Antonio in 1923 of Ephraim Frisch, the new rabbi for Temple Beth-El, and his wife Ruth. For his time, Ephraim Frisch was the rare outspoken clergyman in San Antonio, a courageous leader "who stirred San Antonio's younger generation to strive for a better world."[40] In *Jewish Stars of Texas*, author Hollace Weiner described Frisch as "a rabbi who preached ethics rather than piety, a progressive who backed unions over industry, and a visionary who foresaw the rise of fascism in Europe." Frisch first battled against the effort to ban the teaching of evolution in schools. That issue was burning as he arrived in Texas, when the governor of Texas, at the urging of religious fundamentalists, had tried to block all textbooks that mentioned Darwin's theory of evolution. Frisch fought for civil rights and economic justice for blacks and Mexican Americans, stood up against anti-Semitism, and took on the Ku Klux Klan in particular. In his advocacy, Frisch walked right into the middle of fierce conflict in Texas between proponents of a progressive, liberal society, and religious fundamentalists and traditionalists who resisted change. He persuaded—or some say forced—his congregation and the city to confront those uncomfortable issues. He influenced others, including Perry and Tibe Kallison, to take up the wider causes of social justice.

Frisch's equally influential wife Ruth was the daughter of the legendary Rabbi Henry Cohen of Galveston, whose impact as a scholar and humanitarian reached throughout Texas and beyond. Although Ruth Frisch shared her husband Ephraim's liberal views, she led quietly and diplomatically while he relished a role as the outspoken activist for liberal causes. A fountain of enthusiasm and diverse interests, Ruth Cohen Frisch inspired and energized the Temple's teenagers and young adults—especially Nathan's two youngest, Tibe and Perry, both of whom were drawn into the Frisch orbit.

At the Frisches' urging, Tibe Kallison became a religious school teacher at Temple Beth-El, and also worked as a substitute teacher in San Antonio public schools. The diminutive Tibe's interests ran to literature, theater, and progressive politics. And in all those endeavors, she was greatly influenced by Ruth Frisch, who became her closest friend and mentor.

When Mrs. Frisch organized the Temple League in 1925 to encourage San Antonio's teenage and young adult Jews to involve themselves in cultural and civic activities, Tibe Kallison was elected as the League's first chairman.[41] Intent on introducing their young congregants both to classical culture and to the culture of a modern liberal society, the Temple League sponsored amateur plays, vaudeville productions, instrumental musical recitals, debates, and book reviews, as well as socials at the Frisches' home and dances at the temple.[42] And with Tibe Kallison, they had an enthusiastic leader, eager to learn and become part of a larger world.

Eleven months younger than Tibe, Perry Kallison became a Frisch protégé as well. The youngest Kallison enthusiastically joined the Temple League Players, a theatrical group organized by Ruth Frisch. For a young man with near-deafness in one ear, the result of a childhood illness, theater became a transforming experience. His high school debating expertise had given him confidence to perform in public; now he was thrilled to be able to create what he called "another man" on stage. In 1925, Perry costarred in the "Lost Silk Hat," a one-act play. The next season he turned comedian in a production of "Duky," a recent Broadway sensation. Both plays performed to sold-out audiences at the Alamo Heights High School auditorium, and Perry, generally a soft-spoken, thoughtful young man, metamorphosed under the stage lights into a larger-than-life persona with comic timing and a knack for impersonation. Perry also began to shine offstage. As scoutmaster for the Temple's Boy Scout Troop No. 32, he assumed a post that allowed him to take dozens of youngsters for hikes and campouts in the countryside, often to the Kallison Ranch. Along the way, he gained the skills and fitness demanded by scouting, and reinforced the values of "duty to God and my country" that would inform the rest of his life. Guided by Rabbi Frisch and his wife Ruth, young Perry quickly rose to leadership at Temple Beth-El, proudly serving as an usher at the 1927 opening of the Temple's new building at Ashby and Belknap Streets.

The new Temple Beth-El, with its domed roof made of Spanish tile, was still another visible symbol of San Antonio's growth and prosperity during the 1920s, as the construction industry raced to keep up with the demand in San Antonio for fancier, taller, and more imposing new buildings. In 1926, the Aztec and Majestic theaters opened, each with an ornate interior and ceiling lights imitating stars in a night sky. Visitors to downtown San Antonio in 1927 looked up with fascination at the animated sign on the roof of Joske's Department Store—an electric cowboy twirling a lasso and roping a steer. The twenty-one-story Milam Building completed the same year became the largest concrete building in the nation. In 1928, construction began for the thirty-one-story Smith Young Tower, and the city held its first international exposition and livestock show. In 1929 the Alamo National Bank building and Nix Hospital were completed and opened.

Amidst the optimism, prosperity, and skyrocketing stock market, no one could have imagined—or predicted—that after the completion of the Alamo National and Nix Hospital, major construction in downtown San Antonio would cease for the next thirty years. The 1920s buoyancy abruptly ended when the stock market crashed in October. Fortunes were lost, banks failed, meager savings vanished. October 29, 1929, is now remembered as the start of the most devastating depression in America's history.[43] In San Antonio, the Kallisons tightened their belts.

SEVEN

The Great Depression

THE STOCK MARKET CRASHED on "Black Tuesday," October 29, 1929, just after Texas had come through a stunning decade of rising prosperity. Its citizenry had grown by nearly 25 percent, to a total of 5,824,000. A bumper crop of cotton had been sold, and the twin economic pillars of agriculture and oil were thriving. On the Edwards Plateau, home of the Kallison Ranch, the cattle and goat industry established Texas as the nation's leading producer of hides, mohair, and Angora wool. The Great Depression took San Antonio and its optimistic citizens by surprise.

Nathan grew concerned and apprehensive as he read about the unbelievable losses of homes, fortunes, and everyday jobs that were causing such great suffering in state after state. Yet the growing crisis seemed far away from his hardworking family's success in San Antonio. Even a full year after the stock market crash, the *San Antonio Express-News* was still reporting that the local economy was sound. Late into 1930, news stories debunked "talk of depression and money shortage" and bragged that San Antonio was "one of five cities in the country in which men of billions were looking to invest their money." Economists, the newspaper editors declared, were predicting "better times in store for Texas and the rest of the United States."[1]

The reality of hard times, however, soon could not be ignored. When the Depression finally came down hard on San Antonio, Nathan and his sons Morris and Perry watched from their store in dismay as thousands of destitute citizens stood in long lines across Main Avenue in front of the Bexar County courthouse, waiting to receive welfare payments of $3 per family or small amounts of surplus farm products. The San Antonio schools were forced to lay off several hundred teachers and to pay the remaining faculty with scrip in denominations of twenty-five cents, fifty cents, and one dollar— IOUs that might never be redeemed.[2]

Homelessness followed joblessness as the local economy crumbled. Shantytowns called "Hoovervilles" sprang up on the outskirts of San Antonio and in thousands of other cities and towns across the nation. Built by homeless squatters, they were nicknamed derisively for President Herbert Hoover, whom many blamed for the crisis and its attendant miseries. Compounding wretchedness for its own poor, San Antonio was the only major city in the United States that refused to provide aid to out-of-work and starving citizens. Although the Bexar County government did distribute relief funds and food supplied by the state and federal governments, the Bexar County political machine allocated some of those funds to feather its own nest, using relief money to bloat its payroll to 252 patronage employees. In addition, aid came with strings attached. As Bexar County Relief Commissioner Tex Alsbury testified before an investigating committee: "We told them [social workers] if they wanted more money to give out, that they better vote with us, and we got them to get the precinct vote. The people were out of work and money. They were hungry and they lined up to vote."[3] By July 1934, there were 14,484 families on relief.[4]

Especially hard hit was San Antonio's mostly poor Mexican American population, second largest in the country after Los Angeles—83,000 of the city's 230,000 residents in 1930. City agencies generally denied relief to Mexicans. What aid these citizens did receive came from a few middle- and upper-class Mexican organizations, and from Our Lady of Guadalupe Church, headed by Father Carmelo Tranchese, a charismatic priest and champion of the poor.[5]

Nathan and Anna listened to the nightly news on their living room console radio. The "better times in store" never came. The Depression was dealing an enormous blow to the nation's economy and to millions of its citizens, whether they lived in cities, small towns, or on farms and ranches. Investments disappeared. Although stories about New York stock brokers and bankers leaping to their deaths out of skyscraper windows are more myth than fact, statistics show that the suicide rate in 1929 was almost double the rate at the start of the decade.[6] The 1929 crash had erased 90 percent of the value of all stocks, wiping out the lifetime savings of millions of people and devastating American industry and business. The size of the nation's economy, measured by the US gross domestic product, declined almost 50 percent between 1929 and 1933, falling from $104 billion to $56 billion. Unemployment soared from just over 3 percent in 1929 to 25 percent in 1933, leaving thirteen million workers—one-fourth of the labor force—without jobs. Another 25 percent of American workers saw their salaries cut and working hours reduced.

The Great Depression's cost on human lives was incalculable. Individual family living standards plummeted. Scholars estimated that one half of all American children during the Great Depression "did not have adequate food, shelter, or medical care," with many suffering from rickets, a disease caused by severe malnutrition.

"To save money, families neglected medical and dental care. Many families sought to cope by planting gardens, canning food, buying used [stale] bread, and using cardboard and cotton for shoe soles," according to an article in *Digital History*. "Despite a steep decline in food prices, many families did without milk or meat. In New York City, milk consumption declined a million gallons a day."[7] By the 1930s, thousands of schools operated on reduced hours or closed entirely—with three million children leaving school, two hundred thousand of whom fled home and started riding the rails.

Nearly one half of the nation's twenty-five thousand banks failed and shuttered their doors. Bank closures erased the savings of Americans, their downfall hastened by a "run on the banks," with customers withdrawing deposits and stuffing cash under mattresses at home. The devastation of the Great Depression did not spare any area of the economy or sector of the country. Wreckage of the industrial economy was especially evident in the great manufacturing centers. One half of all workers in Cleveland, Ohio, were jobless; in Toledo, four out of five workers were without jobs as industries shut down or cut their production.

Protests and violence flared in different parts of the country as union workers fought for higher wages and the unemployed begged for jobs. In 1932 a so-called "Bonus Army," forty thousand strong, mostly composed of World War I veterans and their families, marched on Washington, DC, and camped across the Anacostia River from the Capitol. The unemployed veterans demanded that service benefits due to them in 1945 should be delivered in 1932. Congress rejected their demand. President Herbert Hoover eventually ordered the US Army to destroy their jerry-built shanties and to run the protestors out of town.

For farm and ranch families from coast to coast, the Great Depression had become an unmitigated disaster. Most painful for Nathan Kallison was to hear the tragic, heart-rending experiences and travails of the ranchers, farmers, and farm workers—loyal customers, neighbors, and friends throughout South and Central Texas—who had confided in him, knowing they would find a sympathetic ear.

The state's wheat prices tumbled from $2.04 to $0.33 a bushel, cotton from $0.17 to less than $0.06 a pound. Thousands of farmers lost their farms and had no place to go. Their plight was exacerbated by their Roaring Twenties over-exuberance, when too many farmers and ranchers had speculated on "making a killing" by overplanting their land and crowding too many livestock on too few acres. This practice then exposed their land to the full fury of the devastating drought and dust storms that swept Midwestern and Southwestern states in the 1930s, destroying 100 million acres of farmland.[8] The

"Dust Bowl," as the area became known, sent more than two hundred thousand desperate families to California, where they had heard they could use their farm knowledge to find work harvesting abundant crops. Most found only misery.

Nathan learned firsthand from his customers the awful truth behind the stories he was now reading in the San Antonio newspapers: in 1934, crops had failed on more than six million acres of Texas farmland. Another three and a half million acres were abandoned or left to lie fallow. After the banks failed, thousands of Texas farmers lost their land (as well as their homes) in foreclosure sales. As elsewhere in the country, these auctions held on courthouse steps often were marked by threats and violence as angry farmers banded together in attempts to block the sales.

With the situation growing more desperate by the month, Nathan Kallison made his ranch a haven for homeless rural people who had lost their own land and livelihoods. At one point in the desperate 1930s, as many as twenty displaced families and farm workers at a time found refuge living in tents on the Kallison Ranch. One family even lived on the concrete floor at the end of the cattle delousing vat. Nathan cherished his country neighbors who he knew loved the land as much as he did. He understood the dilemma of farmers who were trying to survive when the value of their crops and animals had plummeted to less than the cost of raising them. But he required that the men work, even at small tasks, and he paid them a small stipend. He knew they valued the dignity of being able to work. If a family refused to work, though, they were asked to leave.[9]

One Depression-era family the Kallisons befriended stayed on. Walter Sachtleben, broke and homeless after losing his goat ranch in Kendall County, asked for help. Without hesitation, Nathan offered him a job at the Kallison Ranch. Sachtleben moved there in 1934 with his wife Leona, their two young children Florence and James, and Walter's father and mother, Oscar and Mary Sachtleben. An earnest worker, Walter Sachtleben quickly became the ranch manager, and his father Oscar worked as the "straw boss" supervising workers in the fields—including those who were helping out in return for a place to stay.

Florence Sachtleben Hoffmann was only five years old when her family moved to the ranch. "When we got to Nathan Kallison's ranch, we were starving," she recalled. "We had no place to go. Daddy had lost his land and couldn't sell his goats. He had to shoot them." Nathan Kallison was "a strong but also very gentle man," she said. "Everyone respected him and called him 'the Boss.' He was independent and determined to succeed on his own terms," Sachtleben said, "but he was a fair man with a great sense of honor."[10]

The Kallisons paid Walter Sachtleben thirty dollars a month, the same amount the United States government paid its Civilian Conservation Corps (CCC) workers, and gave his family the use of a two-bedroom wooden house on a hilltop toward the north end of the ranch. The house, which also served as ranch headquarters, had no electricity, as was the case with many rural properties in Southwest Texas in the 1930s. "When winds whipped across that hilltop at night," recalled Florence Hoffmann, "the drafts penetrating through the house often were strong enough to move furniture around." Concerned about the young Sachtleben children, Nathan Kallison hired a mason to build a stone room and fireplace onto the north end of the house, providing a warm, secure room for the family. Nathan gave the family a desk from his store so the children would have a place to do their homework. In a shed outside the ranch house, Kallison installed a Delco battery pack unit, powered by a small gasoline engine. When switched on in the afternoon, the nineteen-battery unit produced enough electricity for several hours of light in the evening. "My mother used a special iron with it, a few minutes at a time," recalled Florence Hoffmann. "She thought it was a luxury. It was a lot better than trying to iron a white shirt with irons heated on wood coals. Not easy at all."

Mrs. Hoffmann recalled a weekly ritual in which Nathan and his son Perry drove out to the ranch from San Antonio on Sunday morning. Their first stop always was Tudzin's country store, three miles east of the ranch, where Nathan bought a Sunday newspaper for her father and a bag of candy for her and her brother James. It was obvious that Perry Kallison shared his father's passionate interest in the ranch. "He was one heck of a young man," Florence added. "If anyone needed work or a place to live, Perry would say, 'send them out to the ranch.' Perry was interested in anyone who loved the land and cattle."

Every day, Florence and her brother walked six miles from their hilltop home on the ranch to the two-room Culebra School on Culebra Road. Perry gave little Florence a pair of boots, and her brother James a horse. Young Florence Sachtleben wore the boots constantly and Perry called her "Boots," a nickname that stuck for decades, even after she married. She simply became "Boots" Hoffmann.

With Perry's guidance and working with Sachtleben, the Kallisons took special care to limit the size of their cattle herd to avoid overgrazing their pastures. In truth, their ranch enterprise survived the Depression partly because the family's livelihood did not depend solely on ranching. If the ranch produced enough to cover expenses, the Kallisons were satisfied. Nevertheless, the combination of sustained drought during the Dust Bowl years and ruinous prices tested their patience.

The damage of the Great Depression was not distributed evenly through the population. Census statistics revealed that the lives of 40 percent of Americans suffered little during the Depression. Some Americans actually prospered. Others earned enough to support their families because they provided vital services—doctors, for example, or merchants, such as the Kallisons, who sold the basic goods people needed most. Others survived well out of sheer luck. The Kallisons had overcome great hardships earlier in their lives, they reminded themselves. After having escaped poverty and persecution in Russia, Anna and Nathan had managed to start a business on

Chicago's West Side ghetto during the depression of 1893-1896, they told their children. So they remained tough, determined, and optimistic even when faced with another blow to their livelihood.

Nathan and his sons were determined that they would find the means to keep their store viable and help their desperate customers at the same time. In Nathan's philosophy, those two goals were inseparable. With Morris now in his early thirties and Perry in his late twenties, Nathan Kallison stayed in business when the stock market crashed by advertising and selling absolute necessities at rock-bottom prices. By extending liberal credit with few (if any) conditions, Nathan and his sons further strengthened the bonds of trust and loyalty developed over more than three decades with his farm and ranch customers, who now were struggling to stay afloat. Sharpening his merchandising skills as a pioneer "discounter," Nathan and his sons bought "in bulk," purchasing railroad carloads of barbed wire and other needed farm supplies from manufacturers at bargain prices, savings they then passed on to their customers. Rather than turn away clients, the Kallisons extended long-term credit with no collateral or guarantee that they ever would be paid. For its cash-strapped customers, for example, Kallison's advertised the sale of Grunow refrigerators, Voss clothes washers, and Florence gas ranges to be paid out over terms of five years, with no money down and "as little as fourteen cents a day" in payments.[11]

Just as Kallison's store was advertising its appliances on credit, the Gunter Hotel coffee shop was running ads promoting its "special delicious" three-course dinners for fifty-five cents. For just fifteen cents in 1935, San Antonians could raise their spirits with a visit to one of the city's eight downtown movie theaters. The theaters did a strong business. Clark Gable was starring in "Call of the Wild" at the Plaza, Laurel and Hardy entertained in "Bonnie Scotland" at the Texas, and the Majestic offered Dick Powell and Ruby Keeler in "Shipmates Forever," along with a live stage show starring the Weaver Brothers.[12] As elsewhere in the country, Texans sought cheap entertainment to divert their attention, at least momentarily, from their economic worries.

Ironically, San Antonians who earned even modest incomes were better off, in some respects, than they were before the Depression because the price of many goods and services had tumbled. Real estate values declined sharply, and affluent or moderately well-to-do San Antonians found bargains available for homes in the new suburbs of Olmos Park, Alamo Heights, and Terrell Hills. The Kallisons took advantage of the opportunity.

During the Depression years, Kallison's store focused on merchandising essential items that their customers most needed. Morris Kallison, now the store's general manager, announced in 1931 the opening of a tire and accessories department, which sold United States brand tires and tubes and Super-Dynamic batteries, both installed free with "prompt and efficient service."[13] The new auto accessories department also offered both the replacement parts and repair services for electrical appliances. In 1933, the store added the better-known Goodyear tire line, providing free installation of tires and batteries with a "five month deferred payment plan." The promotion was based on trust and faith—repossessing a tire or battery after five months of use was not a practical option.[14] There was a certain irony to the opening of the tire and accessories department. Even though harnesses for sale still hung from the walls, Kallison's saddlery was now history. A generation after the automobile edged Nathan out of the harness-making business, it was helping his family survive in tough economic times.

Touting itself as the "largest carload buyers in the South," a 1938 Kallison's ad featured cattle supplies, vaccines, dehorners, ear tattoo outfits, horn weights, wool bags, and well supplies."[15] The store slogan, composed by Morris, now became: "Whatever you need, Kallison's has it—and at the right price." The store began selling water heaters for $25.88 apiece with ten-year guarantees.[16] In another promotion, offering "just more proof that we undersell them all," the store announced a Saturday night sale from 8:00 to 10:00 p.m. offering men's overalls for ninety-five cents a pair.[17] Working men lucky enough to have jobs, and the farmers seeking jobs, lined up to buy these essential work clothes.

Although Nathan Kallison was a tough competitor, his skill in navigating the Depression depended most of all on the personal relationships he had built with hundreds of his longtime customers. A 1933 newspaper article, "Kallison Builds Big Business on Holding Friends," offered an explanation:

> People who bought from N. Kallison in the early years found out that his policy of "satisfaction or your money back" meant just that, and the habit of trading at the big general store became more and more widespread. Hundreds of cattlemen and ranchers made it a point to stock up on all of their general needs at this store when they made their periodic trips to the city from distant points in Southwest Texas. Today, the "second generation" of these and many pioneer families of this city continue to shop at Kallison's like their fathers and mothers before them. Fair treatment and friendly service are traditional with the store and have, indeed, been the biggest factor in its growth and development. . . . Kallison prizes the wealth of friendship which has resulted from the conduct of a business which aimed from the first to be of real service to the community.

"Some people want to get rich in too much of a hurry," Nathan Kallison told the *San Antonio Express-News* reporter. "They just won't take time to be friendly and kind, to give good service, and a little more in old-fashioned friendship of the kind that has made Kallison's."[18]

The nation's approach to weathering the Depression changed dramatically after Franklin Delano Roosevelt was sworn in as president on March 20, 1933. Four years earlier, Texas had handed

Republican Hoover a huge victory over Democratic candidate Al Smith, whose Catholicism was unacceptable to a majority of Texans. In 1932, however, Texas returned to its Democratic roots to give Roosevelt a resounding victory over Hoover. The Kallison family, unlike many other well-heeled local businessmen, enthusiastically supported the new president's programs. "We started off 1933 with some doubt as to whether we were going to emerge from the Depression which has caused so much havoc already," Morris Kallison told a *San Antonio Light* reporter. "True, we were having a new president in March, but we didn't know we were getting a great one! . . . The outlook for 1934 and the years beyond," Morris announced, "can only be much brighter than the threshold of any year since the 'boom' era." The Depression continued to deepen in 1934, however, as unemployment rose to 25 percent. The nation's gross national product plunged to one half of its 1928 levels. That year, myriad New Deal programs the new Roosevelt Administration had immediately launched in 1933 began to reach millions of out-of-work American families—and also directly benefited the Kallisons' business.[19] The Works Progress Administration (WPA) and Public Works Administration (PWA) provided jobs to unemployed workers and boosted the local construction industry with projects of lasting benefit to San Antonio. These included restoring the city's Spanish missions and building the charming San Antonio River Walk. The National Youth Administration program, administered in Texas by twenty-seven-year-old Lyndon Baines Johnson, gave part-time main-tenance and clerical jobs to thousands of college and high school students in San Antonio and throughout the state. Nationally, Civilian Conservation Corps provided jobs to two and a half million men. At its peak, it provided twenty-seven camps in Texas for workers who built thirty-one state recreational parks and several city and county parks, while seventy other camps housed civilians working in forests and on soil conservation. Most of the men in the CCC were paid $30 a month, with the requirement that they send $25 of that to their families.[20]

One unusual program involved federal, state, and local efforts to help the people of Southwest Texas. A government-owned Relief Canning Plant in the heart of San Antonio—operated by the Bexar County Board of Welfare and Employment, the Extension Department of Texas A&M College, and federal relief programs—proved a win-win-win proposition for the area. With Civil Works Administration (CWA) funds, government relief agents purchased cattle for slaughter from local farmers and ranchers unable to sustain their livestock on the parched earth. The beef was processed in the Relief Canning Plant, which operated around the clock, providing work three days per week for as many as 1,150 persons. When operating at capacity, the facility produced thirty thousand cans of meat per day, which was distributed to the area's relief recipients.[21] At Thanksgiving in 1934, plant employee Mrs. Janie Williams, a widow with five dependents, said, "I am glad that our government is giving needy people an opportunity to work for the aid given to them instead of direct charity. It enables needy people . . . to maintain their self-respect."[22]

At the outset of the Roosevelt presidency, the Kallisons participated in one of the earliest and most controversial of the president's New Deal programs aimed at lifting the country out of the Depression. Three months after FDR's inauguration, Congress passed the National Industrial Recovery Act (NIRA), ushering in "a unique experiment in US economic history." It called for America's industries to regulate themselves by creating "codes of fair competition" in an effort to protect consumers, employers, and competitors. Created shortly thereafter by executive order, the National Recovery Administration (NRA) dealt with voluntary, industry-wide agreements concerning work hours, pay rates, and price-fixing, since the recent legislation had suspended anti-trust laws. Businesses that opted in displayed an emblem signifying NRA participation—the Blue Eagle.[23]

Kallison's immediately adopted the NRA program. According to an optimistic Morris Kallison, who referred to the previous few years as the worst of the "late" depression, "Not only have more customers been patronizing the store, but the average sale has increased 15 to 20 percent. This is a sure sign that not only are more people working, but they are spending more money."[24] The program was short-lived, however, with the Supreme Court striking down the NRA's compulsory price-setting agreements in 1935.

But the Roosevelt program that most directly affected the Kallison's store, as well as hundreds of its customers, was the enactment of the Federal Housing Administration (FHA) program. In 1934, the FHA provided low-interest federally guaranteed loans to help people repair their present homes or to build new ones. The ink had barely dried on the FHA law when the Kallisons embraced and offered customers its benefits. In 1934, Kallison's opened a loan department to service FHA loans, and with Morris's direction, set up a construction business to perform FHA work. Morris, who by this time had developed a strong interest in real estate development, seized the opportunity: "Kallison's store has millions of dollars available for modernization and new construction," Morris Kallison announced. "Not only can we supply money, but men and material necessary to complete such jobs are available, on short notice. As an example of the speed at which transactions can be handled at Kallison's store—for a loan application made today, work can start tomorrow."

Billing itself as the "Wonder Store of Texas," the Kallisons advertised FHA-backed three-year home improvement loans of $100 to $2,000 for painting, roofing, home decorating, and plumbing. "Act Now," the ad said, "No Red Tape, No Security, No Mortgage, No Wait."[25] The program was such a success, Morris told the San Antonio Express, that the store in 1934 had the best year in its history, with sales 35 percent higher than its second best year, 1932.

In a late 1935 survey of San Antonio business leaders, Morris Kallison reported, "It is a matter of pride for us to have a report from the Bank Credit Corporation that we have led the whole United States (in the FHA program) during the last four and one half months in the amount of remodeling units, with over one thousand separate remodeling loans made."

Mother Nature's wrath also had a hand in the remodeling business. The most severe hail storm in San Antonio's history struck on Tuesday, March 5, 1935. It denuded vegetation, stripped bark from trees, and pounded crops, compounding misery from dust storms and the Depression. "Several thousand homes were battered in the thirteen terrifying minutes that dumped almost a half-foot of two-inch hail," reported the *San Antonio Evening News*. Windows, street lamps, car windshields, and theater marquees shattered. "The chipped glass on the street and sidewalks resembled confetti." Propelled by a fifty-six-mile-per-hour west wind, hailstones splintered shingles, shredded car tops, and destroyed roofs. Scores of people were injured, and the storm caused a million dollars in damages.[26]

To help the city rebuild after the storm, Kallison's ordered railroad carloads of building supplies. One twenty-car order of Texaco roofing was believed to be the largest of its kind placed by any local firm in connection with the storm.[27] After the disaster, despite increased demand and decreased supplies in San Antonio, the Kallisons (unlike some other merchants who rushed to capitalize on the disaster) did not raise their "rock-bottom" prices for needed supplies—including roofing materials. According to Nathan's grandson Jimmy Kallison, "They viewed the value of their customers' friendship and trust as more important than making a quick windfall profit."

Morris showed his flair for marketing as he promoted Kallison's FHA home improvement programs, which he said would help the unemployed. A 1930s Kallison's newspaper ad featured a picture of Morris in front of a microphone "broadcasting sensational news" from station KDS (Kallison's Department Store). "There are a lot of good plumbers out of work. We've decided to do our share and help these men earn some money to support their families. Buy any plumbing fixture and materials in our large supply. We will supply Master Licensed Plumbers to do the installations for you at absolutely NO LABOR COST TO YOU. You buy the materials and we pay the plumber. Do your share in helping unemployment, and replace all worn-out, unsanitary, or old-fashioned fixtures. Come on folks. Let's get busy and set the wheels humming again."[28]

Spurred by Morris's self-confidence, drive, and showmanship, Kallison's kept expanding the FHA-backed home improvement program, finally offering as much as $50,000 in five-year, interest-free loans for purchase from the store's stock of building supplies, which included Texaco roofing, Pee Gee paints, lumber, plumbing supplies, electrical fixtures, and wallpaper. Ads for the loans not only targeted homeowners in San Antonio but also out-of-towners from Bandera to Yorktown living within a five hundred-mile radius.[29]

Following his father's earlier—and lucrative—investments in real estate, Morris also honed his skills as a budding developer during this period. In a 1936 project financed by the new FHA loans, Kallison's teamed with builder Mel Starnes to build seven new homes with "every modern convenience, comfort, and dependable construction" on Chicago Boulevard and on Lee Hall and Catalina Streets.[30] When the FHA loan program allowed loans of at least $3,000, Kallison's then celebrated San Antonio's centennial with a special offer: a beautiful "five-room mansion built from top to bottom with Kallison's super quality materials. We will finance the deal at the lowest cost in building history," the ad read, "and you repay in monthly installments . . . just as if you were paying rent." The cost of the homes, "completely built," was $2,850.[31]

While the Kallison family learned to prosper during the Depression years, they also extended help to those who could not. San Antonio's elderly, especially, were suffering. At that time in America, few retired workers, including those at Kallison's, received pensions from their employers. Whatever savings they had managed to accumulate were soon depleted or exhausted. (The new Social Security Act would not provide benefits until 1940.) During these painful years, Kallison's store instituted its own version of a "retirement plan." The store simply kept loyal, longtime employees on the payroll, albeit at reduced salaries. Salesmen no longer able to walk the aisles rested instead in a row of chairs on the north wall of the store, near the furniture department. They stood by to help out or advise when they could, but no one monitored their activities. To puzzled customers, one store employee said, "it looked like the Kallisons were providing day care for an old folks' home."[32]

In hiring workers during the Depression, Nathan, Morris, and especially Perry often paid less attention to people's job qualifications than to their desperate need to find work. That same spirit guided Perry's relationships with the store's suppliers. Whenever he could, he tried to help other small businessmen, especially those struggling to gain a foothold in San Antonio during the Depression. In the mid-1930s, Perry decided to buy part of the store's large supply of khaki trousers from Bill and Nathan Sinkin's new Sunshine Clothing Company, rather than from its larger rival, Finesilver Manufacturing Company. A 1910 immigrant from Pinsk, Russia, Nathan Sinkin had come to San Antonio as a street peddler, then ran La Nacional, a small dry goods store in the "Little Jerusalem" neighborhood on Commerce Street. During the Depression, young Bill Sinkin, just out of college, sold the khaki trousers his father had begun to manufacture to Kallison's and other retailers for $9 per dozen. Kallison's then re-sold them to needy consumers for $1 apiece, making a profit of twenty-five cents per pair. Seventy-five years later, Bill Sinkin (ninety-eight years old in 2011), a philanthropist and business leader in San Antonio for six decades, still remembered the boost that Perry Kallison gave his company. "Perry was a nice guy, a gentle, trustworthy man," Sinkin recalled. "He was kind and produced quietly—but he was a good businessman."[33]

During the Depression years, the Kallison family business prospered as Perry and Morris took more initiative in managing the family enterprises. Morris, with his showmanship, expanded the store's outreach through media and through social, business, and political contacts in the urban arena. Perry, whose own showmanship created a friendly rural personality for himself, reached out comfortably to ranchers and farmers. The two worked in concert, respecting the authority and instincts of their father. The three men spent their days at the store, Morris and Perry always deferring to Nathan—and calling him "the Boss."

The family lived frugally, but well. Morris and Ruth, with their son Jimmy, born June 1921, and daughter Jane, born July 1928, moved into their new house down the street from Nathan and Anna in Olmos Park. Ruth, now a full-time homemaker, became a doting daughter to Anna, especially since Anna's elder daughter Pauline had defied her mother by marrying a widower who was seventeen years older.

As a student at the University of Chicago during the 1916-1917 school year, Pauline had lived with the Greenblatts, who had three daughters themselves—Lillian, Rose, and Hannah, whom Anna Kallison had helped to raise many years before. The Greenblatt girls had married—Lillian to a textile manufacturer named Isadore Neustadt, who now ran his own woolen business. Tragically, Lillian Neustadt had died giving birth to their daughter, whom Isadore named Lillian after her mother.

One of the Greenblatts' other daughters, Hannah, long since known as "Aunt Hannah" to Pauline and Tibe, was raising the baby as her own child when Pauline visited the Greenblatts in 1927. It was then that Pauline met the baby and her father Isadore. On her last day before returning to San Antonio, where she had left several suitors her own age, Pauline received a telegram from Isadore imploring her to stay. She went home with the intention of returning, only to discover that Anna refused to consider Isadore Neustadt as an appropriate husband for her lovely daughter. After many tearful sessions, Pauline packed her bags for Chicago, where she and Isadore were married in the Greenblatt-Sigmund home. Anna and Nathan refused to attend.

The Great Depression caught up with Pauline in Illinois, where she and Isadore lived until 1930, the year his textile business failed.

Nathan relented, welcoming Isadore into the store and building a new house in Olmos Park for the couple. Anna never welcomed him at all until January 1932, when Suzanna Neustadt—known as Susan or Suzy—was born at Santa Rosa Hospital in downtown San Antonio.

Meanwhile Tibe, the younger daughter, was beginning to be dubbed an "old maid" by 1930. She did have an active social life, however: it was filled with parties and dates with a series of young suitors whose company she enjoyed, but she met none with whom she wanted to spend the rest of her life. Nor were any of the young merchants in the city eligible enough in her mother's eyes. Tibe's spirits brightened when she worked with Rabbi Ephraim Frisch in his continuing efforts to create a wide variety of programs for teenagers and young adults at Temple Beth-El. With admiration for Tibe's quick mind and her burning idealism, Rabbi Frisch selected her to join him as coteacher for the confirmation class in the Temple Beth-El religious school. She also enthusiastically worked as a substitute teacher in the San Antonio public schools, having been informed that she didn't have the necessary credentials to become a full-time teacher.

Then in 1934, Rabbi Frisch's wife Ruth, Tibe's mentor and best friend, died tragically of cancer at the age of forty-four. Soon a grieving Rabbi Frisch asked Tibe to become his wife. Gently, she explained that she shared his grief for Ruth Frisch and admired him greatly, but couldn't marry him, a man twenty-two years her senior.

Friends in San Antonio, invited or not, began to act as potential matchmakers for Tibe. College classmates from other cities, most of whom were already married, joined in the search. Then a friend from Dallas who was visiting told her about a new man in that city. "He's handsome, he's charming, he's a wonderful dancer. He's witty, with a 'line' those East Coast men have. You'll have a good time with this man . . . but don't marry him," she advised.

"He was a very good dancer," Tibe recalled. Benjamin Jerome Lasser charmed Tibe with his sense of adventure, his sophisticated eastern manners, his feeling for those less fortunate, and his idealistic hope for the future. After joining the army at age seventeen, Ben Lasser had served in the 1916 expeditionary force to chase Mexican outlaw and folk hero Pancho Villa, who was eluding capture along the Texas border. Lasser later served in combat in France during World War I, emerging from the army as a sergeant major. Lasser was now an adman, head of the Dallas (Southwestern) sales region for Fairchild Publications, publisher of *Women's Wear Daily*.

"We wanted to write books together," Tibe later recalled. Over her mother's objections, in 1930, at the age of twenty-seven, Tibe Kallison was married to Ben Lasser in a formal ceremony and reception at the Menger Hotel in San Antonio. They moved to Philadelphia, where Ben had been transferred. Her new husband spent much time traveling his larger East Coast territory. Until now, Tibe had known only San Antonio and "Aunt Hannah's Chicago." Philadelphia was less than comfortable. She and Ben lived in a downtown apartment building, where she tried to learn to cook. (Having bought a nice plump kosher chicken to roast per Anna's recipe, she didn't know to remove the insides first. The odor was so foul she had to set the roasted bird outside her window until she could assail the butcher for selling rotten meat!)

The deepening Depression was creating intense pressures on Ben Lasser, as it was on all salesmen, whether for advertising or anything else. His large territory, which covered several states, kept Lasser on the road for days at a time—sometimes weeks. Tibe found few friends among her northern Jewish neighbors, who were mostly working women with accents and manners unlike well-to-do Texans.

Alone in the apartment, she read books from the library, attended lectures at museums, and volunteered as a tutor at a nearby school. The passionate pursuit of social justice fostered by the Frisches was not on the agenda at the Orthodox synagogue in her neighborhood. Then one day she met a woman in her building, a Jewish judge who initiated the kind of intellectual conversation Tibe felt she needed. They agreed on many liberal government projects that President

Roosevelt had proposed to help needy citizens. The judge invited her to attend some meetings of like-minded people. Tibe was impressed by the sincerity and passion of the highly-educated Socialists and leftist liberals at the meetings.

"When the women on my floor asked where I was going at night, I answered, 'to a League meeting.' They thought I meant the Junior League." Her life as a Socialist activist was cut short, however, when her mother Anna phoned in 1931 with the frightening news that Tibe's father had suffered a mild stroke.

Tibe told her husband Ben, "I need to go home and take care of Papa. And the store needs you to run the advertising." She convinced Nathan and her brothers that Ben would be an asset to the business. Anna was delighted that her daughter was coming home. Tibe and Ben moved in with her parents, and Ben went to work in Kallison's store. Their son Nathan, named for his grandfather, was born in September 1932 in Santa Rosa Hospital.

Two years earlier, on Memorial Day 1930, Nathan and Anna Kallison's youngest, Perry, met Frances Rosenthal of Fort Worth. Tibe had invited Frances, an avid horsewoman, to a picnic and swim party at Landa Park in New Braunfels, thinking Frances and Perry might be a "match." When Perry asked Frances to join him the next day at the Hillcrest Country Club, he learned they had much in common—not the least of which was a passion for horseback riding. He discovered she was inquisitive and intelligent, had attended Vassar College in upstate New York, and graduated from the University of Chicago. In that and subsequent conversations he found out that her love of family, sense of social justice, and commitment to Reform Judaism were as strong as his. They were married in San Antonio on March 8, 1931, at the Menger Hotel.[34] Frances became Perry's partner in all of his religious, community, and ranch activities. On January 3, 1933, Frances gave birth to their daughter Maryann Kallison.

In the wake of his mild stroke, and as the Depression deepened, Nathan had purchased four homes in the new Olmos Park neighborhood and drew his entire family around him. Within three blocks of each other, this Kallison enclave represented Nathan and Anna's passionate desire to further strengthen the bonds within their close-knit family. All four Kallison homes were built of native Texas limestone in the Spanish colonial style, with red tile roofs. They had ample front and back lawns for the Kallison grandchildren to play games and for their parents to gather on Saturday evenings for outdoor parties. In Morris and Ruth Kallison's expansive backyard, softly lit by strings of colored lights, family and close friends—mostly other merchant and professional Jewish families from Temple Beth-El—would dine on enchiladas, tamales, and guacamole salad, and talk about how their downtown businesses were faring. The Depression was a constant subject, as well, with a mixture of gratitude and worry at their fragile good fortune.[35]

Anna Kallison, at age fifty-eight, was a forceful family presence. She often shared her unsolicited views on store management and child rearing with each of her four children and their spouses as she surveyed her family domain in Olmos Park. Anna was especially hard on her sons-in-law. "What are Isadore and Ben doing to help the store?" she would ask Nathan. Isadore Neustadt had won Nathan's favor as a knowledgeable businessman. His dignity, urbane manner, and expertise in management and merchandising made him a valuable asset. Much older than both Morris and Perry, Isadore impressed the brothers with his keen mind and respectful approach to customers. Anna, though, was wary of anyone in the store who was not of her own flesh and blood. Ben Lasser, living under her roof, felt her sting, and also felt cramped by the brothers' reluctance to turn over all advertising to him, an "easterner." On weekends, he preferred playing golf to riding horseback or inspecting cattle—which rattled the Kallisons' intense work ethic.

Early in 1934, the Lasser baby, Nathan, developed croup and was hospitalized. Tibe was distressed to learn that the child had been exposed to tuberculosis. She called her husband at the store and urged him to rush to the hospital. Instead, Ben Lasser left town without a word and checked himself into a sanatorium. A few days later, when Ben telephoned Tibe to let her know where he had gone, she was livid. She knew his older brother had died from tuberculosis, but he had never told her that he had survived an earlier bout of the disease himself. Anna was adamant. Tuberculosis had been Anna's greatest terror, her reason for leaving Chicago. "You have to divorce him now—and never let him near the baby!" she ordered her thirty-one-year-old daughter. "And even if he lives, he'll never make you a living." Fearful and furious, Tibe filed for divorce, asking for—and being granted—a decree prohibiting Ben from visiting their son. When he recovered, Ben continued to come to the Kallison door, but was refused entry. He subsequently sued the family for alienation of affection. In a 1972 account, Benjamin Lasser stated that Perry settled with him for $25,000, with the stipulation that Ben leave San Antonio and never attempt to see or contact his son.[36]

Tibe wanted to go to Chicago in 1934, hoping to return to graduate school and to a job counseling poor, expectant mothers at a Chicago hospital. Anna objected, however. Worried about how Tibe would survive as a single mother on her own, Anna had insisted, "You cannot move to Chicago. You have a child to raise." Tibe was conflicted—torn between her fierce loyalty to her strong-willed mother and her own desires and dreams to become a professional woman and political activist dedicated to helping the poor and disadvantaged. She was the best educated of the four Kallison children, the only one with a college degree and graduate studies as well, and she wanted to participate in the liberal causes of the 1930s. She was strong-willed and opinionated, but in the end, as always, she bowed to her mother's demands. Tibe and two-year-old Nathan remained in San Antonio, moving with Nathan and Anna into the parents' new home on Thelma Drive in Olmos Park. If she was frustrated by failure to fulfill her own desires, she kept those thoughts to herself. She busied herself with caring for her son and her parents, teaching Sunday school at Temple Beth-El, serving as a volunteer, and pursuing a modest social life in San Antonio's small Jewish community.

The Kallisons had barely recovered from this family drama, the embarrassment and its cost, when a far greater loss befell them. A block farther down the street, Pauline and Isadore Neustadt lived with their daughter Suzanna, now called Susan. Tragedy struck there in 1935. Isadore, who at first had been met with angry disapproval, had finally won over the entire family with his knowledge of merchandising, penchant for hard work, and long hours at the store. He was known for his warm and caring nature, and was held in high regard by all of Kallison's employees. Always robust and healthy, without any warning he suddenly fell ill and died of pneumonia. Isadore's death left Pauline alone in her new house with a three-year-old daughter. Both she and Tibe, each of whom had been married "late" at twenty-seven and twenty-eight, were now left alone, each with a fatherless child.

Three blocks away from Thelma Drive, Perry and Frances Kallison lived on Stanford Drive with their daughter Maryann and young son Perry Jr., known as Pete, who was born in 1934. The youngest Kallison grandchild, Frances Rae (known as Bobbi), was born to Frances and Perry in 1940, completing the Kallisons' third generation with eight grandchildren. Anna, usually with a grandchild at her side, strode through her neighborhood visiting her family. She literally marched, her head held high, her shoulders back, as she instructed her little companions about the importance of good posture. She was an enemy of both sloth and sloppiness. Shirts were to be tucked in, hair combed, shoes shined, and laces tightened. These standards, she instructed her four grown children, were to be enforced by them as well.

Although Anna entertained her friends with games of mah-jongg and bridge in the new fieldstone home, she felt left out of business life at Kallison's store. In frustration, she would instruct a succession of bewildered young grandchildren to go down to the store and serve as her floor-walkers to spy on the sales force. "Get down there and see what's going on!" she would tell a grandchild. "They're stealing us blind." Anna's uninhibited and open criticisms annoyed her sons, but she was a shrewd observer, aware that store security and inventory control were not high priorities for either Morris or Perry.[36]

In their affluent enclave, the Kallison women felt protected from the ravages of the Depression years and concentrated on raising upper middle-class American children with high ideals and a strong work ethic. They contributed to good causes, while carrying on an active social life with card games, book discussions, music or speech lessons for their children, and occasional trips to Chicago. The family, with all of its triumphs and tragedies, was the center of their lives.

Adjacent to the green, flowery Olmos Park suburb, however, was the other grim reality: the west side barrio, where thousands of desperately poor Mexican Americans lived in flimsy shacks, most lacking water and indoor plumbing. In sharp contrast to the Kallisons and their friends who had even thrived in the Depression, those San Antonians faced joblessness and dire poverty every day. Despite President Hoover's proclamation that "Nobody is actually starving. The hobos are better fed than they have ever been," people in San Antonio and elsewhere died of hunger. With meat and milk beyond the budget of struggling families, malnutrition—particularly in children—became widespread.

At some point, miserable conditions on the west side were bound to cause an eruption of some sort. It occurred most dramatically eight years after the 1929 crash. San Antonio's single biggest industry was the pecan-processing business. And the first citizens to protest income disparity in San Antonio were not the unemployed or homeless, but the thousand Mexican American workers who received pitifully low pay for shelling the nuts by hand. All over the west side, they cracked the hard shells and picked out the nut meats, either in local factories or at home in their own dilapidated shelters.

It took organized labor, so despised in the South and Southwest, to bring about confrontation between a conservative, anti-union business community (indifferent to conditions on the west side), and the barely-existing workers who asked for decent wages. In 1938, labor union representatives and radical activists organized by the Workers Alliance (founded in New York by a coalition of Socialist Unemployed Leagues and Communist Unemployed Councils) set up headquarters in an old funeral home in San Antonio. They set about organizing the Mexican Americans, whose employers found Depression labor so cheap they paid the pecan-shellers as little as four cents a pound for their yield.

The first protest, on June 29, 1938, was a sit-down strike staged at the Gunter Hotel. Suddenly, the San Antonio police stormed the WPA headquarters in the hotel where the protesters sat. With billy-clubs and drawn pistols, they removed the unarmed workers, hauling many of them off to jail. A few hours later, with no search warrant, uniformed policed ransacked the strikers' headquarters. With axes, they smashed typewriters, furniture, even a piano.[37]

The brutal raid outraged San Antonio's small band of liberal reformers. They were backed by Rabbi Ephraim Frisch of Temple Beth-El and by other close personal friends of the Kallisons. In a fiery letter to the newspapers, also mailed to Temple members, Frisch sought to persuade (some said to force) his congregation and the city to confront the miserable treatment of the Mexican American pecan workers. "They are working in conditions as deplorable as those in the notorious sweatshops of New York's garment district," he charged. The rabbi castigated the police for the raid and defended worker's rights. His letter warned that a city tolerating poverty and low wages would reap "a harvest of industrial strife." In a longer pamphlet, Rabbi Frisch also criticized "fashionably dressed, immaculately manicured, and well-fed ladies" oblivious to the poverty surrounding their "swanky luncheons."

It was lost on no one that some of the business owners whom Frisch excoriated were members of his own congregation—most notably Julius Seligmann, cofounder of the Southern Pecan Shelling Company, the largest pecan-shelling firm in the United States. Frisch's letter "brought coals of wrath" down on him from several Temple members, Frances Kallison later recalled.[38] "The people [in

Temple Beth-El] exploiting the workers were very resentful of his sermon," she said. But the businessmen's protests failed to silence
Frisch's activism.

The labor strife and social protests posed a dilemma for Tibe, a
Beth-El Sunday school teacher, and Perry Kallison, both now in their
early thirties. Rabbi Frisch and his late wife Ruth had been very inspi-
rational for them as teenagers and young adults. Fired with social idealism by her university studies and inspired by the Frisches, Tibe
Kallison empathized with the workers and quietly deplored their
treatment. She was an enthusiastic participant in the Open Forum, a
Frisch-inspired program that brought dozens of speakers to the city
on wide-ranging subjects. Tibe's favorites were the political and social
activists with whom she identified. She supported attorney Maury
Maverick, a reformer, in his successful campaigns for election in the
mid-1930s as a member of Congress and then as San Antonio's
mayor. Tibe remembered that as a young lawyer, Maverick had written an article lampooning the Ku Klux Klan members whom he
described as "wearers of nightgowns who were 'fully as mentally
developed as an ape.'" Despite her strong liberal views and support
for Frisch and Maverick, however, Tibe Kallison chose not to become
an activist in the pecan workers' fight. The Seligmanns were friends
of the family.

After the strike ended, the pecan workers had won only a tiny
increase. But an unlikely champion did emerge in the Kallison family. In the midst of the Depression, Perry's wife Frances became a
leader in an early effort to bring desperately needed services to the
impoverished west side neighborhood. She joined with Sister Mary
Victory to establish the Guadalupe Community Center, the first program to bring substantial help to the city's Mexican American neighborhood. Sister Mary Victory and other nuns from the Sisters of
Charity of the Incarnate Word established the center to promote family and child welfare. Frances helped them to start a prenatal and
postnatal clinic, and a school lunch project for one hundred fifty
malnourished children. Frances led fundraising for the center, served

as vice chairman, and headed a housing subcommittee, which reported on the prevalence of slum housing on the west side. Later, she
would head a citywide committee to address health needs. All during
the Depression, Tibe Kallison had envisioned her life as one devoted
to social justice. It was Frances, instead, who worked to achieve that
goal.

EIGHT

The Ol' Trader

WHILE PAULINE AND TIBE were seeking their independence in Chicago, Morris traveled to New York, where he bought a souvenir newspaper announcing "Morris Kallison Buys Brooklyn Bridge"—a joking reference to his dream of owning a real estate empire. But Perry—so committed to the store and the ranch, as well as to education, civic involvement, and social-justice activism—rarely left San Antonio for a vacation. In the summer of 1936 however, Perry and Frances, now in their early thirties, took a rare month-long road trip across New Mexico, taking in eleven climate zones and vast expanses of open land. The only signs of commerce, Perry noticed, were occasional trading posts scattered across the stark landscape. Like Kallison's store, the trading posts' offerings were eclectic. Food and supplies shared shelf space with native arts and crafts—baskets, rugs, pottery, jewelry—that locals had made to sell or to trade for the staples they needed. Those rustic outposts and their simple barter system sparked Perry's imagination. They inspired him to create a unique advertising platform for the Kallisons' enterprises that would mimic this idea of trading goods at the same time that it made use of modern media—radio broadcasting.

"Through the economic turmoil of the Depression, radio was one of the most important forces keeping the nation together," wrote historian Tom Lewis. "By the thirties, radio had pervaded the consciousness of every American, subtly changing the way they thought and lived. There were 19,250,000 radio sets in America, and it was not unusual for a person to regard the radio as the most prized of possessions."[1]

In the 1930s, radio sets had become more affordable, and merchants offered appealing credit terms to sell them. At the same time, radio manufacturers began selling specially designed "battery-powered farm radios," which meant that rural families did not have to wait for the construction of local power lines before buying their first set.[2]

Author E. B. White described the huge impact that this new medium was making on people living in sparsely populated areas like the Texas Hill Country. "When they say 'The Radio,' they don't mean a cabinet, an electrical phenomenon, or a man in a studio, [but] a pervading and somewhat godlike presence which has come into their lives and homes."

Perry Kallison sensed that presence. He conceived a radio broadcast that would promote the family business while offering a great public service—an on-air bulletin board where listeners could "post" items they wanted to sell, buy, or trade. He called it, of course, the *Trading Post*. In San Antonio and across the nation, he realized that radio had become a powerful tool for promoting products to a rising market of buyers, even during the Depression. Despite massive unemployment and poverty, radio was instrumental among popular media in creating a national consumer culture. Advertisers dictated content. Soap operas, aimed at stay-at-home housewives who bought cleaning products, ruled the daytime airwaves. To enhance sales of Kallison's diverse merchandise, Perry convinced the family to sponsor a radio program as an outreach to rural customers.

In the beginning, a professional radio announcer anchored the *Trading Post* broadcast. But the fellow was "inclined to the bottle," Frances recalled. One morning, he was too drunk to put on the program, and Perry stepped up to the microphone.[3] Affecting the Texas twang and lilting cadence of a longtime cowpoke or rancher, Perry quickly launched into a fast-moving monologue that relayed market reports, cattle prices, and improvements in grass seed. He announced upcoming social events such as the Helotes Volunteer Firemen's Barbecue. And as fast as an auctioneer's spiel, Perry ticked off the names and hometowns of customers who had dropped by Kallison's store the previous day. He also told jokes, which delighted his country listeners. A new radio personality was born— Perry Kallison, the "Old Trader" or as he would say in his down-home, folksy, Texas twang—"Ol' Trader."

People soon began coming into the store to meet him personally and were astonished—on the radio, Perry's voice was that of an ol' boy from South Texas, sounding much older than his actual age. When he bent his head toward the microphone and opened his mouth, the town of Laredo sounded out as *Loh-RAY-da*; Arkansas became *Ar-KAN-saw*; telephone became *tell-ee-PHONE*; and the sport of rodeo (pronounced *ROAD-ya*) rhymed with *San An-TON-ya*. On the *Trading Post*, as Perry explained to legendary country singer/sausage king Jimmy Dean, if you say 'San Antone,' we know you're a Yankee; if you say *San An-TON-ya*, we know you're from good ol' Texas."

For decades, Kallison's store had advertised its myriad merchandise extensively in the *San Antonio Light* and *San Antonio Express-News*, the city's two daily newspapers. Now, the store's unique merchandising appeal was broadcast in the early morning, when Perry Kallison did not just talk about what the store was selling; he was making new friends for Kallison's with farm, ranch, and small town families, listeners from all over South and Southwest Texas. In 1929, Merlin H. Aylesworth, then president of NBC (the parent company of KTSA's rival station WOAI), had noted that the most effective commercials create "such a friendly feeling in the listener . . . that he is very likely to remember favorably the industry that has provided him with good entertainment." Creating friendly feelings came naturally to the "Ol' Trader."[4]

Within the reach of the 50,000-kilocycle station KTSA in a 300-mile radius around San Antonio, Perry Kallison became a "neighbor" to tens of thousands of listeners. His role ranged from newscaster—

announcing farm prices and developments—to community booster, promoting a series of worthy causes that could help people across the region. Then as a public service, Perry also announced individual goods or services that his listeners wished to buy, sell, or trade. One morning, for example, H. L. Gregory wanted to buy one hundred cottontail rabbits to ship to South America, offering to pay $1 to $1.50 each.[5] On another occasion, Perry announced that one old rancher, a widower, was looking for someone to do a little light housekeeping, and possibly become his wife. Then, on a day when temperatures dipped below freezing, Perry would remind listeners that Kallison's had "heaters, hats with ear flaps, 'long-handle' underwear, corduroy chaps, and blanket-lined jackets."[6]

At Kallison's store, traffic multiplied. Inside, everybody lined up to chat with Perry, who took to cocking his Stetson so that it cast a shadow over one eye. Customers signed their names in a clothbound ledger book, jotting down items they wanted to sell or trade. They made note of recent births, graduations, and upcoming anniversaries, all of which, like their items to sell or barter, would be faithfully announced on the *Trading Post.* Many farmers also came to ask Perry for advice about agricultural problems. From the broadcasts, his listeners knew that the Kallison Ranch tested new products and was winning awards for soil conservation and for its cattle, which made them all the more eager to trek into town for a word with the radio rancher. "The Ol' Trader" made them feel that he very likely would be experiencing the same successes or failures as they were.

"A lot of neighbors are comin' in reportin' the cattle are itchy and scratchy and are rubbin' the fence posts," Perry reported. To cure the itch, caused by ticks or other parasites, he recommended applying a topical ointment with a handy gasoline-powered sprayer priced at $79.95. At the same time he was plugging commercial products from his store, he also was dispensing sound veterinary advice. His "neighbors" came to depend upon Perry's knowledge. As Perry Kallison's regional reputation grew, he began visiting livestock shows around the state to familiarize himself with people and trends in the farm and ranch industry. His nephew Jack, Morris's younger son, would ride with Uncle Perry to small-town stock shows in Yoakum and Cotulla, where "all the people greeted Perry by name, and he knew everyone," Jack Kallison recalled.

In the center of the store, the silvery-haired Mr. Davis presided over Perry's *Trading Post* headquarters. As Perry's official greeter, he helped visitors list items for sale on the radio. He always handed out small lollipops, called "suckers," to their children. Nearby, a fresh pot of coffee was always percolating. "You just come by, drink coffee with us," the Ol' Trader invited his radio listeners. There was no charge for a cup of the brew. Perry did suggest, however, that folks drop donations into the "coffee pipeline." The coins went for causes such as an iron lung for Samantha "Sammy" Franklin, a farmer's daughter in Poteet who was fighting polio. For Sammy's lung and other humanitarian requests, generosity to the coffee pipeline would be rewarded with "a preferred stockholder certificate for demonstrating sincere belief in the precept that it is 'More Blessed to Give than to Receive.'"

As needs arose, Perry created other funds to support specific causes. One such effort was "The Dusty Fund" to help Herbie Stiles, a forty-eight-year-old blind man who needed a new guide dog. "Someone had poisoned Herbie's old seeing-eye pal Dusty," the Ol' Trader reported, explaining that the late Norwegian shepherd had come to Herbie eight years before, via the *Trading Post*. Loyal Dusty had guided his master "through traffic, and stayed with him day and night" while Herbie played his accordion on the streets of San Antonio. "How can a man be so mean as to destroy Dusty?" Perry asked his listeners, urging them to "send in their dimes or their dollars" or whatever they could afford to help Herbie buy a new dog.[7]

If anyone ever needed communication and a sense of caring community, it was the remote farm families and small-town citizens touched by Perry Kallison's friendly early morning voice reaching out across Depression-wracked South and Southwest Texas. The program soared in popularity. From the outset, the *Trading Post* provided an unusual, much-needed service. The nation was still suffering in the midst of the Great Depression, made worse in the Southwest by a long, punishing drought that shrank farmers' crop yields when prices already were hitting rock bottom. Furthermore, the farmers of South Texas felt—and were in fact—extremely isolated: farm-to-market roads were unpaved and often treacherous, and electricity was non-existent in many rural areas. But farmers still listened to their battery-powered radios.

The 7:00 a.m. broadcast became a vital link connecting farms and ranches beyond the reach of telephone lines and daily newspaper routes. Like President Roosevelt's effective fireside chats of the day, Perry's radio program imparted a sense of "belonging" to a heretofore isolated people. In his evening broadcasts, Roosevelt sought to reassure Americans during the Great Depression and on into World War II. The President and the Ol' Trader each combined information and advice with homespun wisdom. Both communicated in such a uniquely personal way that their loyal listeners felt an intimate bond with them.

The editor of *Cattleman* magazine described the empathy that the Ol' Trader aroused in his listeners: "From the feedlots in the Panhandle to the orange groves in the Valley, in hard times and good times, Perry Kallison has always been on the air to pat a fellow on the back for a job well done, or to encourage another when living off the land was something difficult to accomplish."[8]

Decades later, those who had listened to Perry's broadcasts could still recall his voice, his unique pronunciations, and how eagerly their family rituals included the early morning gathering around the radio to listen to the Ol' Trader. When the show later aired on KMAC, Lou Rooney, the station's news director, toured the San Antonio environs interviewing listeners as part of the station's license-renewal process. "I talked to county judges, sheriffs, businessmen, and just plain folks," he recalled. "As soon as I mentioned which station I was from, they would say something about Perry's program. I didn't realize what a public service he performs until I got out and talked to the people. He provides a service they can't get anywhere else—radio, TV, or newspaper. I came away impressed."[9]

Early on, the *Trading Post* became a central part of Perry's life, marking the beginning and end of long work days. Before leaving the store at night, he gathered up the *Trading Post* ledgers, stuffed his pockets with notes for other broadcast items, and headed for home. On the days he made it to Stanford Drive in time to eat with his family, it was not unusual for his meal to be interrupted. In fact, the phone generally started ringing during the dinner hour. Often, the caller would be a mortician with news of a death, asking the Ol' Trader to broadcast the time and location of a funeral.

After supper, in his home's second-floor den, Perry would then scribble in longhand on yellow legal pads. He wrote the script for his next morning's broadcast, updating it with the obituary notices, whose sad news would be delivered during the closing moments of the broadcast. Perry would never announce that someone had died. Instead, he would state, in a very solemn voice that "Bill Hastings of Canyon Springs has gone away." Then he would tell listeners where and when to pay their last respects. Working late into the night like a wire service reporter, he also scanned the local newspapers, picking out important information to share with his listeners. Exhausted, he finally would fall into bed.

Rising at 4:30 a.m. the next morning, he would put the finishing touches on his script and head for the store, arriving no later than 6:30 a.m. He took great pride that Kallison's had consumer-friendly hours—opening early and closing late. On several occasions, he would discover an unkempt man who had spent the night at the store's back door. Perry always brought the man into the store, fixed him a cup of coffee, and headed for his broadcast booth.[10]

During one program—just around the "second cup of coffee time"—he told his listeners, "You know we have right here this morning a settled Latin American man. He's worked on the vegetable market. He'd do mighty good in a vegetable or produce house. He can do warehouse work. He says he's good at figures and writes a good hand. He wants work. He's here right now. Take any kind of job. C. E. C. Fuentes is here right now. You might call up Kallison's Capital 7-2304 and ask for C. Fuentes."[11]

During hard times as well as good, Perry Kallison was on the air. And terrible times came to Texas. The Depression, the killing drought, and the Dust Bowl exodus—followed by World War II— denuded the region of farm labor. Later, in the 1950s, farmers would suffer through another sustained dry spell. But Perry would always encourage his listeners, whom he called "neighbors." "Hang on to that ole cow's tail," he would tell them, "and she'll pull you through the drought and buy your children shoes."[12]

All the while, the *Trading Post* was continuing to bring together the interests of Kallison's Big Country Store and the Kallison Ranch. Toward that end, station KTSA sponsored a Future Farmers of America livestock judging day, which was held at the ranch. At the San Antonio Stock Show, Perry Kallison held forth on the air at a "Kallison's Trading Post" booth. At the same time, Kallison's ran a newspaper advertisement for Tox-i-Ton, a medicine designed to kill internal parasites in animals, and urged readers to come by the *Trading Post* booth to get the latest information about the cattle medicine—for which Kallison's store served as the local dealer. In South Texas agricultural life, whether attending a rodeo or livestock exhibition, picking up *Cattleman* magazine, or listening to the *Trading Post*, it was hard to miss the Kallison name. As Nathan Kallison had envisioned, the Kallison family's business and ranching interests reinforced each other.

On Saturday morning broadcasts Perry now delivered more of what he called "sermonettes" to honor the Sabbath. In those talks, he began to offer his listeners his own form of homespun philosophy about the world, the nation, and the role that citizens should play in it. Typical of his Saturday morning sermonettes was one from October 25, 1947.

Now it's been hot and dry in Texas before—old timers will tell you that back yonder it was pretty rough too, but everybody has got to keep a-goin' about their work, getting land ready, dustin' in some oats, shapin' things up to be able to feed their cows. Now, if you look back you'll agree that crops have been comin' pretty easy—the Lord has been doing a good job of takin' care of us all. But we all get to the point that we get careless. We get to a-believin' that it's all our just due. We kinda forget that all we have is just lent to us—a loan for us to use wisely, share with others, and not to get to a-believin' that it was all our own doin', forgettin' that we have had help from above. So sometimes it's a good idea to get down to appreciatin', to go over to the church house, to listen to a sermon, 'cause a preacher has more time to give thought to lots of subjects that we, in our everyday livin', don't have time to digest. So just keep a-workin' harder than ever, 'cause there's lots of green grass a-growin' in other pastures that are good to graze the soul on too. And this is Perry Kallison, your ol' neighbor from over here at Kallison's, the big ol' country store. See you come a' seven o'clock on a Monday mornin'.[13]

The homespun Saturday talks, delivered from his heart, captured Perry's essential modesty, his belief in the goodness and bounty of America, his feeling of the importance of his own moral and religious faith, which stressed tolerance and helping those in need. He also stated his resolute conviction that farmers and ranchers serve only as stewards of the land, and must care for it as carefully as for their own souls. He delivered his sermonettes in simple language that anyone could understand. In another dialect, they might have been delivered from the pulpit at Temple Beth-El on those Sabbath mornings.

The Ol' Trader's reports to his listeners included vital information about the rich social life and entertainment that flourished all over his wide listening area. He announced upcoming celebrations, dances, and benefits. For New Year's Eve 1955, the *Trading Post* program offered suggestions about where rural Texans might celebrate the New Year. With great enthusiasm, Perry mentioned dances in San Antonio at the Knights of Columbus Hall, Silver Spur, and Polo Grill—and in the surrounding towns of St. Hedwig, La Vernia, and Leakey. He told listeners "The Texas Tune Twisters are playing at Blacks Drive-in," and "if you run out of money, there's free barbecue from 8:00 to 10:00 p.m. at Griffin's Drive-In, ten miles south of Route 13 on Highway 281." There would also be an all-night gathering of the Bexar County Singing Convention at the Monte Vista Baptist Church and a party 'til dawn at Rural Murray's on Medina Lake. The celebration at Twin Sisters Hall featured the Hill Country Boys and free coffee at midnight. With concern for the revelers, Perry added: "It's a good idea to be a-drinkin' that good ole black coffee, you know. And be careful on the highways. Texas, we're sorry and ashamed to say, is second in the whole United States for loss of life on the high-ways. . . ."[14]

In a way, Perry patterned his radio program after the legendary Will Rogers, the Oklahoma-bred wit, raconteur, and homespun philosopher. He didn't have Rogers's biting, ironic wit, but his listen-ers laughed at his jokes. One morning the Ol' Trader reported that Mrs. Lasswell from Bulverde in the Texas Hill Country had come in to Kallison's the previous day to buy some of the store's new metal neck chains with numbers attached. "I'm not sure," Perry said, "whether she had got the chains for the cows or to put around the neck of her husband Marshall."[15]

Responding to Perry's warmth and humor, his "fan mail" didn't always fit in an envelope. "The neighbors take good care of the Ol' Trader," he shared with his audience. "Mrs. W. P. Elott thought I need-ed a good chicken for my soup," he said. "So she sent me one of her good fryers—plucked, trussed, froze up, and wrapped in cell–ee–PHANE."[16]

When Perry was away or not able to fill the broadcast booth him-self, his nephew Jimmy Kallison stepped in. Jimmy, who now handled the store's advertising, was a broad-shouldered, broad-gauged World

War II veteran with wide-ranging interests that included collecting antique clocks, snuff boxes, and guns. He reveled in quail hunting and attending bullfights in Mexico, and traveling with his effervescent wife Ruthie. On the radio, he did an excellent rendition of the Ol' Trader's style and brought to the show his own wry sense of humor. During one broadcast, Jimmy told about Hiram Joiner, a "famous scientist feller," who "was trying to cross a talking parakeet with a black panther. 'For goodness sake, what do you expect to get?' they asked. Hiram answered, 'I don't rightly know but if it starts talking—you better listen.'" Jimmy's jokes connected with Perry's listeners.

In times of war or peace, poverty or plenty, Perry Kallison stuck to his basic philosophy of what life should be all about. Although generous in appraisals of his fellow human beings, he also was not averse to recounting to his listeners the values he held dear: brotherhood, patriotism, and the responsibilities of citizenship. America and its citizens had been blessed with freedoms and the natural resources to prosper, he reminded them, but we need to safeguard these good fortunes.

For Perry, protecting the land was more than just a question of the economics of sound agricultural practices. A serious conservationist and environmentalist before those terms were household words, Perry Kallison heeded, and advocated, the Biblical calls to care for the land. "The good earth provides all of our needs," Perry announced. "But the world over, we neglect the earth—and here in America we are perhaps more guilty than elsewhere."[17] He saw stewardship of the land not only in religious terms, but also as part of the country's national security. And he saw the United States as a country whose blessings were a combination of the goodness of its people, the abundance of its natural resources, and the human freedoms protected by the Constitution. In Perry's view, all of those blessings were also fragile—to be revered and protected, or they could be lost. Defending America was more about values than about military might and economic strength, he insisted.

"America is great because of our natural resources," he reported in one Christmas broadcast, "and our moral fiber is still strong—our sense of doing right. As an old Mexican who kinda raised your Ol' Trader used to say, 'Él tiene un buen corazon.' He has a good heart. May the heart of our country ever beat in sympathy with those in need. And this Sunday morning over at the church house, be mighty thankful that God placed you here and not in the many other countries in the world where happiness is unknown."[18]

As a rancher—and rural philosopher—Perry's view of the land and its people was always closely tied to "Mother Nature" and the changing of the seasons. In a July broadcast: "The peach crop in the Hill Country is on the windup, the hay balers are baling hay. And all the men who bale hay and combine the maize would like it to stay dry. All they need is sunshine. [But] the rancher would like a good rain." And then, of course, he slipped in a plug for the store: "It's fence building time and we have a roll of Gaucho barbed wire, an eighty-yard roll for $8.95."[19]

The radio program had begun as an innovative way to promote Kallison's Big Country Store—and it did just that, along with advertising the other family enterprises. But more than that, it became Perry's passion—a vehicle to express his love for Texas, its people, its proud place in America, and his lifelong commitment to the "Golden Rule." In his radio persona, he had adopted a voice in the accents of his native Texas, which became like that of a kindly uncle to hundreds of thousands of "neighbors." As he became more and more engaged in the store's business, the Ol' Trader was "doing well by doing good." And as his hands-on involvement with the ranch grew into a real penchant for raising cattle, he became a student of responsible agriculture for himself as well as for his radio audience. Soon, the "doing good" so absorbed the man within the persona, Perry Kallison became more than a rising radio broadcasting star with a merchandising magnet. Throughout the rest of his life he would translate Nathan Kallison's personal values into his own existential acts. He would be widely regarded with admiration as a steadfast, stalwart Texan—a trusted leader, and one of the best-known and most respected citizens in Texas.

NINE

World War II: The Texas Home Front

SERGEANT YORK was playing downtown at the Texas Theater that Sunday afternoon. Ten-year-old Jack Kallison and his eight-year-old cousin Nathan were watching the actor Gary Cooper as the famous World War I hero—the kind of soldier they wanted to be if they only had a war. When the movie ended, the boys walked out onto the sidewalk to find people scurrying about, passing the word: *Japan!* "Bombed Pearl Harbor!" Some were crying. "They sank our ships!" "Are they headed for California?" A few soldiers in uniform were running down Houston Street, trying to get back to Fort Sam Houston the quickest way possible. For the Kallison boys, Gary Cooper's black-and-white war had become a sudden reality. Would the Japanese planes attack San Antonio? Would they be as brave as Sergeant Alvin York? Terrified, the youngsters rushed to catch a bus home—to safety, they hoped. They found Morris and Ruth listening to every word on the radio broadcast. America's involvement in a second world war had just begun and it would change their lives—and the entire country—forever.

The grave voice of President Franklin Delano Roosevelt described that early Sunday morning surprise attack on December 7, 1941 as "A Day that Will Live in Infamy" when he announced a declaration of war against Japan. The news about the "sneak attack" in Hawaii and the Philippines swept through San Antonio as it did throughout all of the United States. In the nation's capital, a Washington Redskins football game was interrupted for urgent

announcements that all military and civilian defense personnel needed to return immediately to their bases and offices. A similar emer-
gency summons went out to military personnel from the large bases
in and around San Antonio. Three days later, on December 11,
Japan's Axis partners Germany and Italy declared war against the
United States.

Thousands of young Texans made plans to volunteer for military
service as soon as recruiting offices opened on Monday morning.
And at the University of Texas in Austin, Jimmy Kallison, a senior
majoring in business administration, prepared to enlist in the Army
Air Corps. Already fearing an inevitable war against Germany, he had
earned his pilot's license as a civilian and was ready to fight. He chose
to become a pilot, Jimmy reflected later, because war movies had convinced him he wanted no part of bloody infantry combat. The war
would be bloody indeed, he reasoned.

As the United States entered the war, Jimmy's Uncle Perry stated
to his radio audience what was at stake: "Comes a great war. And the
all-American team has 140 million players, each doing his duty," he
began. "Our country shall be great so long as we have a soul—of
goodness . . . as long as we have a desire to feed the starving . . . so long
as we maintain our churches—and all of the teamwork to produce
the best cattle, build the packing houses, create the markets." In 1943,
Frontier Times magazine would praise the *Trading Post* program in a
story headlined "Doing a Real Service."[1]

Perry and Frances, Morris and Ruth, Tibe, and Pauline would
gather around Nathan and Anna's table after the broadcasts to discuss
the impending danger from across two oceans. In the newsreels
shown before Nathan's favorite "shoot 'em up" westerns and in daily
radio news programs and newspapers, they had followed the 1930s
Japanese war buildup and apparent victory over its larger, much
more populous neighbor China, which was appealing to America for
more military aid and weapons. For the Kallisons and most
Americans, Asia was too far away to engage more than sympathy. The
family was riveted by the news from Germany, however, as they

learned about Adolph Hitler's National Socialist Party and its state-sponsored anti-Semitism. Nathan and Anna, now comfortable in Texas and in their sixties, were filled with daily dread, remembering their own harrowing, narrow escapes from the Russian czar in their youth—and the friends who were brutally beaten or killed because of their religion.

From stories of Jewish refugees from Germany and the countries already devoured by the Nazi invasion and from Jewish publications such as the *Jewish Journal of San Antonio*, the Kallisons and Jews throughout America grew painfully aware of the German deification of the Aryan race and their intent to "cleanse" Europe—and the world—of Jews and other "undesirables."[2] In the 1930s, rabbis spoke from their pulpits, wrote, petitioned, and begged the United States government to open its doors to Jewish immigrants. From the early 1930s onward, Perry and Frances Kallison became outspoken sponsors and participants in the efforts of the American Jewish Distribution Committee to help bring German Jewish refugees to the United States. They admired San Antonio Jewish families who sponsored refugees and brought them into their homes.[3]

During the Depression, however, President Roosevelt and the US State Department had turned a blind eye to the inscription on the Statue of Liberty to "Give me your tired, your poor, your huddled masses yearning to breathe free . . . " From American Jewish national organizations, the Kallison family had learned of the heartbreaking voyage of the SS *St. Louis* that in 1939, with 907 Jewish refugees aboard, was turned away by the United States.[4] In the newsreels at the Majestic or Texas movie theaters, Frances and Perry, Morris and Ruth, Tibe, and Pauline were sickened by the robotic goose-stepping of the thousands of German soldiers, raising their arms to "Heil" Adolph Hitler. Nathan and Anna sought information, but little attention in the newsreels and newspapers was paid to the plight of the Russian and other Eastern European Jews.[5] From December 1941, reporting centered on the US military, its battles, and the sacrifices those on the home front needed to make.

In Texas, the military played a major role in the nation's economic recovery from the Great Depression, as it had during World War I. Now new bases sprang up around San Antonio. Older army and air corps centers quickly expanded. Fort Sam Houston became an induction and training center for tens of thousands of soldiers, and Kelly Field soon grew into a massive supply and maintenance depot, with twenty-five thousand civilian employees. San Antonio took pride that its air force base held the largest airplane hangar in the world. The new San Antonio Aviation Cadet Center (formerly part of Kelly Field) was involved in training pilots, navigators, and bombardiers, as well as numerous other military personnel.[6] Randolph Field, called "The West Point of the Air" when it was founded in 1930, transitioned into a school to train instructors for all of the air corps' pilot training programs.[7] The new post hospital at Fort Sam Houston, named Brooke General Hospital in 1942, treated wounded airmen and soldiers, providing both convalescent and psychiatric facilities.[8] The San Antonio economy benefited from billions of dollars of military construction, and emerged as the nation's largest military complex outside of Washington, DC.[9]

Participation by Texans in World War II almost matched the Lone Star State's outsized ego. It produced 750,000 Texans who served in the armed forces, including 12,000 women. Texas A&M University alone provided more officers for the armed services than the two US military academies combined.[10] Thirty-three Texas soldiers won the Congressional Medal of Honor, including Audie L. Murphy of Kingston, an army lieutenant fighting in Germany and the most highly decorated American in the war.[11] Admiral Chester Nimitz, a native of Fredericksburg, from a pioneer German American family, commanded the Pacific Fleet.[12] Outstanding wartime leaders included General Walter Krueger, a native of Germany and resident of San Antonio, commander of the Sixth Army in the South Pacific, as well as General Claire Chenault, a former high school teacher from Commerce, Texas, who organized the "Flying Tigers" to fight with the Chinese against Japan. And although General Dwight D. Eisenhower had been mostly raised in Kansas, his place of birth was Denison, Texas, where he lived until the age of two.

Both Walter Krueger and Claire Chenault were friends of Morris Kallison. During World War II, many other military men and women based in San Antonio who shopped at Kallison's store became friends with the whole family. Morris and Perry, both in their forties and ineligible to serve in the military, assisted the war effort from the home front. With problems of rationing or otherwise surviving shortages of essential items, Perry Kallison used the *Trading Post* to bring buyers and sellers and "swappers" together. Barbed wire, metal tools, and farm equipment were in particularly short supply. Across the country all sources of steel were concentrated in making weapons to fight against the widening Axis of Germany and Japan. The *Trading Post* also brought news of local servicemen. Perry reminded his listeners to "support our boys overseas," appealing to his rural audience to contribute to the Community War Chest campaign and to buy war bonds.

Despite shortages of many basic farm supply items, especially anything made of steel or other metals, both Morris and Perry scrambled to find what their ranchers and farmers needed. In *Cattleman* magazine, the store advertised in "Ol' Trader" vernacular: "Why be 'throwed' by wartime shortages? Stop by Kallison's country trading post for hard-to-find items! We got corralled all kinds of ranch 'n farm supplies—wire, plumbing, hardware. Next time you're in San Antonio, folks, tie up at Kallison's—where ranch folks been tradin' since '99."[13] Addressing the problem of wartime shortages, a 1943 Kallison advertisement in the *San Antonio Light* displayed a picture of a decrepit barn with this advice: "Your farm and ranch buildings are war buildings now! Don't let them become dangerous and inefficient for the want of proper and regular repairs." To repair barns, Kallison's offered thirty-five-pound-weight roofing for $0.89 a roll and quality ferronite roof paint for $2.95 a gallon.[14] As it had during the Depression, Kallison's store managed to thrive during the war.

The economic impact of World War II was immense both for San Antonio and for the entire state. Between 1940 and 1945, twenty army combat divisions trained more than 1.2 million troops at Texas's fifteen major army camps. An estimated 200,000 airmen, including 45,000 pilots, 12,000 bombardiers, 12,000 navigators, and thousands of aerial gunners, photographers, and mechanics prepared for combat at forty military airfields, with a cluster of the largest ones located in and near San Antonio. Along the Gulf Coast, the greatest petrochemical industry in the world was built to refine fuel for the American war effort. Enormous aircraft factories grew up in Garland, Grand Prairie, and Fort Worth. Shipyards were opened in Beaumont, Port Arthur, Houston, Galveston, and Corpus Christi. Steel mills arose in Houston and Dangerfield. The total output of manufacturing in Texas increased fourfold from $453 million in 1939 to nearly $2 billion in 1945, employing thousands from Texas and from out of state—men ineligible for combat. And for the first time, women, personifying the legendary "Rosie the Riveter," were brought in to provide skilled labor. Farm output soared, with every available acre planted to meet demands for food at home and for allies overseas.[15]

As in World War I, but perhaps to a lesser extent, lingering flashes of prejudice against German Americans emerged in South Texas. Anna Kallison and her children always strongly refuted that charge. The Kallisons were quick to cite war heroes Krueger and Nimitz and others to exemplify the patriotism of German Americans. After learning that the German American woman from New Braunfels who delivered eggs to their homes had been boycotted by some of her longtime customers, the Kallison families of Olmos Park doubled their orders of farm-fresh eggs. Despite the family's horror at the Nazis systematically exterminating their fellow Jews, they drew a distinction between Adolph Hitler's heinous Nazi crimes against humanity and the behavior of German American gentiles.

The US Office of War Information was pumping out a steady stream of unparalleled propaganda to motivate Americans to exert their passions and hard work to defeat the evil Axis Powers. Nazis replaced American gangsters as the villains of American films. The Japanese and their soldiers were even more harshly portrayed as "the Japanese Ape," as "near-sighted, buck-toothed, evil, rat-faced enemies" who slaughtered infants with their bayonets. More accurate were charges that the Japanese brutally mistreated American soldiers held as prisoners of war.

With those propaganda-induced fears in their minds, a group of Nathan's young grandchildren suddenly came face to face with their first German soldiers at the Brooke Army Medical Center Officers' Club. Invited to dinner by a family friend, the youngsters discovered that the white-jacketed young men serving them at the club were German prisoners of war![16] The young Kallisons were terrified that the waiters might put poison in their food. After staring at the waiters, however, the cousins discovered that the German prisoners serving them looked very much like young American men. A strange feeling—almost sympathy—was reported by each child.[17]

The propaganda against Japan, however, played strongly on the incipient racism still existing in mainstream America. Japanese American citizens, including residents from farmers to college professors to prominent businessmen whose ancestors had immigrated to the US a generation or more earlier, were rounded up like prisoners of war and shipped to barracks in remote camps. It was called a "patriotic precaution"—a fate much harsher than, say, a German American woman's eggs being boycotted. Under the auspices of the Department of Justice, the Immigration and Naturalization Service (INS) ran three internment camps in Texas—in Seagoville, Kenedy, and Crystal City. The largest of the three, Crystal City, housed numerous Japanese families from Latin America—many from Peru—who were brought to the United States for "repatriation" under the guise of "securing the Western Hemisphere from internal sabotage and to provide bartering pawns for exchange of American citizens captured by Japan." In reality, many Japanese as well as Germans and Italians living in Latin America were deported to the United States by their adopted countries not because they posed a security threat, according to the Texas State Historical Association, but "as a result of racial prejudice and because they provided economic competition for the other Latin Americans."[18] Closer to the Kallisons' home, the name of the Japanese Tea Garden in San Antonio was changed to the Chinese Tea Garden.

All the Kallison women kept active in the home-front war effort. Ruth worked as a social worker, helping soldiers with their family problems. Both she and Tibe served as Gray Ladies, visiting wounded soldiers in the area's military hospitals. Pauline volunteered as an airplane spotter, trained to identify and report on enemy planes that might fly over San Antonio. Her team stood watch on the rooftop of a downtown office building to report any German Messerschmitts or Japanese Zeros.[19] The entire family was relieved that Jimmy Kallison, the oldest grandson, was assigned as a flight instructor, despite his ardent wish to pilot fighter planes or bombers. As the Army Air Corps was rushing to mass-produce fighter and bomber pilots, his commanding officer had already decided that Jimmy, with previous civilian training and calm competency, would make an ideal flight instructor.

His assignment also allowed him to marry his high school sweetheart. In 1943, Lieutenant James Kallison wed Ruth Friedman at the St. Anthony Hotel. In World War II haste, their wedding was squeezed into the lieutenant's demanding flight schedule. After the morning wedding and reception, Jimmy had to report back to base. The bride ended up spending her wedding night at the St. Anthony, not with her bridegroom, but with her best friend Marie Holland. As Jimmy was transferred from base to base, Ruthie—so called to distinguish her from his mother, also named Ruth—packed and repacked a dozen times to follow her husband.[20]

The Kallison women, along with the rest of the family, entertained troops at the Kallison Ranch every weekend, bringing out dozens of soldiers and airmen who were on leave. Invitations to the ranch were announced on flyers distributed by the USO at area military bases. With Frances Kallison in charge, a barbecue would be prepared, beef or pork smoking slowly on a mesquite grill. Sometimes a goat would roast on an outdoor spit. A particular thrill for Nathan and Anna's grandchildren were the Sundays when busloads of airmen from Randolph Field and other nearby military facilities rolled out to the ranch in buses to drink beer, eat, ride horses, and enjoy a few hours away from their preparations to go into battle. The youngsters eagerly followed the Army Air Corps men around, admiring their khaki uniforms and hounding them with questions about the planes they were flying. Thus inspired, the Kallison boys would carve balsa wood models of those World War II airplanes and pretend to be pilots like their hero, Cousin Jimmy.

One special Kallison Ranch gathering was an Independence Day party on Sunday, July 4, 1943. Perry and Frances were hosts for military personnel and their dependents. As they had during World War I, the Kallison family worked closely with the Jewish Welfare Board (JWB) throughout the war to serve the military personnel, including Jewish soldiers, sailors, Coast Guard, and airmen. Chartered buses brought soldiers and their families to the ranch from the Calcasieu Servicemen's Center at 214 Broadway, and everything at the ranch was free—except for the fifty-cent round-trip bus fare.[21] Arranged by the Armed Services Committee of the JWB, a USO participant, the patriotic party was especially festive. The Kallisons brought in western musicians wearing cowboy hats and boots who strummed guitars and sang of tumbleweeds or broken hearts—and always "God Bless America." With a crew of local girls standing ready to dance the Texas two-step with soldiers, Pauline, Ruth, Frances, Tibe, and Ruth and Morris's teenage daughter Jane were hostesses. Together with the troops, they ate barbecue, drank colas and beer, and listened to stories about home told by young men from all parts of the country.

Some of the young airmen and soldiers soon became close family friends. Anna Kallison's daughters and daughters-in-law acted as surrogate mothers, in a way, by writing to the servicemen's parents, or pinning wings on their lapels at graduation ceremonies from flight school. And in hushed tones, they answered telephone calls that brought word that one of the young flyers had been killed in a training accident—or in combat.

The military presence vastly accelerated the social life of San Antonio's young women. Jobs for secretaries and nurses opened at the bases, and other opportunities for actual armed service positions brought women who volunteered as Women's Army Auxiliary Corps (WAAC) into close encounters with soldiers and airmen. From those encounters at the bases and dances at the downtown USO, romances blossomed. Exposure to a wider field of eligible Jewish bachelors was welcomed by the Kallison sisters during wartime San Antonio. Entertaining the troops became more than just a patriotic obligation. Many of the officers they met at the ranch or at High Holy Days hospitality events had been called into service because of their professional expertise. On weekends, there were gentleman callers on Thelma Drive. "Pauline and I enjoyed that part of the war, I'm embarrassed to say," confessed Tibe years later.

At one of those social events, the widowed Pauline met Lieutenant Colonel Max Blumer, an orthopedic surgeon from Pittsburgh who had been wounded in Italy. Now on staff at Brooke Medical Center, Dr. Blumer (or Max) came calling. They were married on January 13, 1946, and he moved into the house on Thelma Drive with Pauline and young Susan.[22] At first, Anna had warmed to the notion of a doctor in the family. As with the late Isadore Neustadt, however, in the critical eyes of Anna Letwin Kallison, no one would ever be good enough for her high-spirited, beloved elder daughter. But Dr. Blumer was high-spirited, too—and brought laughter into Pauline's life as they played golf together, went to nightclubs or horse races, and threw parties at home for fellow officers and family friends. Anna kept hoping for the war to be over, Pauline recalled, so that Max could go into private practice and "make some money."[23]

All during the war, the family regularly gathered for dinner at each other's homes. During one of those dinners, the Kallison children and grandchildren sat tensely around Nathan and Anna's dining room table as dinner was being served. Papa—as Nathan's children and grandchildren called him—was the only person at the table who did not know the "secret" about their meal: the steak on his plate had come from the Kallison Ranch! Nathan, everyone knew, would have choked on his food if he learned that he was eating one of his prized cattle.[24] Although by law farmers and ranchers were allowed to consume all foods they had raised, as a rule, the Kallisons used their own ration coupons to purchase meat at the butcher's shop.[25] Their pedigreed Polled Herefords were raised for breeding purposes.

Wartime rationing became a way of life with government-issue stamp books for meat, sugar, shoes, rubber, auto parts, and finally gasoline. It was an effort to ensure that limited supplies were distributed fairly. To show patriotism and conserve their food rationing stamps, tens of thousands of Americans planted Victory Gardens. In Texas, reaching jobs and farm markets involved driving long distances, and gasoline rationing stirred controversy. Governor Coke Stevenson denounced gas rationing in Texas. "Gasoline," he said, was as much a necessity as "the saddle, the rifle, the ax, and the Bible."[26]

Younger Kallison grandchildren also tried to help win the war. When the war began, Jane Kallison, Jimmy's younger sister, was taking music lessons from June Rose Fluornoy and playing in her fourteen-member accordion band. The plucky group performed for the troops at military bases around San Antonio, with Jane and her best friend Elaine Davis featured in an accordion duet. At one USO program, Jane and her accordion band played on a stage with famed comedian and actor Red Skelton, whose trademark straight-faced ad libs made them giggle. Afterwards, Jane reported to her envious friends that Skelton had winked at her. GIs called asking to date the lovely young woman—until they learned that she was only fourteen years old. Not entertainers, the Kallison children Jack, Susan, Nathan, and Maryann, tried to make themselves useful by collecting tinfoil and scrap metal used to make weapons. They also collected used cooking fat in rancid-smelling barrels to be made into lubricant for greasing the insides of gun barrels. Susan Neustadt and her cousin Maryann Kallison pulled a toy wagon through Olmos Park collecting tinfoil and scrap. Encouraged by their grandmother and their parents, the children also bought savings stamps, filling their stamp books until they had $18 to buy a war bond—redeemable ten years later for $25.

During the late 1930s, Nathan Kallison had suffered another stroke, the second of several that would eventually claim his life. Stricken at work in his downtown store, he was rushed by ambulance to the Nix Hospital, only blocks away on Navarro Street. As San Antonio's state-of-the-art medical center, the Nix complex combined hospital facilities with doctors' offices and covered parking. With expert care from his team of doctors, Nathan recovered quickly. At home in Olmos Park, he received nursing care from Anna, his daughters, and his daughters-in-law. His sons ran the family store and ranch.

After the second stroke, Nathan and Anna felt confronted by mortality. They discussed how they wanted the businesses they had built over four decades to be left to their children. Together, they decided that all their assets—Kallison's store, the Kallison Ranch, and their commercial properties—should be divided equally among their four children—Morris, Pauline, Tibe, and Perry. They made these gifts early in 1941, while they both were still active and before America entered World War II. At the time, they were especially concerned about protecting the widowed Pauline and divorced Tibe, each then the sole support of a nine-year-old child. It never occurred to the aging parents that those arrangements might cause difficulties, although Morris and Perry spent their lives running the store and ranch, and neither sister played any role in managing the businesses.

Nathan and Anna's decision to divide all their assets equally among their four children intensified an already simmering conflict within the family. Morris, the eldest son, who was dedicated to pursuing his own dreams of developing a downtown real estate empire, now spent more time on his own projects. His failure to include his sisters in his new ventures angered Anna, who felt he was violating the family ethic of "one for all." At times their disagreements grew into shouting matches, one ending with Morris standing in the front yard of his parents' home, yelling back and forth with his mother, who stood at the window of her bedroom.

In these family arguments Morris and Tibe, both strong-willed, vied for their parents' approval. Tibe typically prevailed. Perry, devoted to the store, ranch, and radio program, was torn between loyalty to his parents and sisters and to his wife Frances, who felt that the rewards of his labors should go to their own family.

With the exception of the front-yard shouting match, the family turbulence remained behind closed doors. Despite private resentments and disagreements, the Kallisons lived up to their public personae—a warm, welcoming family who worked hard and played well together. Resentment simmered, however, as the weakened Nathan ceded control to his sons.

In retirement, Nathan had more time to spend at his beloved ranch, making the weekly Sunday trip there with Perry. He also enjoyed his Saturday trip to the double-feature westerns at Uptown Theater—a two-story, stucco Spanish Colonial Revival style building with a Moroccan foyer on the northwest corner of Fredericksburg Road and West Ashby.[27] A succession of grandchildren shared his fascination with exploits of his favorite movie cowboys—Hopalong Cassidy, Gene Autry, Roy Rogers, and Tom Mix—along with newsreel films showing vivid scenes from battlefields in Europe and the South Pacific. Both the cowboy fighting and wartime battle scenes deepened their immersion in the palpable mythology of Texas manhood.

While Anna constantly provided her grandchildren with detailed and valuable instructions about how to behave properly and to live well (lessons also laid on by their mothers), Nathan's relationship with them was more like that of an easygoing older friend who expressed interest in their activities and enjoyed their company. Years later, his granddaughter Susan Neustadt Miller would recall his sweetness and generosity. He taught mostly by example—but did impress upon Jack, Nathan, and Pete one important value he believed in. Gripping a grandson's forearm with his hand—and his grip did remain powerful—he would quietly but firmly instruct, "You've got to be strong, boy!"[28]

Every summer, Nathan and Anna accompanied Pauline and Tibe and their two children, Susan and Nathan, for a week's stay at a beach hotel in Corpus Christi or Galveston. Always an early riser, Nathan would wake at sunrise and head for the Gulf of Mexico. Wearing a two-piece woolen swim suit, he'd wade out into the Gulf and vigorously splash cold salt water on his face. Always tagging along with him was his delighted grandson Nathan, called "Nicky" by family and friends, the only other early bird in the family party. Every day he avidly followed the war news with Papa as the two listened to the radio and treasured their time alone together.

On December 3, 1944, as American troops were pushing toward victory in Europe against Nazi Germany, Nathan Kallison suffered a third and final stroke. He died at seventy-one, in bed at his home on Thelma Drive, surrounded by his loved ones. The family knew very little of Nathan's early life—only that he had arrived in America fifty-four years earlier, as a seventeen-year-old apprentice harness maker from Russia who could not speak a word of English. It was a past he put behind him, one that the successful family saw little reason to explore. Only later would they appreciate his vision and how hard he had worked to fulfill it. They benefitted greatly from Nathan's personal success in business, which brought such security and pleasure to his family. His sons tried to follow his example in business and ranching, serving the people of his community, bringing together farmers and ranchers and city people searching for better ways to live. The next day, on the *Trading Post* broadcast to farmers across South Texas, Perry Kallison began his morning radio program:

In 1899, came a young man to San Antonio. He had very little in the bank. He had a will to work—a will to be part of the country. Nathan Kallison could have been a success in whatever he might have started out to do—because when he planted a wheat field to raise a crop, he planted deep. When he built a fence, there always was a stout corner post. When he made a friend, he was always true. He would advise farmer friends "to put the seed in the ground and the money in the bank." Dad Kallison would have made a pretty good judge too, because he knew what was right and what was wrong. And usually, he was mostly right. The old timers still come around and they miss the Boss—because he was the kind of man always handy to have around—because his feet were always on the ground.[29]

Seven months after Nathan's death, Germany surrendered to the Allied Forces—the event Nathan had prayed for while listening to those news programs and watching newsreels. And three months later, Japan surrendered as well, only days after American bombers had dropped the newly minted atomic bombs on Hiroshima and Nagasaki. Among the 406,000 Americans killed in the four years of World War II, Texas had lost 22,000 young men. The Kallison family, especially Morris, Ruth, and Ruthie, were forever grateful that Jimmy was not counted among them. Just as the war ended, Captain Jimmy Kallison and his nine-member B-29 bomber crew were finally poised on the West Coast, only days away from heading for Okinawa to fly bombing missions against Japan. Relieved that he and Ruthie could at last live a normal life, Jimmy went back to work at Kallison's. But as a reserve officer, he soon was called back during the Korean War. He spent that war testing decommissioned World War II airplanes for the new US Air Force, to find out whether they were still airworthy. Later he flew transports to Europe and around the world. He always had a passion for flying, but he never had a chance to see combat. After the Korean War ended, Jimmy wanted to stay in the Air Force.

Yielding to his father Morris's strong urging, however, he joined the family business, bringing to the store much-needed modern management skills.

Nathan's death and the end of World War II marked the end of an era for the Kallison's modest empire. Now led by Morris and Perry, Kallison's would open a new chapter in the boom that followed victory in the war, and return to a new kind of peace. A Kallison advertisement noted the return of scarce items to store shelves: "All kinds of farm and ranch supplies that've been missin' since Hirohito broke loose, are back at Kallison's again. Come on in and stock up on what you've been missin'."[30]

TEN

The Best Years

WITH THE NEW POSTWAR America open for business again, Morris and Perry Kallison's ambitions now grew broader than Nathan had ever envisioned. In the euphoria created by the parallel victories over Germany and Japan, and after four years of unparalleled sacrifice on faraway battlefields, supported by patriotic discipline at home, there was no limit to what Americans thought they could accomplish. Enjoying a comfortable level of unpretentious prosperity in San Antonio, the Kallison brothers immediately began planning to expand what Nathan had built.

The end of World War II had released a surge of pent-up demand for all kinds of consumer goods and services that had not been available while the entire country's industry was dedicated to producing weapons and materials for the armed services. Fifteen million servicemen and women returning to civilian life created immediate needs for housing, automobiles, and every other American consumer product. When the GI Bill of Rights was signed into law in 1944, new and even broader opportunities opened. Millions of war veterans would be able to attend college, buy homes, and start businesses. And American agriculture, devoted to raising food for the war effort, now was challenged not only to meet new demands at home, but also to feed hungry people overseas whose countries had been devastated by the war.

Morris and Perry Kallison saw all of those challenges as opportunities which they eagerly sought to seize. Their decisions would result in the Kallison enterprise's finest era, during which the family-owned business would compete successfully with retail giants Sears, Roebuck & Company and Montgomery Ward, as well as with farm implement stores, specialty retailers, and even with Joske's, at that time part of the Allied Stores chain and one of the nation's leading department stores. Because of the wide range of merchandise the store offered, Kallison's was unique in Texas.

The San Antonio business economy was still led by older mainstays, though—in banking, the Frost National Bank and the National Bank of Commerce of San Antonio; in manufacturing and distribution, Pioneer Flour Mills and The Roegelein Company; in building and maintenance, Steves & Sons, Friedrich Air Condition & Refrigeration Company, and Alamo Cement Company; and in merchandising, Joske's, Frost Brothers (fine women's clothing), and Wolff & Marx (general apparel for men, women, and children).[1] Kallison's Big Country Store covered almost all retail categories with its wide range of merchandise.

Like many other cities in America, San Antonio had prospered quickly during the postwar years, but it no longer reigned as the state's dominant city. While it was lying somnolent during the 1930s and the Dust Bowl, its economy had been surpassed by Dallas and Houston, cities that grew even during the Depression. Well to the south and slightly west of Dallas, the "Alamo City" lacked the central location and transportation network that had positioned Dallas to become Texas's financial and merchandise center. San Antonio also lacked the deep channel port, surrounding oil fields, and petrochemical plants that propelled the rise of Houston. Nevertheless, Morris and Perry, along with other downtown businessmen, worked tirelessly to persuade new industries and businesses to come to San Antonio. Aside from some food processing and garment manufacture, however, growth and prosperity in San Antonio still depended primarily on its large military establishment—the source of one-third of all jobs. Economic success also banked on the city's tourist attractions, the construction industry, and on agriculture from the surrounding counties. As the country transitioned from wartime to a peacetime economy, the resourceful Kallisons sought to profit from each of the city's strengths.

One opportunity appeared immediately. The federal government was pumping billions of dollars' worth of surplus military equipment into the market, creating a new type of retail outlet, the "army surplus store." Everything from American military jeeps and trucks to uniforms, helmets, and canteens were now available for civilians to purchase. Always ready to experiment with new products, Perry and Morris jumped in. They ordered hundreds of surplus gas-powered army generators, believing that they would be extremely useful for their rural customers. Offered for $178 to $480 each, depending on size, the generators were advertised by the government as capable of powering ten sixty-watt lamps, two pumps for water in the house or barn, a small chicken brooder, and a milking machine. Even in 1946, quite a few Southwest Texas farmers in surrounding counties still lacked electricity.

Unfortunately, when the surplus generators arrived at Kallison's store, many were rusted and worn from hard use and exposure to weather. They simply did not work. The Kallisons sued the US government to get their money back—unsuccessfully. The store ended up with hundreds of generators with no value except as junk metal. The useless generators were followed by a big order of surplus army gas stoves, a similar effort that also fizzled. The stoves were left to collect more rust in Kallison's warehouse. They watched in dismay as "army surplus" became a big new retailing venture elsewhere, but it was one the Kallison brothers never mastered.

Kallison's store had much better luck with another undertaking, however. With millions of veterans coming home, America suddenly was facing a severe housing shortage. Congress quickly responded by authorizing the Wherry and Capehart housing programs, which provided federally subsidized rental housing for thousands of military families who could not find or afford housing in the booming civilian market. Taking advantage of those federal programs,

Kallison's leased or sold furniture for hundreds of government-financed houses located on or around San Antonio's military bases, including a housing development called Billy Mitchell Village, adjacent to Kelly Field.[2] In addition, the postwar building boom brought customers to Kallison's Builders Supply Company, expanding the store's depression-era business beyond the Federal Housing Administration's (FHA) home renovation and new construction programs.

After four years of scarcity, the Kallison brothers moved aggressively to sell many of the new products pouring into the prosperous postwar marketplace. They decided that home freezers, introduced in the early 1950s, would have equally strong appeal to their country and their city customers. On August 19, 1953, three thousand enthusiastic women showed up to attend a promotion they advertised as "Kallison's Freezer Kollege." The hundreds who could not jam into the store watched from television sets in the store's parking lot, as an attractive home economist from the General Electric Company demonstrated how to scald fresh vegetables before freezing them, and how to wrap foods properly in tinfoil before storing them in the new freezer. "Red River Dave" McEnery performed for the women, juggling his roles as a popular country western singer as well as the manager of Kallison's appliance department. The women screamed "like bobbysoxers at a Frank Sinatra concert," the newspapers reported, as McEnery called out the names of the six women who had won freezers in a lottery.[3]

Red River Dave, so named because as a teenager he had so often strummed "Red River Valley" on his guitar, was a persuasive salesman who appealed both to city buyers clamoring for bargains and to farmers purchasing as much merchandise as they could pile into the beds of their pickups. He was such a draw at the store that Perry Kallison sponsored a show on WOAI-TV called *Barn Dance*, featuring Red River Dave performing his greatest hits, including a 1937 ballad titled "Amelia Earhart's Last Flight." (McEnery liked to write songs about events in the news—especially about tragic occurrences.) As master of ceremonies for Kallison's *Barn Dance*, Red River Dave McEnery introduced other western singers, square dancers, and vaudeville acts—interspersed, of course, with a persuasive pitch for the latest home appliances from Kallison's store. Farm and ranch families eager for all the latest labor-saving products for their homes flocked into Kallison's downtown store to buy washing machines, refrigerators, kitchen ranges, freezers, and air conditioners—"just like a Sears 'n Roebuck store," said one rural customer, admiringly. Free giveaways for the new products were announced on *Barn Dance* television and on Perry's *Trading Post* radio show. The promotion to launch the new Serta Perfect Sleepers luxury mattress line, for example, brought hundreds of customers into the store to register for the drawing.[4]

Determined to compete with both department stores and appliance dealers, Kallison's, often advertised as "The Big Country Store," next held a widely promoted grand opening in 1957 for its new and expanded home furnishings and appliance center, "Kallison's Kitchen Paradise." This department advertised the newest General Electric kitchens and appliances and Youngstown sink cabinets. Again, with its door prizes, entertainment, and candy for children, "Kitchen Paradise Day" drew a large audience who listened attentively to home economists demonstrate how the latest devices, such as electric mixers, combined with a few interior decorating touches, could transform an ordinary kitchen into a "magazine-picture model kitchen."[5] And for a time Kallison's even offered a home freezer food plan.

In those promotions, Kallison's became part of a national scheme to reboot the postwar economy. Those glamorous kitchens shown in national magazines and touted in the store were a central element in a marketing strategy by government and industry that was designed to spur both peacetime manufacturing and incite consumer desire. This plan was also aimed at luring "Rosie the Riveter" wartime working women back into their homes. Their factory jobs were needed by returning veterans, the peacetime planners reasoned. With the "home and garden" and new women's magazines poised to elevate home-making into an art, with "how-to" articles on decorating living rooms, building comfortable home additions, using sleek new appliances, planting elegant but easy-care landscaping, and cooking up mouth-watering recipes in their new "gourmet kitchens," America's women would leave their wartime factory jobs and go home to their new roles as "model wives and homemakers." This planned exodus into new, hastily built suburban homes would then leave space in the labor market for World War II servicemen eager for peacetime work. It was an effective offensive. With television as a new media outlet, advertising became a creative and powerful industry that could offer dramatic promotions such as those Morris and Perry Kallison were embracing.

With the consumer era in full swing, bigger was better, whether in home freezers that could store a whole prime steer, or in automobiles, which grew longer and sprouted fins. Americans were proud of what their industrial ingenuity was bringing to the public. Even in the midst of the Cold War, with the United States and the Soviet Union locked in a deadly missile race, there was intense competition over consumer achievements. In a famous 1959 "kitchen debate" between Vice President Richard Nixon and Soviet leader Nikita Kruschev at a first-time Moscow trade show, the two men argued over the merits of a model American kitchen sponsored by the United States government.[6] Krushchev claimed that under Communism, his country also could produce modern kitchens—but accused America of being overcome by gross materialism. Nixon pointed to American personal freedoms in a democracy. The Cold War had shifted from a deadly race about nuclear weapons, it seemed, to a debate over which country—and system of government—best provided for its citizens.

General Electric and Westinghouse spurred the Kallison's sale of their newest appliances, providing the store with special discounts and credit arrangements offered to their best distributors. With generous credit terms from the appliance manufacturers, Kallison's was able to stock large varieties and quantities of the latest home appliances and television sets. At its peak in the 1950s, Kallison's sold more new television sets than Joske's, the older department store. Morris and Perry, who seldom took vacations, even escorted Ruth and Frances to New York and Europe on trips sponsored by General Electric as bonuses for achieving great sales.

Even as they were presenting the dazzling new home appliances, though, the Kallisons always carefully calculated ways to consider the basic needs of their original core customers—farmers and ranchers of Southwest Texas. Advertising regularly on the farm pages of both San Antonio daily newspapers, the store still projected its downhome appeal: "Been so dry and so hot," began one 1948 spread, "that sheep-herder Wade claims his popcorn started popping in the field. His cows thought 'twas snowing, got a chill, caught a case of 'newmonia.' We still have a lot of Fairbanks-Morse windmills, galvanized cisterns and pump jacks, both electric and gasoline, at Kallison's Big Country Store."[7] Kallison's farm sales soared.

For many of those farm and ranch families, a visit to Kallison's store was still a special occasion for both adults and children. Families often came to the store from the stockyards after they had sold cattle or goats and had money to spend. Rancher Gary Schott recounted his experiences as a boy visiting the store with his brother and father on Saturday mornings in the 1950s: "The smell of leather would hit you as you came in the door," he recalled. "We'd play on the saddles by the front door. Then, we'd get on the Fairbanks scales to see if we had gained any weight. Perry Kallison would greet us with peppermint sticks, as friendly as could be. He knew everyone's name."

The boys would follow Perry and their father Howard Schott, a fourth-generation Texas rancher, around the shelves while Schott examined cattle medicine and other items needed for his ranch. "Perry didn't bug you to buy something, but after you had picked out what you wanted, he'd take you over to the cashier and announce, 'Mr. Schott wants these things; please take care of him.'"

The Schotts' store experience would not be complete until the next morning, added Gary Schott. After their early chores were finished, the family would gather around the breakfast table to hear the

Ol' Trader's seven o'clock radio program: "Perry would announce, 'Well, Howard Schott and those two boys of his were in the store yesterday,'" he remembered. "And hearing our names called made Daddy so happy."[8]

Kallison's store and Perry's radio program also helped the Schott boys earn some spending money: "Perry would announce, 'Well, tomorrow will be Tuesday, and Old John will be here in the parking lot to buy furs. If you have furs to sell, bring them in,'" he explained. The Schott boys had put out their trap lines to catch raccoons and ringtails.[9] They skinned them, then stretched and nailed the skins to the barn to dry. On the announced day, in Kallison's parking lot, they sold the hides to Old John, who sometimes also gave them a bag of the pecans that he was selling to passersby.

Nurturing old friendships and making new acquaintances remained an essential component of the store's appeal. It was also fostered by an integral part of Perry's personality. Being greeted by the Ol' Trader, shaking his hand, and hearing their names on the radio were important to family ranchers and farmers who lived in sparsely settled rural areas in the Hill Country and Southwest Texas. Perry was tirelessly promoting business for the store as its "goodwill ambassador," but business aside, he derived both energy and great pleasure from those diverse personal relationships.[10]

By the mid-1950s, Kallison's had evolved into a large hybrid enterprise, one that had constantly redefined itself over the previous half century. It defied any easy description. It was not a sleek, modern department store, yet it could compete with those stores in selling a variety of home appliances, furniture, and clothing. It looked like a farm and ranch supply store that extended itself into whatever categories of merchandise that Morris and Perry thought their customers might want. In many ways, Kallison's was an expansion of the traditional old country general store that tried to meet the needs of its isolated rural customers. The concept was similar to the one that Sam Walton later would employ in small towns when he began to build what eventually would become Walmart, the world's largest retailer—but Kallison's was entirely unique in its personal, rustic approach to merchandising.

The Kallisons—fathers, sons, and eventually grandsons—kept adding new lines of merchandise, with minimal regard as to whether they fit neatly into any particular niche: farm supplies, appliances, furniture, hardware, men's and women's clothing, lumber and building materials, cooking and glassware, gifts, even Christmas decorations. When Morris's daughter Jane's bridegroom Seymour Dreyfus joined the store in the early 1950s, Perry Kallison assigned him to open a furniture department in an empty basement space underneath the clothing department. In his eagerness to provide the store's initial furniture inventory, Perry directed Dreyfus to buy furniture at retail prices from a local store—one with which Kallison's would be competing. When a building adjoining the store then became available, the Kallisons expanded the furniture department to fill it, offering "a houseful of furniture for $295." For that bargain price, a customer could get a full, matching suite of furniture for a living room, dining room, and bedroom.[11]

The Kallisons' guiding merchandising principle was first to find out what their customers wanted. Then they'd see whether they could supply it. It was an old Kallison tradition. If a customer asked Nathan Kallison for an item that his store didn't stock, Nathan was known to ask the customer to wait while he scoured the neighborhood to find it. To the consternation of his children, Perry Kallison continued his father's practice of rushing out to find whatever item his loyal customers wanted. The Kallisons tried to keep up with new trends in merchandising, but their underlying focus was to satisfy their loyal core of customers, a loyalty often passed through to a second or third generation.

When the ever-expanding store ran out of space, the Kallisons would rent or buy the closest nearby building they could find. The one-room harness shop eventually covered sixty thousand square feet, nearly a full city block on South Flores Street between Dolorosa and Nueva. Merchandise that couldn't be squeezed into the main store was offered for sale from a half dozen other locations in the neighborhood.

At its peak, Kallison's store listed 125 employees on its payroll—many of whom were quite well known in the community. The Big Country Store's unique flavor was seasoned by a motley group of characters who added spice to the sales force. "Perry Kallison had a do-gooder streak," recalled Seymour Dreyfus. "He tended to hire unfortunates with a good story to tell, willing to work long hours for low wages. These included hopeless alcoholics, drifters, old friends seeking relief from the boredom of retirement."[12] Singer and TV performer Red River Dave sold a lot of appliances, including freezers already stocked with steak and vegetables. Mr. Reed, a ninety-year-old gentleman, always immaculate in coat and tie, sat at a desk near a side entrance with the assignment of "watching the door." The sporting goods department was run by "Hound Dog" Ferguson, a chain-smoking fellow with a passionate interest in 'coon hunting. Otto Stahl, a big heavyset man, ran the paint department, ringing up sales to customers who ranged from homeowners wanting to paint a door, to painting contractors from all over the city. Mr. Dixon, who ran the plumbing department, was missing most of his front teeth, but still managed to tell dramatic stories to his customers about his days as a soldier in the trenches of France during World War I.

In a small balcony alcove, Marvin "TV" Smith, a former carnival circus performer who had been crippled by polio, expertly repaired television sets. His wife, a former sword swallower in the same circus, also worked at Kallison's. Sometimes during the store-sponsored Saturday night *Barn Dance*, Mrs. Smith would perform her act on television—swallowing an illuminated florescent light bulb as well. Sign painting and store layout were handled by Max, a talented man with a drinking problem, who once set the store on fire when he fell asleep while smoking a cigarette, Dreyfus recalled. Julian Asheim, a savvy jack-of-all-trades manager, especially enjoyed stocking the store with children's toys at Christmastime.[13]

No matter how many departments the store added, however, the identity of the enterprise remained Texas Country, the Old West. Arnufo Carter, a wizened and diminutive Mexican American, reigned as the store's expert on and star salesman of western hats. If a customer wanted to buy a cowboy hat, Carter scrambled up a narrow staircase to his second floor loft storeroom and brought down a dozen different sizes and styles of Stetsons, Resistols, and other premier brands. After a customer selected a hat, Carter would shape it artfully with his handheld steamer to fit the personality and desires of the buyer. "He was the 'pro's pro' of hats," recalled Morris's grandson John Dreyfus, "and he sold a lot of them." For customers, visitors, sales clerks, and the Kallison family alike, the Big Country Store offered a hearty dose of nostalgia for a rapidly vanishing rural Texas that was steadily being displaced by San Antonio's expanding suburbs. The store's atmosphere in the 1950s and early 1960s seemed to be drawn from another era, even though its merchandise included the latest in home appliances and color television sets. Kallison's customers and visitors were colorful as well: downtown employees on lunch breaks, ranch hands in their jeans and Stetsons, and blue-collar workers looking for bargains. Proximity to the Bexar County Courthouse across the street lent a special character to Kallison's, which not only served its courthouse clientele, but also provided a shortcut through the store from the courthouse steps to their favorite little Flores Street cafés—The Cantonese at South Flores and Dolorosa Streets, which featured both Chinese and Mexican food, among the most popular.

A procession of judges, deputy sheriffs in uniform, court bailiffs, clerks, assorted politicians, and hangers-on used the Kallison's shortcut, often pausing along the way to exchange gossip with Perry or with Morris, who was now becoming known as an influential political insider. Occasionally, some in the courthouse crowd passing through would even spot something they "needed." Another constant presence was "Apple George," a thin, wiry, and boisterous old man who hawked a basket of apples between the courthouse, city hall, and Kallison's store. Thought to have been shell-shocked during World

War I, Apple George complained without restraint about whatever his current peeve happened to be. On one occasion, Morris Kallison mischievously directed Apple George's attention, and subsequent ire, toward C. A. Harrell, the San Antonio City Manager in 1952-1953, a political foe Morris disliked.[14]

Customers came into the store from its two east entrances on Main Plaza, facing the Bexar County Courthouse, or from South Flores Street. What had started out on Main as a hitching post for horses and wagons, and later was used as a parking lot, soon was packed with rolls of barbed wire, windmills, lumber, farm equipment, and implements. Entering the store from Main Plaza, customers first saw a large set of scales used by salesmen to weigh nails, bolts, and other hardware, items which were stored nearby in large wooden barrels. On the right side of the store was the paint department; clothing was sold in the back. On the left side of the store remained the saddle and harness department. And in the center, under the balcony, stood a large iron safe from which Perry dispersed cash each morning to the various cashiers throughout the store.

On the balcony above the sales floor, Mr. Hunter, a silver-haired man with a green eyeshade, kept the store's books, and generally was the best source of information on inventories, balance sheets, payroll, and "how the store was doing." Nominally, Perry and Morris shared responsibility as the store's top executives, but beneath them authority and responsibility were dispersed in a way that would have defied any detailed organizational chart.

Nathan Kallison's enterprise, ambition, and vision were instilled in his two sons, who vowed to expand upon his legacy. By the mid-1950s, Morris and Perry had worked together successfully for twenty years as the store's managing partners. Like their father, they were independent and determined to succeed on their own terms—and to

Above left: Anna Kallison with her four children, c.1918. Standing, left to right: Anna, Morris, and Pauline; Perry and Tibe are seated in front.

Above: Tibe (left) and Pauline (right) at the University of Texas at Austin, 1918.

Left: US Army Sergeant Morris Kallison during World War I, 1918.

Above: Kallison home on San Pedro Avenue, c.1920.
Opposite, top: Teenager Perry Kallison in 1918.
Opposite: Pauline (front) and Tibe (center left) with Tibe's
University of Texas roommates, Austin, 1919.

Left: Pauline Kallison, 1921.

Below: San Antonio River's flood swamped the downtown in 1921, killing fifty-one in the West Side barrio and causing millions of dollars in damage. *General Photograph Collection, MS 362: 069-8530, University of Texas at San Antonio Libraries Special Collections from the Institute of Texan Cultures.*

Opposite, top: Dolorosa Street at Main Plaza, 1925. The Southern Hotel is on the right. *General Photograph Collection, MS 362: 069-8771, University of Texas at San Antonio Libraries Special Collections from the Institute of Texan Cultures.*

Opposite, bottom: South Flores Street, 1926, with the new construction site for the Kallison Block building on the right. The original Kallison's store is the fifth building down on the left side. *DRTL SC926-65-1.*

Top: Nathan Kallison with ranch hands, 1928.
Above: Morris Kallison at Kallison Ranch during 1927 wheat harvest. *San Antonio Light Photograph Collection, MS 359: L-1024-E, University of Texas at San Antonio Libraries Special Collections from the Institute of Texan Cultures.*

Nathan Kallison at the Kallison Ranch, 1927.

Top: Prohibition: on March 26, 1927, federal agents raided the Bottlers Supply Company, a tenant in the Kallison Block, for violating the Volstead Act. Photograph submitted as evidence in *US v. H. L. Worman, Morris Kallison, Nathan Kallison.*

Left: Crest on top of the Kallison Block building. *Photo courtesy Nancy Pettersen, 2013.*

Top: Anna, Tibe, Pauline, and Jimmy Kallison (left to right) beside Anna and Nathan's San Pedro home, late 1920s.
Right: Perry Kallison on his honeymoon in Mexico, 1931.

Top: At Kallison Ranch: Morris, Jimmy, Perry, Nathan Kallison (left to right), 1929.

Left: Perry Kallison and his mother Anna, late 1930s.

Above: Nathan Kallison, c. 1930.

Opposite, top: Kallison's store interior, c. 1930s.

Opposite, bottom: Kallison's storefront, c. 1930s.

Perry Kallison on horseback at Kallison Ranch with Polled Hereford cattle, 1930s.
The ranch house is in the background.

Opposite, top: Kallison's store plumbing department, 1930s.

Opposite, bottom: Kallison Ranch: Nathan Kallison and Bill Shomette with the ranch's championship Polled Hereford bull. San Antonio Light *Photograph Collection, MS 359: L-2412-D, University of Texas at San Antonio Libraries Special Collections from the Institute of Texan Cultures.*

Above: Morris Kallison in Kallison's veterinary supply department, c.1930s. San Antonio Light *Photograph Collection, MS 359: L-3185-B, University of Texas at San Antonio Libraries Special Collections from the Institute of Texan Cultures.*

Right: Morris Kallison and Dorothy Sherwood with Pancho Villa's saddle on display in Kallison's store, c.1930s. San Antonio Light *Photograph Collection, MS 359: L-3185-A, University of Texas at San Antonio Libraries Special Collections from the Institute of Texan Cultures.*

Above: San Antonio Depression-era homes in West Side barrio, c.1930s. *(WPA Photo Control No. RG 69-57-19249-D) Texana/Genealogy, San Antonio Public Library (007-031).*

Left: Unemployed workers gather at Bexar County Courthouse for jobs and relief during the Great Depression, 1933. San Antonio Light *Photograph Collection, University of Texas at San Antonio Libraries Special Collections from the Institute of Texan Cultures.*

seize new opportunities to enlarge the family's business interests. The Kallison brothers, so different in personality and appearance, complemented each other. In the store itself, Morris's strength was a brilliant grasp of marketing, mass merchandising, buying, and pricing. A master of public relations, Perry, who knew hundreds of farmers and ranchers from all over South Texas, became the store's most important sales asset. Outside the store, Morris's primary interests were in real estate development and politics; Perry's in ranching and civic activities, first with Temple Beth-El, then with a growing number of community endeavors. Boosting Texas agriculture was his top priority. The brothers attracted a wide cross-section of Texans into Kallison's. They shared offices on the balcony overlooking the store's sprawling showrooms below. When they weren't on the floor greeting customers, both men were above in their offices meeting with a steady stream of farmers, ranchers, city residents, and politicians from the courthouse across the street and from city hall a block away on Main Plaza.

Morris and Perry were the driving forces in the growing Kallison enterprises—the store, the Kallison Block building on South Flores, the acquisition of other downtown properties, and the Kallison Ranch that Nathan had started, which Perry would manage from the middle 1930s onward. Following Nathan's example, they continued to diversify Kallison's merchandise lines, and like their father, tried to stay just ahead of trends. In their participation in civic affairs, however, the Kallison brothers went well beyond their father in providing public service while advancing the store's business interests. At a time when other businesses had started leaving for the new suburbs, Morris and Perry worked hard to sustain the central city of San Antonio.

Both brothers integrated themselves—effortlessly it seemed—into the very diverse business and community activities of San Antonio. Particularly in local politics, each reached beyond the boundaries many Jews of that era did not cross, either because of the barriers of prejudice, or because most felt more comfortable in the shelter of the Jewish community—a community that also remained an important interest of Perry's. Both Morris and Perry presented themselves as men filled with bonhomie, ambition, and a confident projection that declared "I belong here. I am Texas."

Clearly, the pairing of their very different personalities was a strength in the business, but the traits they shared were just as crucial to their success. Each brother was able to make friendships easily, and they shared the goal of making Kallison's store not just a destination shopping place but also, as they described it, "a welcoming meeting-place for country and city people alike." Together, Nathan's oldest and youngest made a good team.

Neither man deviated from Nathan and Anna's stern family work ethic: long hours and few vacations. To accommodate their farm and ranch customers as well as Perry's early morning radio program, the Kallison brothers arrived at the store before seven every morning. Even though there were few customers that early, they opened the store at exactly seven and stayed open until six or later in the evening. On occasion, Perry would announce the store's expanded hours in his broadcasts: "And you don't have to wait 'til nine or ten o'clock for the Big Old Country store to open up like you do for the fancy-doodle places. Here at Kallison's the doors open wide at seven o'clock. And you can come right in dressed as you are."[15]

The store's hours, along with that relentless work ethic, carried over to the next generation. When Kallison sons and sons-in-law entered the business, they continued another family tradition: driving to work together. In the early 1950s, with either Morris's son Jimmy or son-in-law Seymour Dreyfus driving, they would pick up Perry and Morris before daybreak, and the four of them would open the store together, always in time for the roosters to crow on Perry's radio show. With their father gone and their mother policing the home front, the business camaraderie and the empire building were solely the realm of the men.

ELEVEN

The Brothers Kallison

A STRANGER COMING IN to Kallison's would never guess that Morris and Perry were brothers. Aside from their seven-year difference in age and their great disparity in appearance—broad-shouldered Morris with his dark eyes and shock of black hair; blue-eyed Perry, shorter and balding—the brothers' interests were as wide apart as their personalities. Morris, the elder (who was quite vain about his good looks and wore tailor-made suits, highly polished shoes, and a diamond ring on his finger), dressed the part of a city executive on the way to his club. His club, proudly, was the Masonic Lodge, in which he had achieved the thirty-second degree. "He was very smart," said his lawyer Jesse Oppenheimer, "and competitive and ambitious." If Morris ever regretted not finishing college, no one could tell. He was flamboyant, ebullient, energetic, and attractive. He loved local politics—and the city soon recognized him as a "kingmaker." He also loved money, and the power he believed it brought.

Both Kallison brothers were outgoing, meeting people easily and collecting scores of friends. Perry's charm was quiet and more thoughtful. He thoroughly enjoyed his role as the Ol' Trader, and relished the friendships gained by that acquired personality. His radio show with its "sermonettes" allowed him a platform to express his philosophy and his opinions—like an editorialist or a rabbi. Since his high school days in the thrall of Rabbi and Mrs. Frisch, he had centered his life in the philanthropic and organizational work of Temple

Beth-El. The Jewish community, locally and internationally, was at the heart of his social commitments. But it was the Kallison Ranch, his herd of cattle, and his passion for the Texas agricultural economy that captured Perry's deepest feelings. He dressed as a Texas cattleman—brown jackets with yoked shoulders, embossed leather boots, and the ever-present Stetson to protect his thinning hair, scalp, and fair complexion from the sun. He had inherited Anna's blue eyes and round face, a face that was open and earnestly inquisitive into the lives of others, including strangers.

As partners throughout their lives, Morris and Perry had worked in tandem under Nathan's tutelage and direction. What they shared most was a deep respect for their father, "the Boss," and his commitment to and appreciation for hard work. Morris and Perry Kallison each made a considerable impact on business and community life in San Antonio. Outside the store, however, their principal interests continued to diverge after Nathan's death. Perry gravitated to the ranch, where he could engage his passionate feeling for the land and his expertise in cattle breeding. Morris focused his considerable energy on building his own downtown real estate empire, as well as becoming a behind-the-scenes power in city politics. As time passed, disagreements, at times bitter, arose between the brothers. Perry felt that his older brother Morris neglected the store while focusing on his separate real estate holdings. Although Morris later included Perry in several of his real estate deals, the growing family rift was compounded by Anna Kallison, the widowed matriarch. She deeply resented Morris for not including his sisters Tibe and Pauline in his new ventures. Conflicted in his own loyalties, Perry tried to play peacemaker as the chasm widened between Morris and his mother, Pauline, and Tibe. Arguments sometimes grew heated, with Morris stalking out of his parents' home.

From an early age, Morris Kallison sought the spotlight. In his suits of silk, mohair, or summertime white linen, he was always noticed. "A striking figure," reported the society pages. His abundant head of hair, its dark glistening waves always carefully combed and pomaded, was his pride, especially when it began to show streaks of silver gray. He would often stop in at a beauty college in a building he owned to enjoy a facial and to have his hair coiffed by the instructors.[1] With his smartly-tailored clothing and forceful personality, Morris Kallison drew attention, which was his intention. He drove big cars— Cadillacs—with his monogram on the dashboard. He was seen by many acquaintances, and also by his grandchildren, as a larger-than-life character, one with a magnetic personality and the ability to persuade others to agree with his ideas and plans. Determined to stand out from the crowd as a successful businessman, real estate developer, and community leader, Morris projected flair and brash-ness. Although he and his family were nominal members of Temple Beth-El, Morris was not actively involved in Temple affairs. He focused on conquering the wider secular world around him.

Working on weekends at a desk in his home den, Morris first began his real estate career by buying cheap houses, remodeling them, then reselling them. Eventually he focused on purchasing and redeveloping downtown office buildings. It was in the "good years" of the 1940s and 1950s that he would build his own "Kallison empire." Most Morris Kallison properties featured air conditioning and free parking, new 1950s amenities he hoped would keep busi-nesses in the inner city. As many ambitious developers began fleeing to the lucrative suburbs, Morris dabbled in that market as well. Although he understood the new market and proved in several suc-cessful projects that he could prosper in it, Morris focused resolutely on downtown San Antonio. He believed that he could spark a revival. His efforts to restore many old properties and erect new buildings provided a bright presence in a downtown that increasing-ly appeared seedy and deserted. First, he redeveloped the neighbor-hood immediately south of the Bexar County courthouse, near Kallison's store.[2] His distinctive projects included the Kallison Business and Professional Building on South Main Avenue, the Kallison Industrial Building on Santa Rosa Street, and the Kallison-Walsh Building on West Nueva Street.

When Morris Kallison began to develop downtown real estate in San Antonio after World War II, no major construction had taken place in the city's central business district since the Great Depression struck the nation in 1929. And aside from Kallison, local builders and financers still wouldn't risk investing in the downtown. As he surveyed the community's building needs, Morris recognized that the downtown would continue to be depleted as many city retailers inevitably followed their customers to the growing suburbs. Where he could make a difference, Morris reasoned, was in developing and modernizing buildings for tenants who needed to remain downtown—the county and city governments, federal government agencies, and private businesses that did business with the government. Slowly and patiently, he bought up dozens of rundown properties that were south of the Bexar County Courthouse and located near other government agencies. After assembling the land, Kallison built or redeveloped twelve office or commercial buildings in that area between 1946 and 1961. He called his ambitious project the "Kallison-Downtown-near-Bexar-County-Courthouse Developments." Eventually, in post-World War II San Antonio, Morris would construct twenty-five buildings and remodel nearly two hundred of the city's older downtown structures—becoming a virtual one-man urban renewal force. His efforts served as a brake on further downtown decline.[3]

As a flamboyant and colorful "boss" who didn't shrink from being portrayed as a political kingmaker, Kallison's government real estate projects at times drew harsh criticism from newspaper reporters and columnists who presumed he had benefitted financially because of his political influence. When Morris built the three-story KW (Kallison-Walsh) Building on West Nueva Street near the courthouse, and rented part of it to Bexar County to store the county's voting machines, San Antonio Express-News columnist Paul Thompson asserted in a blistering series of stories that Kallison was charging excessive rent. When Kallison sold the building to the county, Thompson charged that the county had overpaid him. Believing

in the fairness of his dealings and confident of his powers of persuasion, Morris always sought to win over his critics. Eventually,
Thompson and Kallison became friends after the columnist decided
that the developer's downtown projects did benefit the city.

With the help of a weekly meeting called the "Breakfast Club,"
Morris built up a network of friends and business associates. Around
a large table at the Gunter Hotel, Morris would preside over early
morning gatherings of the city's most active leaders. He relished
those get-togethers as a forum for making business deals and playing
local politics. The Breakfast Club soon became a fabled institution in
town.

Over their scrambled eggs and bacon, a club member or visitor
would make a brief talk about issues of business and civic interest.
For example, when a group of military officers and civilian officials
from the North Atlantic Treaty Organization (NATO) visited San
Antonio in June 1956 to inspect its military bases, Morris seized the
opportunity to extol the importance of San Antonio and South Texas
to the visitors. He brought the NATO officers to the Breakfast Club,
arranged tours of San Antonio business and historic sites, and feted
them with a dinner at Kallison Ranch. Among other honored guests
at the "western night" celebration at the ranch, the NATO delegation
met the top brass from the area's military bases and four hundred of
the city's business and political leaders.[4]

As a highly visible participant in local political struggles, Morris
became a central figure in a hotly contested 1950s fight over control
of the San Antonio city government and its bond issues. In 1951, he
opposed a concerted political effort to replace the city's longtime
mayor-and-commissioner system with a city-manager form of government. The San Antonio contest was part of a long-running
nationwide deliberation about how best to govern a modern city. Out
of the early twentieth century progressive movement emerged the
idea that government should best be administered by professionals,
with most permanent employees protected by civil service, and with
elected political officials limited to setting policy. Proponents of the

city-manager plan argued that it would inject needed efficiency and professionalism into city affairs, thus reducing the power of political bosses and patronage.

The San Antonio reform effort initially had begun in the 1930s with the Good Government League, which elected liberal lawyer and political reformer Maury Maverick to Congress, and then to a single term as mayor. Morris's sister Tibe Kallison had been an ardent Maverick supporter at that time. Later, in the 1950s, calling themselves the "Citizens Committee," San Antonio's reform effort was led by a coalition of liberal "good government" advocates and by downtown business leaders who wanted to modernize and expand city services.

Opposing the change were Morris Kallison and his longtime and carefully cultivated political allies, who included former mayors Alfred Callaghan and Gus Mauermann, Judge C. K. Quin, and Sheriff Owen W. Kilday. They were old-style politicians who held power by handing out patronage jobs and favors to those interest groups and neighborhoods who supported them. The Callaghan family had ruled San Antonio politics at various times since the 1880s. Morris Kallison and Alfred Callaghan had grown up together; their fathers were close friends when the elder Callaghan was the city's mayor and political boss. What Morris, Alfred Callaghan, and their business allies feared most was that a city-manager-led government would not just increase city services, but it would also pay for them by raising taxes. They were concerned that higher taxes would hurt downtown business interests—including, of course, the Kallisons'. As the city's largest downtown property owner and individual taxpayer, Morris Kallison had a personal stake in the outcome. But he also strongly believed that San Antonio's effort to attract industry—and to compete with Houston and Dallas—depended on creating a favorable business climate with lower taxes.

In a hard-fought 1951 election, voters finally approved the city-manager plan, but the battle was far from over. Morris Kallison and his allies immediately mounted a concerted 1953 campaign to defeat the entire nine-member city council that had been elected under the new city-manager government. If they couldn't succeed in revoking the city-manager plan, they reasoned, at least they would try to control it. Newspaper stories described Morris as a member of the "Big Three," along with oilmen Al A. Jergins and Strauder G. Nelson. Together, the three men organized a rival slate of candidates whom they called the "San Antonians." Morris's group displayed its campaign slogan "Lower Taxes" by mounting an eight-foot billboard atop the Kallison's Feed Store at West Nueva and Flores.[5]

In politics just as in business, Morris worked diligently to make friends, to avoid making enemies, and to embrace old foes as new allies. There was little surprise, therefore, when his insurgent group picked former mayor and hotel executive Jack White as the group's candidate for mayor, even though Kallison and White had repeatedly clashed in earlier campaigns. *San Antonio Light* political columnist "Don Politico" dubbed the new Kallison-White alliance as "the political wedding of the year."[6]

The fight soon turned nasty. Citizen Committee candidates accused Morris Kallison of being "a political boss, a maker of deals to benefit his own business interests, and a tax dodger." The attacks against Morris Kallison came in part from his proposal as a developer to build a new city hall and jail for the city and county governments on property in which the Kallisons held an interest. Kallison fired back. In a half-page political advertisement headlined "Kallison Answers Charges," Morris denied their accusations of self-dealing, and described his own role in bringing downtown improvements, which included widening major streets, expanding the municipal airport, and constructing a new post office and federal building. "We need bigger men in office than those who have perpetuated these vicious charges and who play such petty, cheap politics," Kallison wrote. He urged support for his "San Antonians" slate of candidates. The next day, the "San Antonians" swept the election.[7] Columnist Don Politico approvingly dubbed Morris "the sage of South Flores Street," and applauded his plan to raise city income by taxing profits of the city-owned municipal utility company called City Public Service (CPS)—a concept the city later partially adopted.[8]

While Morris Kallison's views were praised by some newspaper editorialists, they were reviled by others. In 1955, addressing Morris's opposition to a bond issue, the *San Antonio Express-News* called him and his cohorts "diehard remnants of the disgruntled obstructionists who for ten years have fought a losing battle against city-manager government and every related civic effort for community progress."[9]

A lifelong Democrat, Morris ultimately became disillusioned with partisan politics, deciding that the primary consideration shared by both political parties was winning elections. "When you put them (Republicans and Democrats) both in the same hat and shake them up, there's not a quarter's worth difference between them," he told the *San Antonio Express-News*. As the Cold War deepened, he saw America living in an era of false prosperity. "If we were to have peace tomorrow, we would find ourselves in the greatest depression we've ever known. The war hysteria and buildup has created the prosperity in the country and it will have to stop sometime."[10]

Although some critics continued to describe Morris's politics as self-serving, his family and coterie of friends knew that he truly cared about San Antonio. With his singular vision of rebuilding downtown San Antonio into a great commercial city, Morris said he backed those political candidates who he felt shared his aims for the city's vibrant growth. His political allies included colorful personalities like Texas State Senator Virgil Edward "Red" Berry, who allegedly once controlled gambling in San Antonio. Morris was effusive in his praise for Berry when he introduced him to members of the Kallison family.

As he acquired fame and notoriety, Morris clipped news stories about his activities, and showed them to his friends. "Isn't this terrible?" Morris said, shaking his head as he handed his attorney Jesse Oppenheimer a story critical of his political views. "But Morris loved it—all the attention," commented Oppenheimer.[11]

"I like to make San Antonio boom and bloom," Morris told the

San Antonio Light. His hobby was "creativity in designing buildings, in remodeling them, and in taking a little bit of nothing and making something out of it."[12] Kallison and his architects aimed for clean, modern designs in his new buildings and called for landscaping that included at least one palm tree. As a member of the City Planning Commission, he opposed a proposed downtown plan that dubbed San Antonio the "Athens of the West" because the plan's landscaping did not include a single palm tree.[13] The San Antonio Conservation Society honored Kallison for his efforts to beautify his own downtown properties, and the General Services Administration praised him for providing quality rental space to the federal government at reasonable prices.

Morris Kallison saw himself as decisive, a man of action. Sending a 1964 Christmas greeting to President Lyndon Johnson, Morris shared his own views about leadership: "There are three kinds of people: those who make things happen, those who watch things happen, and those who do not know what has happened. May 1965 help us to make good things happen."[14]

He saw himself and President Johnson, whom he supported, as belonging to the group that "make things happen."[15] Like Lyndon Johnson, Morris exerted a forceful personality, with strong powers of persuasion. LBJ was known for the "Johnson treatment," in which he would grab a man by the lapels and stand nose to nose with his victim while convincing him to choose whatever plan Johnson supported. In conversations, Morris's approach to persuasion was often similar—but without grabbing lapels. He would lock eyes in a penetrating, intense stare, which some found intimidating. The combination of his concentrated eye contact and his gregarious personality did hold people's attention, however. And in contrast to his sleek cosmopolitan panache, Morris, like LBJ and other men of their time, could pepper his speech with the down-home Texas talk of earlier eras. To get to the essence of a situation he'd say, "That's how the cow ate the cabbage" or "Things got down to the lick log."[16] Judging whether politicians were honest or could be bribed, Morris would insist, "I can tell whether they'd take or not!"[17] And as for leadership: "It's not what time you get up; it's what time you wake up."

Morris Kallison was also known as master of the grand gesture. He thrilled his first grandchild Nancy Kallison on her sixteenth birthday with the gift of a bright red Chevrolet Impala Super Sport, which he deposited in the driveway of her parents Jimmy and Ruthie's home on Park Drive. When Nancy's brother Kal turned sixteen, however, his grandfather gave him $25. Girls, it seemed, got special treatment.

On Sunday afternoons, accompanied by the same Kal Kallison, then a teenager, Morris liked to drive his Cadillac all over the city, inspecting his own properties and looking for new real estate opportunities. On those outings, young Kal observed his grandfather's habits and superstitions. Faced with a black cat about to cross the road in front of his car, Morris would back up his car, turn around, and take another route to avoid the cat's path.[18] "He would warn us not to put a hat on a bed—because it was bad luck," Kal added.

As a father and grandfather, Morris was not known for sentimentality. His children reported instances of deprecating, even harsh words directed at them. Morris expressed his love in glass and steel. He named his downtown buildings for family members: the Morris K Apartments, the James K Building after his son Jimmy, and the Kathy K Building, named for his granddaughter Kathryn Dreyfus, the first of three children born to his daughter Jane. Another was named for his longtime real estate manager Marjorie Calvert, who adored him.

In total contrast, Perry Kallison, the younger brother, developed a consistent and conservative style. He wore unpretentious brown suits for dress occasions, blending in as comfortably with other downtown merchants as he did with the farmers, ranchers, and small-town denizens of rural South Texas—his customers and friends. On scorching summer days, he might concede to leave the suit jacket at home, but he still wore the white shirt and tie, often with a tie clip engraved with "President, Texas Polled Hereford Association," an office he held in 1948-49. With a narrow-brimmed Stetson cocked over his eye, covering a hairline that began receding when he was still in his twenties, he looked the part of a classic Texan. But Perry Kallison was no "drugstore cowboy," as he called city folks who dressed in full western regalia but would have been lost on a ranch. Or as he might say of someone pretentious, "He's all hat and no horse."

Partially deaf in one ear since childhood, Perry was an earnest listener, tilting his head to listen with his good ear. He learned by listening intently to what customers—and others—had to say, showing them respect by looking them in the eye and paying close attention. In his own quiet way, Perry made himself into a public personality so effortlessly that it soon became natural to him. Through his *Trading Post*, he had become a revered presence for rural South Texans, who saw him as understanding, empathizing with their wants, needs, and aspirations.

While Morris was holding court with the movers and shakers of commerce and politics in the upscale Gunter Hotel, Perry presided over his own informal "clubhouse," a table in the basement of the downtown Sommers Drug Store on Houston Street. At lunch time, he invited cattlemen and city friends to meet there. On the way to lunch he often would gather up still other friends whom he passed on the way to the drugstore. He was like the Pied Piper, drawing people to him with his unaffected, generous spirit. By the time the lunch hour ended, the soft-spoken Perry would have talked with just about everyone in the room.

Unlike Morris, Perry usually disengaged himself from partisan election politics, preferring a wider sphere of influence. Despite his sermonettes, the Ol' Trader was always careful not to turn his radio program into a political platform, although he did make some exceptions. One was the extraordinary boost he gave to the political career of Lyndon Baines Johnson. The 1948 campaign for the United States

Senate in Texas pitted US Representative Johnson against the veteran Governor Coke Stevenson. As a young congressman from the nearby Hill Country, Johnson had championed a cause dear to the hearts and pocketbooks of the Kallisons. By aligning himself with President Franklin Delano Roosevelt and his New Deal programs, Congressman Johnson had fought successfully for funds to build the hydroelectric dams and power lines that brought electricity for the first time to the farmers, ranchers, and small-town dwellers spread out so sparsely throughout the vast rural Hill Country. Among those who benefited most were the radio listeners who came in from the countryside on Saturdays to shop at Kallison's Big Country Store in San Antonio.

Perry saw Lyndon Johnson's opponent, Governor Stevenson, as a "no-doer," and simply wanted him out of politics. Perry's progressive wife Frances and his liberal sister Tibe supported Johnson for additional reasons. He was one of a handful of southern congressmen who had voted for the progressive New Deal social programs, social security, and the minimum wage, which they championed as advocates for social justice issues. "Now we might get something done with Johnson," Perry told his radio audience.

In the 1948 Senate race, LBJ "wanted to use radio on a scale it had never been used in a political campaign," wrote his biographer Robert A. Caro. Rather than giving stump speeches in front of county courthouses, "he wanted to be on the air himself every day, several times a day."[19]

Candidate Johnson needed airtime. Perry concurred, and invited Johnson to join him on the *Trading Post* show early on August 27, 1948, the date of the Democratic primary runoff between Johnson and Stevenson. On the program, Perry introduced Johnson, heartily endorsing him. The airtime with Johnson, along with Perry's unabashed endorsement, were important because Perry's widespread radio audience on KTSA reached locations that Johnson vitally needed to win: the Hill Country north of San Antonio, the city itself, particularly its large Mexican population on the west side, the smaller

African American population on the east side, and the counties south of San Antonio reaching down into the Rio Grande Valley all the way to the Mexican border. In the election's aftermath, both sides flung serious charges of vote-buying, both in San Antonio itself and in Jim Wells County, where powerful political boss George Parr also support-ed Johnson.[20] When the much-disputed election results finally were certified, Johnson had won by eighty-seven votes, earning him the nickname "Landslide Lyndon." With a spark of humor in his eye, Perry claimed that he provided Johnson with his razor-thin margin of vic-tory. And Johnson was happy to give Perry Kallison credit.[21]

A second important Lyndon Johnson appearance on the *Trading Post* came twelve years later, on the morning of November 8, 1960, the day of the presidential election. In another close race, Democratic Senator John F. Kennedy was running against Republican Vice President Richard Nixon. As Kennedy's running mate, Senator Johnson, now the Senate majority leader, was expected by his party to carry his home state of Texas, whose electoral votes would be critical. The presidential race in Texas was down to the wire. Vice presidential candidate Johnson came to San Antonio, hoping that the *Trading Post* broadcast would swing Perry's loyal South Texas followers to vote for the Kennedy-Johnson Democratic ticket.

Perry's introduction led Johnson to discuss the impact of politics on the livelihood of Texas farmers and ranchers, including the Senator's own ranching operation at the LBJ Ranch near Johnson City. "We sold our calves the other day and we got twenty-one cents (a pound)," LBJ replied. "That wasn't anything like the forty-four cents I got during the Truman Administration, but I guess that's all you can expect from a Republican Administration."

"Our (farm) people are kind of troubled," Perry noted—and ended the broadcast with his endorsement: "We're sure looking for-ward to when the Democrats come in with the power of the presi-dency."

In turn, Johnson was full of praise for Perry, the *Trading Post* radio program, and Kallison's store. "This is a wonderful program," he said. "I believe in the *Trading Post*. I've visited Kallison's. . . . I remember the program twelve years ago, and I think that's one of the things that helped me be elected then (to the US Senate), and I think this program will help me today."[22]

Thanks to their slim victory in Texas on that Election Day, the Kennedy-Johnson ticket narrowly won the 1960 election. Johnson never forgot Perry Kallison's helping him on two critical election days. He thanked him again in 1968: "It's been a long way from there to here, but I haven't forgotten the occasion of my closing talk (on the *Trading Post*) in 1948, nor all the good people like you who were by my side then and now." Letters back and forth between the men revealed their easy friendship and the bond they shared: love of cattle ranching and of the Hill Country land itself, which could be so beautiful, yet was such a harsh, demanding environment in which to earn a living. The northern end of the Kallison Ranch, at the edge of Hill Country, was just sixty miles south of Johnson's LBJ Ranch "as the crow flies."

Perry's appreciation of Johnson was shared by Frances, Morris, Ruth, and Tibe. Following the assassination of President Kennedy in November 1963, all the Kallisons were quick to register their support and suggestions for their fellow Texan. They were horrified that the murderous shots had been fired in Dallas, in their beloved Texas. Shortly after Johnson was sworn in as president, Perry and Frances Kallison and Frances's mother Mary Rosenthal wrote him a lengthy letter praising his first State of the Union Speech and expressing special gratitude for "your administration's humanitarian intention to wage war on poverty." And they urged Johnson to take action to help "another forgotten element of our society, the migratory workers and their families, especially the children."

Even though he had overtly and avidly supported the Kennedy-Johnson ticket in 1960, Perry immediately cautioned his radio listeners at that time not to expect too much from any political leader or from government itself: "Regardless of promises, the country will be running the day after the election. Taxes are going on. You are not going to get something for nothing—regardless of the promises. So after the election, we can all settle down to our knitting. But to keep our country strong, and keep us on an even keel, the big job for each of us is holding the religious faith of our people, our desire to do justice to our fellow man—and see the churches of all faiths standing side by side, each being tolerant of the beliefs of the others. And as we enter the church of our choice, we each have the same common background—and the stairway of all the churches leads to the same God to which we all give reverence. So America is in good hands—it is the hands of her sons and daughters. And the background of our forefathers gave us the strength to carry on."[23]

The "Other Perry," in his downtown persona, shined in a wide range of activities, from leading Jewish organizations and their support for Israel, to heading city and county programs for land conservation. A particular pet project was a proposed livestock coliseum. For years, Perry used his *Trading Post* to champion the notion of a coliseum in San Antonio, an arena that could be used for livestock shows and rodeos. World War II had put on hold a grassroots movement among San Antonio civic boosters to construct an arena large enough to rival that in Fort Worth. After the war, the local effort revived. Perry reminded his listeners that San Antonio was the last remaining cattle center in Texas without a livestock exposition, yet the local government entities refused to fund a coliseum. He worked for years within the San Antonio Chamber of Commerce, single-mindedly urging the city to create the coliseum, arguing that an annual stock show and rodeo not only would help South Texas farmers and ranchers, but would also bring tens of thousands of visitors to San Antonio and add millions of dollars to the local economy. (His partners in pushing support for the coliseum were San Antonio automobile dealers Joe and Harry Freeman, fellow Jews who also were longtime ranchers themselves.) In 1948 the Bexar County commissioners finally proposed a highly contested bond issue to underwrite coliseum construction. Once the $1.7 million measure was on the ballot, it was up to proponents to pull in the votes. Making no pretense of objectivity, Perry began broadcasting Saturday morning sermonettes to convince Bexar County taxpayers to vote for the proposal. They did. The coliseum opened February 17, 1950, with the first annual San Antonio Livestock Exposition and Rodeo. Perry Kallison served as a founding director.

As Perry had predicted, the Joe and Harry Freeman Coliseum helped promote South Texas ranch and farm interests, and served as a major business asset to the city, attracting thousands of visitors to the city for livestock expositions and rodeos. For years, the annual exposition and rodeo were heralded as front page news in San Antonio newspapers and featured on radio and television broadcasts throughout the Southwest.

During livestock shows and rodeos, Perry would broadcast his radio show from an open booth at the coliseum, exhibit his own prize-winning, purebred registered Polled Hereford cattle from the Kallison Ranch, and advertise the store. At the South Texas Vegetable Day exhibition at the coliseum in 1952, Perry and his nephew Jimmy Kallison prominently donated the attendance prize—a brand-new Westinghouse home freezer, a new product featured at Kallison's Big Country Store.[24] At the annual meeting of the Santa Gertrudis International and the Pioneer Breeder's Association at the Coliseum, Kallison's store advertised in the Coliseum's program its sale of "Santa Gertrudis Red"—an exterior paint color for roof, barn, or corral.

Historian Char Miller has noted that the stock show and rodeo at the coliseum was established in 1950 "at a critical juncture in San Antonio's economic history." With the city's economy increasingly tied to its military bases and to tourism, the new coliseum had "a powerful economic impact." The annual two-week event brought to San Antonio tens of thousands of visitors who spent their money freely, including—as Perry had hoped—at Kallison's store.[25]

Virtually all of Perry and Frances's close friends represented the second generation of Jewish families whose parents had migrated from Russia. Among those close social friends were Selma and Phil

Adelman, owners of a downtown men's clothing store; Alma and Joe Davis, who owned a cleaning supplies business; and Henry and Irene Cohen, operators of an oil and gas company. By mid-century, most were moderately well off, and today probably would be classified "upper middle class." None were as wealthy, however, as the Oppenheimers, Halffs, and Seligmans, whose German Jewish ancestors had arrived in America fifty or sixty years earlier than the Jewish immigrants from Russia. But they, too, were friends of the Kallisons.

Perry Kallison's steadfast involvement in religious affairs and the Jewish community had continued unabated since his commitment to Rabbi Frisch as a teenager. Now, as president of Temple Beth-El in 1948, Perry stressed interfaith cooperation, making the temple available to the community and housing a Protestant congregation after its church had burned. When the Orthodox synagogue Rodfei Shalom faced a financial crisis, Perry raised funds to save their synagogue.[26] His interdenominational efforts led to his election as president of the San Antonio Jewish Federation.

In his religious and community leadership roles, Perry dropped his folksy "Ol' Trader" persona, but he remained the same effective advocate for his causes. Both roles had given him insights into bringing a group or a committee into consensus as he steered a project or a meeting into accomplishment. As both a rancher and a citizen of the city, he served as chairman of the Chamber of Commerce Agriculture Committee; one of his favorite engagements was as a longtime member of the San Antonio Livestock Exchange. He had his father Nathan's calm, genial, straightforward manner in dealing with people as he led campaigns for the San Antonio Red Cross or for the March of Dimes program to combat infantile paralysis (polio).

Perry engaged in community service with an almost rabbinical zeal, involving himself with several other community-wide organizations such as Goodwill, Boysville, and the San Antonio Zoological Association—and even finding time to serve on the Bexar County Grand Jury. In those activities, and on any other platform he could find, Perry fought discrimination not only against Jews but also against African and Mexican Americans—anyone he thought was being treated unfairly. For those efforts, the San Antonio chapter of the National Association of Christians and Jews presented him with their Brotherhood Award in 1958.[27]

TWELVE

All in the Family

DURING THE DEPRESSION and throughout World War II, the Kallisons prospered. In the spacious—but not grand— fieldstone homes with wide grassy lawns Nathan had built in Olmos Park, their lives were comfortable; their lifestyles, although considered "upper middle class," were never ostentatious. The Kallison women—the sisters and sisters-in-law—were the "chief operating officers" of those homes. As women of their time and place, their principal concerns were décor and cuisine, entertaining friends at dinner or lunch, games of mah jongg or bridge, planning family vacations, shopping for clothing and food, preparing three meals every day— and foremost, raising their children with strong values, manners, respect, and good educations. Pauline, Tibe, Ruth, and Frances would have listed their primary occupations as "mothers."

Each college-educated woman took her home role very seriously —finding the best schools, summer camps, and museum trips for the eight young Kallison, Lasser, and Neustadt children. In this and other aspects of their lives, they operated in tandem. Living harmoniously in such proximity, they supported each other. But the matriarch Anna remained in command.

Family loyalty was important to all the Kallisons. Morris and Perry held enormous respect for their father. Each brother had inherited Nathan Kallison's passion for hard work and pride in the accomplishment of a job well done. Like many businessmen of their day, Morris and Perry spent long hours at work and frequently attended community meetings late into the night. After Nathan's stroke, his two sons would stop by their parents' home every day on their way home from work. They dutifully reported to Anna on the activities at the store and, at their mother's insistent urging, often sat down to join Anna and Nathan for dinner. Their mother's table was abundant, but not always appetizing. (Her frequent stewed chicken dish was actually dreaded by her sons and grandchildren.) "Eat, eat," she would insist—even though Ruth and Frances had dinner waiting for their husbands at home. In their efforts to serve their father and mother and also to provide for their own families, however, Morris and Perry frequently came home too exhausted or too late to communicate at length with their own wives and children.

At his own dinner table, Morris talked politics and instructed his children in proper behavior. "Sit up straight in your chair," he would admonish them. He signed up Jimmy and Jack (and later, his grandsons) for boxing lessons so they could also participate in the sport he'd excelled in as a young man. He wanted them trained in the "manly art of self-defense," he said. If Morris did stay home for dinner, his wife Ruth and daughter Jane often would drive him to the YMCA afterward for a massage and visit to the steam room. He was a demanding father, impatient and critical if he thought his expectations were not being met.

"He was a kind of stoic, larger-than-life figure," revealed grandson Kal Kallison, a mathematics professor and administrator at the University of Texas. "He didn't show his feelings at all, and was never affectionate physically or with words. He was the polar opposite of Grandmother Ruth, who was always warm and loving. We were really important to her."[1]

Perry and Frances were kindred spirits in their love for the ranch, but Perry's long hours and commitments to his extended family at times strained their marriage. Many evenings, by the time Perry arrived at his home on Stanford Drive, Frances and their children— Pete, Maryann, and Frances Rae, known as "Bobbi"—had already finished dinner and left a plate for him to warm. When Perry did occasionally join them for the evening meal, it would often be interrupted with calls from funeral directors who asked him to announce burial services on the morning radio, or from members of his many civic and religious committees. Soon after dinner, Perry would climb the stairs to his pine-paneled second floor den, where he'd take some more calls and prepare for the next day's broadcast. He might look at an issue of *Cattleman* magazine before heading to bed. By 9:30 p.m. he would be asleep. If Frances wanted to attend a symphony or other cultural event during the week, she would call a friend to accompany her.

"Perry had to be dragged out to social events," observed his daughter Bobbi Ravicz. "His life was focused on the store, the ranch, and his radio program."[2] His nephew Jack Kallison added, "Perry was bored at social functions with people who had no knowledge of farming and ranching. In his own element, he was the star of the show."[3]

If Morris and Perry seemed overly preoccupied with work, Ruth and Frances made up for their absence at home, devoting extraordinary amounts of time to their children. The wives also engaged themselves in multiple community activities, but the children came first. The widowed Pauline Neustadt and her sister, the divorcee Tibe Lasser, devoted themselves to raising young Nathan and Susan—and often helped care for their nieces and nephews as well. All the Kallison women shared childraising tasks for the young cousins. At Frances Kallison's dining room table, "study hour" was an after-school session, not just for her three children, but for their cousins as well. They came from their nearby Olmos Park homes to be drilled in English, history, and math. The children also gathered at the homes of Aunt Ruth, Aunt Pauline, and Aunt Tibe for instruction, guidance, and love. The Kallison women alternated in exposing the eight Kallison cousins to cultural and educational events. For the extravaganza surrounding the movie *Gone with the Wind* in 1939, for example, Frances packed five of the eight into her car and drove them to the Majestic Theater.

Raised by four mothers—Ruth, Frances, Pauline, and Tibe—the children of Morris, Perry, and their sisters grew up in Nathan and

Anna's neighborhood compound like siblings, but without the rivalry. Jimmy, the oldest, was revered: he drove cars, was an Eagle Scout, went to dances, and flew airplanes. Protective of his younger siblings and cousins, Jimmy mentored and encouraged them. His sister Jane, next in line, grew to be a renowned beauty, a Bluebonnet Belle at the University of Texas, where she served as president of her sorority. Later, after raising three children of her own, Jane worked joyfully as a guidance counselor to students at Alamo Heights High School. Fair-skinned and dark-haired, she was known, like her mother, for her sweet nature. The four "stairsteps"—Jack, Suzanna (Susan), Nathan (Nicky), and Maryann—born in the 1930s within a year of each other—were in and out of the others' handsome two-story field-stone homes on Hildebrand Avenue and on Thelma and Stanford Drives. Jack and Nathan tossed footballs and rode bikes; the girls raced to meet each other to play halfway between their houses. Summers were long, pleasurable days of bike rides, long walks, and picnics at the ranch.

The shared mothers kept the children close, guiding the older ones to tolerate and teach the younger. The four mothers took turns chauffering them to religious school at Temple Beth-El, to movies, concerts, school plays, and summer camp. They all took music lessons. Jane and Jack played the accordion; Nathan, the trumpet; Susan and Maryann, piano. They were enrolled in elocution and dance lessons, and Jack starred as best dancer in performances put on by Bud Nash's Dance Studio on Main Avenue.

Tibe (who had reclaimed the surname Kallison for herself and her son after she divorced Ben Lasser) tutored young Nathan all through elementary school, sitting beside him every evening, helping him with his homework. And she conveyed to Jimmy, Jack, and Nathan her passionate interest in public affairs. In *He Soared with Eagles*, a biography of his father Morris, Jack Kallison wrote with affection about his Aunt Tibe and her role as his mentor, recalling how she coached him to victory in a high school debate. Discussions with his "studious, well-read, well-educated" Aunt Tibe about the limited powers of government and the US Constitution informed his remarks. "I will never forget," Jack wrote, "the help . . . my Aunt Tibe gave me to present a cogent and convincing argument."[4]

Ruth Kallison and Pauline Neustadt were renowned as the family's gourmet chefs; Pauline drawing praise for her flaming cherries jubilee and baked Alaska, Ruth for her ginger-molasses cookies and her airy sunshine cake with buttercream frosting. Ruth and Pauline alternated in holding an annual New Year's Eve party, to which they invited all of their close friends, including other Jewish retail merchants or professionals and their wives, many of whom lived in the Olmos Park Neighborhood. Those same families then would entertain each other at Saturday night dinners in their homes, afterwards playing bridge and—interspersed with teasing and laughter—discussing business or politics.

Frances Kallison's culinary efforts, though, were the subject of family teasing, especially concerning the matzo ball soup for the Kallison family's joint Passover dinners. Relatives called it "cannon ball" soup. (Exceptions to Frances's lowly-regarded cooking skills, however, were the three-layer angel food cakes which her six grandchildren eagerly anticipated on their birthdays, and the French toast she served them for breakfast after overnight visits.) "The only thing worse than her cooking was her driving," recalled granddaughter Mara Ravicz Huddock. "She would drive down the middle of the street. Once she even stopped in the middle of Broadway to look at something in a dress shop window."

The four mothers, vastly different in appearance, temperament, and interests, did not confine their lives to the dinner table, however, neither for serving up cakes nor for conducting study hall. Each woman employed domestic assistance—cleaning lady, cook, or caterer—so that their lives had space for substantial volunteer contributions to humanitarian projects and philanthropic institutions. Outside their homes, Ruth, Frances, Pauline, and Tibe each became deeply engaged in community activities. They all participated in the San Antonio and Texas chapters of the National Council of Jewish

Women, with Pauline serving as secretary. Both Ruth and Frances were self-effacing leaders, proud of their accomplishments without seeking credit or basking in the spotlight. Frances became a regional president of the National Council and spearheaded the group's creation of the Happy Hour Nursery, which cared for premature babies who had been born blind. For many years, Ruth Kallison also sought out and conveyed disfigured children to Santa Rosa Hospital for treatment by a plastic surgeon.

Frances, whose inquisitive mind and powerful intellect were her strongest characteristics, was forceful and effective as an advocate for needy citizens. When she graduated from the University of Chicago in 1929, she reported ruefully that she felt qualified only to teach Latin at a girls' school. But over the years Frances Kallison developed into a community dynamo, launching new social service programs that included a visiting nursing service as well as the Guadalupe Community Center's Good Samaritan House in the heart of San Antonio's West Side. After serving alongside her on a civic committee, Texas historian T. R. Fehrenbach described Frances Kallison— favorably—as a "formidable presence."[5] Frances's broad interests and accomplishments extended from helping to found the Texas Jewish Historical Society to completing her master's thesis for Trinity University at the age of sixty-nine. Her topic was the history of Jews in San Antonio. She served as a trustee of the Witte Museum, helped form the San Antonio Archeological Society, and, as an accomplished horsewoman, helped to initiate another new local institution—the Ladies' Auxiliary to the Bexar County Sheriff's Mounted Posse.

The term "posse" connotes a lawman's vigilante supporters riding en masse on horseback in search of an outlaw. But as the Wild West grew tamer, posses evolved into sociable riding clubs who represented sheriffs' departments in ceremonial parades. The female posse, which Frances described in the September 1951 issue of *Cattleman* magazine, was formed in 1947 to promote "superb horsemanship, good sportsmanship, and perfection of mounted drills." Frances's crack drill team rapidly became a popular public attraction.

In April 1948, the posse won a blue ribbon in the San Antonio Fiesta's Western Parade. The horsewomen became a fixture in the Livestock Exposition's opening day parades. Dressed in "smart light blue serge trousers and shirts," the proud equestriennes accented their outfits with white western hats, white gloves, and "flag-red ties." They spruced up each horse with a red and white saddle corona. Frances rode her Arabians with the group for years, particularly strutting in the annual Battle of Flowers parade in downtown San Antonio.

Despite her prominence in San Antonio's humanitarian and cultural activities, Frances, like Ruth, Pauline, and Tibe, chose her social acquaintances from the community within: Jewish women of her age and educational equivalent. Perhaps that choice was also "protective" selection. Discrimination, subtle or overt, still remained.

The Botanical Garden became a special interest that Frances supported devotedly. A skilled gardener herself, she was always experimenting by crossbreeding flowering plants. She regularly grew one of the most ambitious and admired flower gardens in the city. However, she was never invited to become a member of the elite San Antonio garden clubs, nor was her home ever included in the city's prestigious annual Garden Tour. Her daughters resented their mother's exclusion, suspecting it came either from a policy of excluding Jews, from simple social snobbery, or both. Frances simply ignored the snub; elevating her social status was not one of her goals. Although anti-Semitism had proved at most only a minor handicap to the Kallisons in their business affairs in Texas in the first half of the twentieth century, the family was not unaware of the insidious or brazen ways in which Jews were made unwelcome. On a vacation trip through the Southwest with their children in the 1940s, Frances and Perry were stunned to discover that a lovely lodge in Santa Fe where they had planned to stay advised them that it was "restricted," a term then meaning that it did not admit Jews, African Americans, or Mexican Americans.

"They were proud of being Jews and also of being Kallisons, with all that that meant," recalled grandson Li Ravicz. "But their pride reflected their identification with a collective experience (about faith and the family) rather than an individualistic one. Neither Perry nor Frances ever trumpeted their many personal accomplishments. On the other hand, I can recall many times being told that I should be proud to be Jewish—the first monotheistic faith and therefore the most farsighted one—and proud to be a Kallison, as clearly they were. Frances also frequently intoned that I should also be proud of my Texas roots."[6]

In later years, although Perry Kallison was preoccupied with work, both he and Frances nurtured affectionate relationships with their six grandchildren, while impressing upon them their most deeply held values. "Frances quietly advocated manners, education, and pride," noted a close family friend.[7]

Another grandchild, former journalist Elenita Ravicz, closely observed Frances and Perry:

> Both grandparents were among the most consistent people I have ever known. Their appearance, their values, their beliefs, and behavior varied hardly at all over time. They were very even keel, not in a good mood one day, and a bad mood the next. Grandfather even hid the matzos for Passover every year in the same place—a drawer in the downstairs bathroom.
>
> Grandfather was extremely Victorian in his morals and values—religion, family, hard work, thrift, community, country. These were the things he valued. He lived by his word and his beliefs. He did not say one thing and do another. If he supported America on the radio, then he entertained troops in his home and at his ranch. If he believed that others should work hard or not be flashy with their money, then he certainly lived that way himself, never driving fancy cars, or even eating the fanciest cuts of meat.
>
> Like most men of his generation, he did not talk much, if at all, about his feelings, hopes, or fears. His interests tend-

ed toward the practical and concrete—business, the weather, farming, ranching, cattle breeding—rather than the abstract. I think that is one reason he related so well to rural people in general and farmers and ranchers in particular. He didn't want to escape from reality or live in the future, or delve into the past. He wanted to figure out what was going on, how things worked, and how they could be made better.[8]

Despite his seriousness of purpose, Perry clearly had a whimsical sense of humor and a penchant for puns that were an endless source of amusement for his grandchildren. When the San Antonio Zoo held a contest to name a new giraffe, he suggested that his grandchildren submit the name "Zoosie." They won the contest. With a twinkle in his eye, he gave his children and grandchildren nicknames he found amusing. Daughter Frances Rae became "Bobbi," after the bobby socks that she and other girls wore in the 1940s and 1950s. He called grandson Alan Friedman "Ally Kally," after his middle name of Kallison. When granddaughter Marisol Ravicz, also known as Robi, was quarantined with mumps for several weeks at her grandparents' home, Perry nicknamed her "Mumpsy Girl" and "my Star Boarder." He called his grandchildren "my dividends."

Frances also had a lighthearted side. She regularly carted all of her grandchildren both to the circus and to the rodeo, and her interest in the circus went beyond a sense of duty. "I think she always enjoyed them more than we did," said Robi Ravicz. "She was very vocal in her enthusiastic support for the performers—cheering them on with her booming voice."

Both Perry and Frances were meticulous about how they dressed. He put on a suit and tie to work, and wore it to dinner when he returned home in the evening. He disapproved of men in white-collar jobs who did not wear coats and ties. And they both frowned upon men growing beards or long hair. Throughout her long life, Frances retained her own unique understated style regardless of the current fashion mode. And she always wore a pair of white gloves.

Like their father before them, Morris and Perry expected their children and grandchildren to work in the store at an early age, as they themselves had done as children. Although their offsprings' labor was no longer an economic necessity, Morris and Perry felt that it was important to instill in them the family's strong work ethic. They believed that some of the younger Kallisons might grow up to help them run the family business, perpetuating Nathan's vision. At age twelve, Morris and Ruth's younger son, Jack, spent his summer vacation as the store's shipping clerk. Young Jack inherited the job after the regular shipping clerk became ill. (By that time, in 1943, the store had its own fleet of trucks to deliver large items to its many rural customers.) As a pre-teen Jack Kallison made the truck assignments and was thrilled to ride out through the city and countryside with the truck drivers, who taught him how to drive. His cousin Frances Rae (Bobbi) Kallison, Perry and Frances's younger daughter, would ride the bus from home to the store, where, at thirteen, she operated the store's old-fashioned telephone switchboard. She felt so important, she recalled, whenever she announced on a loudspeaker, "Perry Kallison is wanted on line two." As an eleven-year-old, Tibe's son Nathan was assigned to sell products from a special display of fancy soaps. These apprenticeships were assigned to the next generation as well. Morris's teenaged granddaughter Nancy worked as a cashier in the hardware department; her cousin John Dreyfus, son of Morris's daughter Jane, spent one summer selling boots in the western wear department, where the teenager observed with awe how old-timers sought the honor of shaking hands with Perry Kallison, by then a public figure through his cattle breeding associations and his radio program.

The feed and seed department served as a particular testing ground for Kallison children, as well as for the children of family friends. Kallison's had expanded its feed and seed department in 1949, moving it across Flores Street into its own space in the Kallison Block. It was stocked with grass seed, fertilizers, pesticides—and a menagerie that at times included baby chickens, rabbits, and large-breasted turkeys (which Kallison's promoted as "Baby Beefs"). The young Kallisons liked the fluffy chicks and furry bunnies, but hated the smells and their cleaning chores. Under the headline "From Little Seeds Do Big Beef Grow," Kallison's advertised "the largest stock of grass seeds in the Southwest." A large photograph of Gold Mine, grand champion son of a Kallison Ranch prizewinning bull, highlighted the ad. Like their father before them, the Kallison brothers reinforced the store's identification with their now-famous ranch. "The Big Country Store knows your needs as farmers and ranchers because we are ranchers," was one newspaper advertisement's 1946 headline.[9]

"When you are ten years old, if you were Morris Kallison's grandson, you are old enough to work," recalled Kal Kallison. As a ten-year-old, he spent the summer in the feed and seed department, where he was paid $1 a day to sell baby chicks, package seed into small containers, and record sales on a cash register. "The store was a magical place," he recalled. "It had everything—western wear, appliances, and at one time, it even sold groceries."[10] At thirteen, Kal was promoted to his grandfather's real estate office. "I would take phone calls from people renting property and would write down their complaints. My instruction was to listen to people as long as they wanted to talk."[11]

After her husband of forty-nine years had died in 1944, the widowed Anna focused her attention on her daughters and their children. Sometimes the attention was painful. Although Pauline was happy with her new husband, Dr. Max Blumer, Anna never approved—which caused Pauline anguish. He didn't meet the family's strict work ethic. "He spends too much time on the golf course and not enough practicing medicine," she would complain. "He just married you for your money." "What do you want me to do? Divorce him?" Pauline screamed, in tears.[12] Pauline's daughter Susan Neustadt was a daily visitor to the grandparents' home up the street, where her

Aunt Tibe and cousin Nathan still lived. A year apart in age, the two children of the Kallison sisters had been raised as sister and brother.

Tibe, in her forties, still had not remarried, and Anna, scrutinizing each beau who came to call, cautioned her not to make another "mistake." Mindful of her mother's pressure on Tibe, her rabbi and close personal friend David Jacobson (who had succeeded Frisch) kept his eyes open for a "suitable" suitor. Shortly after World War II ended, Jacobson was called to serve as chaplain at Sampson Naval Air Station in Seneca Lake, New York. A close navy friend, Commodore Harry Badt from Washington, DC, introduced Jacobson to Dr. Jacob Kotz, a visiting friend and physician also from the nation's capital. Kotz was a highly-regarded obstetrician-gynecologist and a widower. The rabbi instantly liked Dr. Jacob Kotz, known to his family and friends as "Jack."

"I have someone you need to meet," he told Jack Kotz, who, taking the initiative, came to San Antonio to meet Tibe Kallison. They had much to talk about: like Tibe, Jack had been a precocious student, and at age twenty-two served as a battlefield surgeon in World War I. He too had parents who came to America from Russia at the turn of the century. He was head of his department at George Washington University Hospital, and deeply involved in research in cervical cancer, at that time the number one killer of women in America.[13] What surprised everyone in the family was how Anna took to this courtly, cultured stranger who had come calling.

Tibe took to him as well. Three months after their first encounter—and her subsequent trip to Washington to meet his family—they were married at the Menger Hotel in San Antonio, the site of her first wedding sixteen years earlier. She and her son Nathan, just turning thirteen and a Texan to the core, moved to Washington, DC, and a new identity.

After Tibe remarried and moved away, Anna focused her attention on Pauline, not always happily. Alone in her large home, the matriarch missed her earlier involvement in the store. She also missed Tibe, the child who always obeyed her every order and bowed to her

A *San Antonio Express* advertisement, May 3, 1936. FHA financing helped families buy homes even in the midst of the Depression.

Top: Perry and Frances Kallison's children. Seated: Maryann (left), Bobbi (right); Standing: Pete.
Above: Kallison grandchildren Susan, Nick, Jack, Jane (left to right), 1938.
Opposite, top: Perry (left) and Nathan (right) Kallison at ranch, 1938.
Opposite, bottom: Pauline Kallison Neustadt (right) with daughter Susan at ranch house, 1939.

Above: Jane, Morris, and Jack Kallison (left to right), 1940.

Left: Anna Kallison (right) with her daughter-in-law Ruth (left), 1940.

The historic Riverside Building, 1940, owned by the Kallison family.
It was located at the East Commerce Street River Bridge.

Left: KTSA *Trading Post* Broadcast Request Form. On the air each morning, the "Ol' Trader" passed along messages from his listeners.

Below: Perry Kallison with barbed wire rolls on Kallison's store's back lot, 1940. *Zintgraff Studio Photograph Collection, MS 355: Z-2505-1-F, University of Texas at San Antonio Libraries Special Collections from the Institute of Texan Cultures.*

Above: Frances Kallison at Kallison Ranch with one of her Palomino horses, 1940s.

Right: Frances (center), Maryann (left), and Pete (right) Kallison dressed for the Ranch.

Below: Frances Rae "Bobbi" Kallison (Ravicz) astride "Good Old Hilda," 1945.

Above: Lieutenant Jimmy Kallison, flight instructor in US Army Air Corps during World War II, 1942.

Opposite, top: Perry, Pete, and Nathan Kallison with farm manager Walter Sachtleben (left) at Kallison Ranch, 1942.

Opposite, bottom: Grand Champion, Beeville Fat Stock Show, Spring 1946. Weight: 1250 lbs. Sold for $1/lb. Left to right: Pete, unknown, Perry, and Jimmy Kallison.

Opposite, top: Dining tent at Kallison Ranch party, May 18, 1947.

Opposite: Kallison Ranch front gate, 1948.

Top: Aerial view of Kallison Ranch party, May 18, 1947.

Right: Frances Rosenthal Kallison, civic leader, author, and horsewoman, 1948. San Antonio Light *Photograph Collection, MS 359: L-3569-F, University of Texas at San Antonio Libraries Special Collections from the Institute of Texan Cultures.*

Top: Kallison's store in the 1950s. San Antonio Light *Photograph Collection, MS 359: L-5139-C, University of Texas at San Antonio Libraries Special Collections from the Institute of Texan Cultures.*

Above: Ku Klux Klan cross burning in front of the Jorrie family's furniture store, 1955. *Courtesy of Marilyn Jorrie.*

This is to certify that

_____ is a

★ ★ ★ **Preferred Stockholder** ★ ★ ★

Old Trader Coffee Pipe Line...

This certificate is awarded to the above individual in appreciation for contributions to humanitarian causes.

The Kallison "Coffee Pipe Line" of the Old Trader is devoted to improving the welfare of our fellow men.

As a Preferred Stockholder, the bearer of this certificate has demonstrated sincere belief in the precept: "It's more blessed to give than to receive!"

President

Top: Perry Kallison and actor Dale Robertson in Kallison's store, 1959.
Above: Preferred Stock Certificate for charitable donations via the *Trading Post*'s "Coffee Pipe Line."

Opposite top: Kallison's Warehouse Showrooms, 1963. San Antonio Light *Photograph Collection, MS 359: L-5139-B, University of Texas at San Antonio Libraries Special Collections from the Institute of Texan Cultures.*

Opposite: Rodeo at Kallison Ranch, which drew thousands of spectators, 1963. *Zintgraff Collection, UTSA's Institute of Texan Cultures, Z-1534-1, courtesy of John and Dela White.*

Top: Kallison Tower on Main Avenue, Morris Kallison's last project, 1964. *Zintgraff Collection, UTSA's Institute of Texan Cultures, Z-134-41600, Courtesy of John and Dela White.*

Right: Perry Kallison in an Israeli bunker during an air raid drill, 1970.

Top: Perry (right) and Pete (left) Kallison holding the ribbon at opening of the new Kallison's Western Wear in the Kallison Block building, 1968. San Antonio Light *Collection, UTSA's Institute of Texan Cultures, L-6350, Courtesy of the Hearst Corporation.*

Above: Nick Kotz and Perry Kallison at the ranch, 1972.

admonitions. Pauline, on the other hand, had a will of her own—and Anna's ever more frequent criticisms of Dr. Blumer kept the ebullient older daughter quite miserable. Dr. Blumer and his golf still did not meet with Anna's approval.

Although Tibe came back at times to visit her mother, the absence of a daughter and grandson in her home had left Anna unhappy and fearful. And then, her graceful and gregarious older daughter Pauline—her favorite child despite her complaints—was diagnosed with breast cancer. The family was devastated, holding the news from Anna as long as they could while Pauline challenged her disease with all that modern medicine had to offer at the time. Tibe persuaded her mother to fly to Washington for visits—which Anna began to enjoy, basking in the warmth her new son-in-law showed her. With Anna out of town, Pauline was freed for a short time from her mother's constant antagonism toward Max Blumer.

Pauline was fifty-four when she died at home on March 8, 1953. Jimmy Kallison had driven Susan home from the University of Texas at Austin to be by her dying mother's bedside. There she stood while her stepfather, on his knees, begged Pauline to sign over all her property to him. She did not do so. (He took her jewelry instead, according to her daughter.) Pauline was buried in Temple Beth-El Cemetery, near her father. Susan graduated just months after Pauline's death, and moved to Washington to live with her Aunt Tibe. Living with her deteriorating grandmother was not an option.

Tibe made frequent trips back to San Antonio to comfort Anna, who was overtaken by unbearable grief and loneliness, as well as by an increasing paranoia. She took Anna on winter trips to Florida and brought her to Washington, DC, several times a year, where the calming presence of her son-in-law temporarily eased her pain—until the aging Anna could no longer travel. Returning to San Antonio, unable to cope with losing her elder daughter and diagnosed with "hardening of the arteries," Anna slowly retreated into her own world. Live-in nursing aides stayed by her side at home, but Anna's primary caregiver became Ruth Kallison. Ruth, who was known as the "kindest person in the family," came to see her mother-in-law every day, supervising the aides, securing medical help, taking care of the large, empty house. When disagreements arose in the Kallison family between parents and children, brothers and sisters, Ruth never took sides. She extended her love and care to all in the family.

Tibe's visits to her mother became fewer and farther apart as Anna entered full dementia. In Washington, she was creating a joyful new life of her own, and one for her orphaned niece Susan as well. With Jack Kotz as her companion, Tibe was never happier. He gave her the nickname "Tibby" which she adopted as her legal name. They traveled widely, read Carl Sandburg's six-volume biography of Abraham Lincoln to each other at night, listened to classical recordings together, and attended the symphony, opera, and Broadway shows. Tibe was embraced by the doctor's wide and diverse circle of friends—prosperous Jewish doctors and other professionals, college professors, prominent government officials, newspaper editors and correspondents. As a frequent hostess and glamorous guest in Washington's "Cave Dweller's" community of upper class Jewry, the diminutive Tibe enjoyed a more sophisticated and richer cultural life.[14] Most of her new friends were "cultural Jews"—attending religious services once or twice a year, but dedicated to Jewish ethical values, including service to their community. She dedicated herself to supporting philanthropic programs to help needy children and the newly created nation of Israel. In the summer, she took adult courses in history, philosophy, and art at Brandeis University outside of Boston.[15] In Washington's postwar atmosphere of mounting Cold War paranoia and anti-Communist McCarthyism, outside her family Tibe kept quiet about her strongly liberal views, but remained committed to them.

The remaining family in Texas began to resent those evermore infrequent visits when Tibe would "swoop in, give orders, or criticize the way her mother was being cared for, and then fly back to Washington," according to Frances Kallison. "It was Ruth who was the daughter, taking all the time and the responsibility."[16]

With Pauline gone, Tibe away in her new life, and their mother no longer able to communicate, the Kallison brothers had lost the last ties to an earlier generation that had stressed family unity above all. Tibe's ecstatic life in Washington was short-lived, however, after her surgeon husband, always a heavy smoker, was no longer able to practice medicine because of his worsening heart disease. He died in February 1958, after only twelve years of their marriage. There was no option for Tibe but to return home to San Antonio. After Dr. Kotz's death, then Anna's in 1959, Kallison family rifts widened. Morris did not speak to Tibe; they communicated through lawyers and accountants. Perry would call her only on her birthday, as she would call him on his. Although they still conveyed the value of family loyalty to their children and grandchildren, each family had now become a separate unit focused on its own goals and aspirations.

THIRTEEN

No Business for Sissies

C LOUDS OF DUST spread out in every direction from the dirt roads leading into the Kallison Ranch. Hundreds of pickup trucks, new postwar station wagons, sedans, and surplus jeeps drove up on that sunny Sunday afternoon carrying farmers, ranchers, rural neighbors, and city dwellers from all over South Texas. A line several miles long slowly passed dusty cowboys and women on horseback, as they streamed through the entrance gates.

Perry and Morris Kallison had invited friends, neighbors, and customers to a picnic on their ranch on May 18, 1947. More than ten thousand people showed up. They devoured barbecued beef and goat, quaffed Pearl and Lone Star beer, cheered at a rodeo with bull riding and steer-tying contests, and examined a display of the farm products sold at Kallison's store. The Kallison brothers were presenting their guests with the latest innovations in farm machinery to the most improved hybrid seeds and effective weed killers. Seated in tents and around picnic tables in the shade of live oaks, the visitors looked out toward the Hill Country, where a prize herd of Polled Hereford cattle grazed. Around them lay terraced green fields where many different kinds of hardy grass seeds and methods of soil conservation were being tested. The giant picnic was a mini-exposition, at which the Kallisons were marketing new products sold by their store, and at the same time educating the crowd in the breakthrough methods and materials that would revolutionize postwar farming.

With young men returning home and the Great Depression ending, prosperity was again appearing in city and country alike. The victory also released a huge pent-up demand for more and better food, a goal unattainable during four years of crippling wartime shortages and rationing. This time, the postwar American agricultural challenge was to develop the capacity not only to fulfill consumer expectations at home, but also to help feed a war-ravaged world.

For South Texas farmers and ranchers, the added challenge was to figure out how they might earn a decent living in a marketplace distinguished by rapidly changing technology, volatile prices, rising costs, intense competition, and the constant threat of punishing droughts. In South Texas, agriculture never had been an easy life. As Perry Kallison often told folks, "ranching is no business for sissies."

Most South Texas ranchers bore little resemblance to popular movie and television images of swashbuckling "high rollers" and cattle barons awash in money from oil wells, huge herds of cattle, and spreads of land counted in thousands of acres. With few exceptions, these local men and women and their families earned modest returns on large investments of their time, labor, money, and gritty determination to earn their living from the land. To supplement their farm income and support their families, many also worked full time at second jobs. They were the Kallisons' neighbors, friends, and customers.

"Perry Kallison perhaps knows more farm and ranch people in South Texas than any other man and can call most of them by their first names," wrote R. G. Jordan, the *Express-News's* veteran farm writer. "He has done more for all segments of the agricultural economy of South Texas than any other individual."[1]

But after World War II, even as Texas and its agricultural sector were booming and American industry and agriculture were thriving, Perry cautioned his *Trading Post* listeners not to take for granted the country's and Texas's phenomenal growth: "You notice the country is coming south," he said. "The big companies are investing in Texas—not because the Yankees love us. They're moving in because the economic wealth of the earth lies over our way. But history shows that man is greedy. He uses some, wastes more. And while we are in the richest part of the world, waste will finally tell. Our oil will be gone, our water wells will be dry, our land washed away—and not enough to feed our own. Now there is time to save our future," Perry went on. "A soil conservation district in your county is more important than an oil field. A saving of water, under or on top of the ground, means more to our future than anything in the world. So always be a'thinkin' when you plow the ground, when you build a terrace—and stop the soil from washing away. When you stop the waste of water, you are part of an important plan—to save America. God has given you power in use of the land."[2] His words presaged what would become a national environmental defense movement generations later. But Perry worked to improve the land and its products as well as to save it.

In the beginning, the Kallison Ranch had been stocked with range cattle, ordinary Hereford cows distinguished by their red bodies and white faces. In 1932, however, in the midst of the Great Depression—and undaunted by it—Nathan Kallison and his son had made a decision which would determine the future of the Kallison Ranch in the decades that followed. As Nathan and Perry saw beef cattle ranching evolve into a far more specialized and competitive business, they decided to upgrade their operation by selling their "range cows" and developing a herd of higher-quality animals. At the Fort Worth Fat Stock Show in 1932, the Johnson Brothers from Jacksboro, Texas, had convinced Perry that their own purebred Polled Hereford cattle were "the coming breed." These beefy white-faced animals were a new strain of a venerable British breed imported to the Midwest in the 1800s. What was special about this new strain was that the bulls had no horns—a condition described as "polled," describing a smooth head without projections. The breed had large brisket sections (breast and lower chest), which were said to be "tasty," and therefore had a strong commercial value. Without horns, the Kallisons learned, the cows were easier to handle in corrals and feedlots and were less likely to hurt each other or their owners. The big cows also gave birth easily to large calves, requiring less assistance from ranch hands or veterinarians. Beyond their utility, the Polled

Herefords looked distinctive—even endearing—with their white heads, white bellies below their copper-red bodies, and white fluff at the ends of their tails. And well-bred registered Polled Herefords gained weight rapidly, producing high-quality meat that sold for a premium price. For Nathan and Perry, the Kallison Ranch goal was to develop the finest Polled Hereford herd in the country, which then would be sold as breeding stock to help other ranchers upgrade their own herds.

Neither Perry Kallison nor anyone else involved in American agriculture claimed to know all the answers about how ranchers and farmers could prosper in such a rapidly changing America, however. Over the decades, Nathan, Perry, and the nation had seen remarkable progress in agriculture: better tractors, trucks, and other labor-saving equipment, new seed and fertilizers, and better breeds of cows. Yet the costs involved in change, while benefiting some, usually hurt others.

The end of World War II, with all its upheavals in every aspect of life, also ushered in what has been called the "second revolution in American agriculture." The first had fostered a transition from using manpower to animal power, with improved steel plows and use of inventions such as the cotton gin and McCormick reaper. Nathan had noted and learned from each new innovation. But many farmers lagged in adopting new methods, so the advanced agricultural techniques and machinery had made only a few inroads into the nation's farms after World War I. With the resources developed and available following the Second World War, however, Perry became keenly aware that a new technological revolution was on the horizon, with "widespread progress in mechanization, greater use of lime and fertilizer, widespread use of cover crops and other conservation practices."

According to agricultural historians, "use of improved seed varieties including hybrid corn, a better-balanced feeding of livestock, and the use of chemicals for such purposes as weed killers and defoliants" defined the "revolution's" great progress. Change in the countryside included mechanized cotton production with huge cotton-pickers, cows bred to produce more milk for the dairy industry, development of hybrid sorghums for cattle feed, and improved breeds of chickens and pigs.[3]

Nationally, production soared. The US Department of Agriculture, state agricultural colleges, and private industry invented and introduced the groundbreaking technological changes. Importantly, information about new products reached more and more farmers and ranchers who rushed to purchase them, thanks to the work of the colleges, USDA extension services, and the vital role of the rural news media—very much including Perry Kallison's *Trading Post* radio program. As a result of rapid and continuing developments to produce better crops and animals, less and less manpower was required in managing a farm or ranch. With all those new inventions and technologies, however, greater capital investment was needed to farm efficiently.

Increasingly, economists and bankers were emphasizing that agriculture was "a business," just like any other, and therefore subject to the demands of the marketplace. Yet for many of the men and women who owned family farms and ranches in Texas and across the country, their livelihood involved more than being just another business. It represented deeply held values, family traditions, a love for the land, and what they called "a way of life." These were understood, and also deeply felt, by Perry Kallison. In the decades-long debates over government policy and the role of agriculture in American life, an ongoing tension continued to build between the concept of agriculture as "just another business enterprise," or as an important American institution (exemplified by the family farm), worth preserving for its contributions to the economy and to society. The latter definition was an extension of Thomas Jefferson's original ideal about the importance of the land and its people.

Perry Kallison held this second view. Indeed, he understood that farmers and ranchers constantly needed to modernize and to compete vigorously in the marketplace. But American agriculture, its farmers and ranchers, and the small towns that served them, were too important to be left unprotected from the exigencies of a marketplace shaken by overproduction or by volatile weather, which could destroy crops over wide areas of the country with bitter cold or late-season freezes, sustained droughts or major floods. Perry and others who shared his view believed that agriculture needed help from the government when either the economy or weather conditions wreaked havoc on the "family farm"—defined as a sustainable farm owned and operated by a single family. He preached his deeply held values about the land in his Saturday radio sermonettes and to live audiences throughout Texas.

However, Perry Kallison's views on the role of government in agriculture were not shared by many of his best ranching friends, conservatives to the core who railed against any government interference in their business. Despite his strong beliefs, though, he seldom, if ever, allowed disagreements over politics and government farm policy to disrupt his relationships with those other ranchers and farmers with whom he shared important common interests. Agriculture, they all knew, was indeed a business—and a healthy national agriculture was vital to the entire national economy.

In running the Kallison Ranch, however, Perry was a conservative. He had a strong commitment to conservation and believed there was an appropriate governmental role in agriculture, but in his own enterprise he clung to prudent agricultural practices and was, above all, practical. He knew what farmers and ranchers wanted, and what they might achieve. "We are not trying to do anything extraordinary," he told farm editors, "but just to develop this thing on a practical basis and by methods within the reach of the average person interested in farming and ranching."[4]

The Kallison Ranch pioneered in experimenting with different kinds of permanent pasture grasses, for example, that might thrive reasonably well, even in periods of below-average rainfall in the thin South Texas soil, which too often nourished only weeds, underbrush, and mesquite trees. Hybrid seeds developed by Texas A&M scientists and seed manufacturers brought new possibilities for growing hearty grasses and grains with larger yields. Working with the US Soil Conservation Service in 1948, Perry conducted a typical grass-growing experiment in a ten-acre field on the south side of the Kallison Ranch. The field was terraced to prevent runoff and erosion and planted with a California mixture of almost a dozen grasses and one clover. And of course, Kallison's feeds and seeds department sold these hearty, drought-resistant grasses that the ranch successfully tested. In an advertisement in *Cattleman* magazine headlined "Meet the Two Wonder Grasses of Texas," the Kallison's promotion described Buffel Grass as a solution for "worn out soils" with "roots that can extend eight feet deep," making it "excellent for erosion control and soil building," and also extolled the deep-rooted Blue Panicum, a grass with a high protein content.[5]

In addition to agricultural demonstrations at the ranch, Perry was a ceaseless advocate for land conservation. For Perry Kallison, soil conservation was essential for farmers and ranchers to survive in South Texas. In 1961, N. D. Coleman, board chairman of Alamo Soil and Conservation District 330, cited Perry Kallison as the professional man "who has done the most for soil conservation" in the region. Coleman noted that the Kallison Ranch had adopted 95 percent of the soil conservation practices recommended by Alamo District 330.[6]

What was most important about the demonstrations carried out by Perry and other progressive ranch leaders was their influence on other farmers and ranchers. The federal planners of the Extension Service and Soil Conservation programs discovered that a majority of farmers still had remained stubbornly resistant to their recommendations. They were simply not responding positively to an outsider telling them "to try some new scientific methods." The program became successful only when farmers could witness what their own neighbors had accomplished with higher yields of grain and with fatter steers and heifers. Perry Kallison took great delight in bringing visitors out to the ranch—even throngs of them—to share with them what he was doing and how he was doing it.

Whenever there was a program to encourage people to become ranchers and farmers, Perry also participated. After World War II, he volunteered his ranch and farm expertise to a federally assisted program to help returning veterans enter agriculture. Perry brought former soldiers enrolled in the veterans' vocational school in Cuero, Texas, to the Kallison Ranch "for a first-hand study of practical farm and ranch practices." Describing the veterans' program, Perry emphasized that "we are trying to show our mistakes as well as our accomplishments so these boys won't make the same mistakes that we have in some of our practices."[7]

In another US Agriculture Department program to encourage progressive farming, Perry Kallison supported 4-H Clubs and Future Farmers of America (FFA), organizations whose members were farm and ranch children, as well as other youths with an interest in agriculture. He regularly traveled throughout South Texas, attending the annual sales at which 4-H club participants competed and sold their animals. He took pleasure in congratulating and inspiring all the young "ranchers." At the 1946 Medina County Fat Calf Sale in Castroville, Perry bought the prize calf, exhibited by Helen Marie Schuchart, the daughter of one of his ranching neighbors whose Alsatian great-grandparents had come to Texas as part of the Castro expedition in 1845. Sending Helen Marie his payment for the calf, Perry wrote: "I expect you to have the grand champion next year."[8] Earlier, Kallison also had singled out Helen Marie's older brother Millard Schuchart, rewarding him with a cowboy hat and pair of boots after he had won top prize in a cattle show.[9] Perry, the former Boy Scout leader, embraced the farm youth organization's four values: "Head. Hand. Heart. Health." His goal was to motivate the young students to remain on the land and nurture it with sustainable farming.

Beyond encouraging 4-H members such as the young Schucharts, Perry supported the organization itself by purchasing ads in their event programs. A full-page Kallison's store ad in the program for the Medina 4-H Sale: "Best of luck to you fellows from the

Ol' Trader," the advertisement stated. "When in San Antonio, visit the Big Country Store. Drop around to see us. We are always happy to meet you and swap. You know, Kallison's is the largest supplier of farm and ranch supplies in this part of the country."

Perry urged dozens of young people from Texas and beyond to pursue careers in agriculture. Another brother and sister, Jon and Dinah Weil, came as children with their mother in the 1950s from Livonia, Louisiana, to the Kallison Ranch, where Perry sold them two young bulls which they named "Perry K" and "Elvis." That experience launched the youngsters on what would later become successful careers in the cattle business. Dinah reflected decades later that Perry Kallison "looked like a rugged Texan who radiated enthusiasm about ranching and warmly encouraged young people interested in the business. You see him and you know he's a man who has done a lot."[10] In 2011, Dinah Weil's enterprise, 3X-HK Cattle—a "dynamic Red Brahman cattle ranch headquartered in Rosharon, (Brazoria County) Texas"—noted on its website their ventures in Brazil, Costa Rica, Panama, and Mexico.[11]

"Perry Kallison was the kind of man who took a real interest in young people," recalled Lloyd Benke, another 4-H participant, whose family owned a fifteen-hundred-acre spread bordering the Kallison property. After Benke's father's death, he took over his family's ranch at age nineteen. Perry helped and advised him because, said Benke, he "was interested in seeing a young man get ahead."

For years, Perry Kallison also supported the agriculture training programs at Luther Burbank Vocational High School in San Antonio, giving the school and its students calves to raise, and hosting the school's events at the ranch, along with programs for other 4-H and FFA student organizations from around the region. "Whenever we've had a problem or needed something," recalled the director who ran the Burbank program, "Someone would always say, 'Why don't we call Perry Kallison?' And he always came through."[12]

In the years immediately following World War II, the Kallison ranch and store also led efforts to eradicate the native weeds, juniper, and mesquite bushes that continually frustrated South Texas ranchers by overwhelming the grasses their cattle grazed on. In one highly publicized experiment, Kallison's became partners with E. B. Stull of Stull's Chemicals, Incorporated, then manufacturing and selling weed and brush killer. The experiment drew widespread publicity, including a full-page spread in the *San Antonio Light*.[13] Customers flocked to Kallison's store to buy the new herbicide. After showing early promise, however, Stull's chemicals failed to keep down the offending weeds and bushes.

Perry and Morris Kallison were bold in seeking out new ways to make a profit and at the same time benefit the rural customers. However, if a product failed, like those army surplus generators after World War II or the magical weed and brush killers, they were ready to try something else. In fact, their experiment with weed killers was a forerunner to what would become a multibillion-dollar business in selling herbicides to farmers.[14]

By the 1950s, though, the Kallison Ranch was a carefully-planned operation, equally divided between pastureland and farmland used to raise crops suitable for feeding the cattle—crops that included cane, millet, oats, barley, and grain sorghum, a grain that was improved after World War II and flourished as feed for cattle in South Texas. About two thousand tons of silage was stored in the ranch's trench silos, which were designed to store grain economically, without spoilage. The horizontal trenches, several hundred feet long and ten to fifteen feet deep, were made airtight by covering them with dirt and plastic, which would be removed when the silage was needed. The ranch was increasing its silage storage capacity by five hundred tons a year—a safeguard against the periodic droughts. The cattle were grazed alternately in five different pastures. Water for the livestock was provided by seven wells and six water tanks.

In his breeding program for Polled Herefords, Perry helped move that breed of cattle to the pinnacle of its success. In 1950, Texas stood at the head of Hereford producers both in quality and numbers, and the Texas Hereford Association and the Polled Hereford Association, of which Perry was president, were the strongest in the country.[15] He continued as a driving force, later teaming up with Ervin E. Voigt, another innovative San Antonio area rancher, to start the South Texas Polled Hereford Association to help market "better-bred animals" in their region.

In their political views, Kallison and Voigt were a study in opposites: Voigt outspokenly opposed government aid to ranchers, and Perry staunchly supported government assistance. They worked closely together, however, first to build the livestock coliseum in San Antonio, then to further the development of their own Polled Herefords. As Perry Kallison told the *San Antonio Express-News*, "Cattlemen wanted bloodlines that produced more beef for less feed, and better cuts of beef in the carcass." With its research into breeding programs, the Kallison ranch was instrumental in helping other ranchers produce finer herds.

Perry had explained to Frank Reeves, livestock editor of *Texas Ranch and Farm* magazine, that his own goal was to develop animals "that will do well for practical ranchers" who were buying the ranch's registered Polled Herefords bulls and cows to build up their own commercial herds.[16] After visiting the ranch in 1959, Reeves wrote that "the abundance of grass and the cows made an unforgettable picture." He praised the Kallison herd as "an attractive lot of deep, thick-bodied cows of excellent proportions." Perry's wife Frances later reminisced, "Perry fell in love with that breed, and the love affair persisted."[17]

With his emphasis on assisting "practical ranchers," Perry was not afraid to buck any popular tide of the moment. For example, he ignored the 1950s and '60s trend of growing smaller registered Polled Herefords, which were bred to show well and win blue ribbons. "Perry never did that," recalled cattle auctioneer Bert Reyes, who worked with Kallison for decades. "He was trying to raise big, practical cows. Breeds change like women's fashions, but he consistently stayed with his kind of cattle. And when larger-framed cows were again in demand, Perry's ranch was the place to get them."

On the *Trading Post* and his regular visits to Texas A&M's agricultural researchers, Perry virtually proselytized young people to enter the cattle industry. Bert Reyes and his brother Ruben had come to him soon after their graduation from A&M. "Can you give us advice on how to become cattle auctioneers?" they asked him. He steered them to the apprenticeships to begin their careers. "I like their enthusiasm and their commitment," he would tell potential hirers who preferred experienced workers to candidates who wanted training on the job. "I think these boys could make a contribution to the cattle business." For years thereafter, when Polled Hereford auctions were being planned, he tried to see that the Reyes brothers, now auctioneers, got the business, a favor they later would return.

"Perry was not just interested in his own ranch but in all Polled Hereford people," Reyes added. "He knew every farmer and rancher in this part of the country. He always worried that farmers and ranchers were not getting enough for their cattle."[18]

As a leader of the Texas Polled Hereford Association, Perry later became frustrated when the breed's market value began to slip, losing out to black Angus cattle. He thought that this shift was not because the Angus beef was better, but because the Angus industry had done a far more effective job of marketing and advertising their black cattle. Through his association, Perry tirelessly crisscrossed Texas—as well as the entire country—to promote the virtues of the big cattle with red hides and white faces. From the ranch he exported male calves to distant destinations—Venezuela, Australia, and Hawaii (which the "Ol' Trader" pronounced *Ha-WHY-ya*), thus spreading the Kallison reputation even farther via its bulls.

Within a dozen years, the Kallisons had developed their major herd, four hundred prize-winning registered Polled Hereford cattle, one of the larger "quality" herds in Texas. The ranch's specialty then moved up to breeding and selling outstanding registered Polled Hereford bulls and cows. The cattle at the Kallison Ranch were treated as tenderly as if they were thoroughbred race horses. They were brushed and groomed daily in a long, three-sided pole barn that also sheltered them from the sun. That specially designed barn, construct-ed of corrugated sheet metal and telephone poles, was located on the north end of the Kallison Ranch, on a hill that caught the summer breeze.

From the barn and the ranch house located nearby, one had a commanding view in all directions—downtown San Antonio eight-een miles to the east, and the rolling Hill Country stretching out to the north and west—a vista always admired by potential cattle buyers. The ranch's income derived from selling fifty young bulls and fifty heifers a year. Each of the bulls would bring at least several thousand dollars and the cows not much less. Value was judged both by blood-line and by how the animal appeared to buyers. For several decades, the Kallison cattle, with their "better cuts of beef," won prizes and sold for record prices at livestock shows all over the country.

Like his father before him, Perry pursued prizes, which helped enhance the economic value of the ranch's livestock and further pro-moted the store's reputation for knowing the needs of ranchers and farmers. But those prizes were just a bonus. Perry Kallison simply took great pride in the animals he had bred, and shared his enthusi-asm with his family and other visitors to the ranch. He loved to get in the pen with a handsome bull, gently brush the animal's hair, point out the bull's important features, such as his wide, strong, muscular back and well-sprung ribs, and then give the bull an appreciative pat on its rump.[19] His family was greatly amused by the affection he bestowed on his outstanding cattle.

He spoke of his prizewinners as though they were movie stars. The foundation of the Kallison herd was Golden Nugget, a prize bull Perry purchased at a national sale in partnership with Robert Halbert of Sonoma, Texas. Another star, Gold Mine, a son of Golden Nugget, quickly justified his name. By 1967, Gold Mine had sired more top Polled Herefords than any other bull in history. As the years went by, other Kallison-bred cattle won numerous awards and set records. In 1967, Hazel Domino 52, a granddaughter of Golden Nugget, became the top Register of Merit cow of the breed. Golden Diamond, another granddaughter of Golden Nugget, that same year ranked third among all Register of Merit cows. Other cattle celebrities among the herd included Beau Perfection, Domestic Mischief, Advanced Mischief, and Lamplighter. As a newspaper advertisement noted: "The Best Cow Families Make their Home at Kallison Ranch."

Frances Kallison was his ranch partner in every respect. Of all the Kallison women, Perry's wife was the one who "took to" the ranch for more than a Sunday picnic. Not only did Frances host various social events there, she was also deeply involved in the ranch's management. She kept the breed books detailing the ancestry of each cow, recorded each calf's unique number, and named the newborns. A horsewoman as well, Frances raised her noble white Arabians on the ranch, and rode in shows and exhibitions throughout Texas. Across the nation and beyond, she often traveled to livestock shows with her husband. In February 1956, she accompanied Perry to the Pan American Livestock Show in Havana, Cuba, where prize Polled Herefords from Kallison's Ranch were featured.

International success of the Kallison cattle ranch did not extend to all of Perry's attempts to improve Texas agriculture, however. If one subject endlessly dominated conversations in the Kallison homes, it was rain, rain, rain—the lack of it. Periodic droughts not only were ruinous to the Kallison Ranch, but also to the nearby farmers and ranchers who were the family store's most important customers. Their very livelihoods and families were dependent on rainfall.

Throughout its history, severe dry spells have plagued Texas. The Spanish explorer Álvar Núñez Cabeza de Vaca discovered in 1528 that the natives there had been starving for nearly two years when he came upon them. Stephen F. Austin's first colonists lost their first corn crop after settling in Texas in 1822. Thousands of eastern farmers who migrated to Texas on the opening of the western school lands in 1883 fled home during the ruinous drought of 1884-86. But the worst drought in Texas history, even more ruinous than the one that produced the Dust Bowl, arrived toward the end of 1950.[20]

The post-World War II years had raised high expectations of

prosperity for the farmers and ranchers of Texas. In 1950, the Union Stockyards in San Antonio set a record with the sale of one million cattle, hogs, sheep, and goats. Disaster soon followed. That year ushered in a seven-year drought which had actually started in the Rio Grande Valley in 1949, then spread to cover nearly every part of Texas by 1951, and worsened from 1954 to 1956.[21]

"Many fields did not have a blade of grass," Perry recalled later. "Many cattlemen went broke because they could not feed their cattle. There was practically no feed to be had; no hay to be bought. To help the ranchers, the government was buying cattle and paying the price of $16.75 for a cow. The government brought in trainloads of hay and allocated it among the ranchers to help out the situation. But with all of that help, many never survived the losses they sustained in those years."[22]

Like its neighbors, the Kallison Ranch also suffered. Kallison's Big Country Store was in a position to sustain them, though. The store was thriving, with its sale of television sets, washing machines, and other appliances—primarily to city customers—and the Kallisons simply put aside money to support the ranch. Perry's principal concern was about other ranchers and farmers—the damage inflicted upon them and the entire Texas agricultural economy. Summoning the store's managers to a lunch meeting in Sommer's Drug Store basement cafeteria on Houston Street, he spoke about Kallison's farm and ranch customers. "I want you to understand we are undergoing a tremendous drought," he said. "It's hard on our customers. Sympathize with them, try to understand!"[23]

Like his father, Perry tried not to turn away loyal customers in hard times, but to work with them to extend their payments. It may not have been a sound business practice, thought some members of his family, but it was humane, the way he wanted to operate. For Perry and veteran Texas ranchers and farmers, the 1950s drought brought back memories of the Great Depression and the subsequent Dust Bowl, when, combined with the 1930s economic crash, the drought decimated Texas agriculture.

With his wry sense of humor, Perry turned to unusual "prognosticators" to raise the spirits of his *Trading Post* listeners as the drought worsened. "As you know we are hoping that the rains for January will come and mellow the ground for spring planting," he drawled. The Singing Turtle (owned by Mallory Franklin who brings in the weather reports) and old Will Kay who lives in that cave on the banks of the Nueces—both say we're goin' to get rain."[24] But it did not come.

Desperation set in. Four years into the drought, Perry and his neighbors across the area began to receive glowing announcements from professional rainmakers. With panic spreading and farms folding, Perry Kallison organized a plan. Later, when working with the San Antonio Chamber of Commerce farm committee, he recalled the experience:

"A group of us got together, and we raised $50,000 to hire a rainmaker—a man named Barnes from Arizona. He called himself 'Precipitation Control.' The idea behind rainmaking was to seed the clouds with silver iodide—a chemical that causes water to form inside the clouds. But that's not all that Precipitation Control prescribed. We also planted generators with the silver iodide in a stretch of fifty miles across from San Antonio south up into the hills. A Precipitation Control office in Denver supposedly monitored cloud formations. If cloud formations heading toward South Texas looked like they were bearing water, our team would switch on the generators to attract them. It was a big boondoggle," Perry conceded sadly. "They never did any good. And, of course, there was no rain."

Although Texas had long grown accustomed to enduring the dry periods, the prolonged seven-year drought of the 1950s simply devastated small ranchers and farmers, most of whom lacked deep capital resources and other sources of income. The drought also compounded problems caused by the more expensive mechanized agriculture, in which larger farms and ranches increasingly dominated the market. Smaller farmers and ranchers were driven out of the business, forced to sell their land to larger operators or to urban developers. These changes saddened Perry Kallison as he saw "family farming," at the heart of rural America, being wiped out.

When the drought finally broke on May 7, 1957, it broke with a vengeance. Kallison Ranch was flooded, along with most of South Texas. The dormant Culebra Creek, a dry ditch, turned into a raging river overnight. Ponds, called "stock tanks," overflowed, rendering ranch roads impassable. Many cattlemen who had endured such terrible losses of livestock from starvation during the drought were devastated again when their remaining livestock drowned in the raging creeks. Crops, however, were born again. Sugar cane and sorghum grew to gargantuan heights. Ranchers and farmers stood outside in the rain and cheered. Frances Kallison snapped a photograph of one of her lanky nephews, standing in the verdant field, the cane towering over him. Good times had returned to the ranch, and Perry turned again to his favorite pursuit—helping others.

Perry Kallison's willingness to lend a hand reached beyond America's borders. In 1964, when a group of idealistic young Israelis wanted to form a settlement and raise Angora goats in Galilee, the Israeli Ministry of Agriculture sent them to Texas A&M University, where extension agents referred the visitors to Perry Kallison. The Ol' Trader took charge of the project. The fledgling state of Israel hoped to start a mohair industry, and the Israeli farmers had come to the right place.

Together with Frances, Perry had contributed to the 1930s American effort to help Jews escape from Nazi Germany and immigrate to Israel, the United States, and other countries. In 1946, in the wake of World War II, Frances had written to President Truman requesting him to liberalize immigration for displaced persons.[25] Perry, president of Temple Beth-El in San Antonio in 1948, subsequently contributed funds and passionately rallied political support for the birth of the state of Israel. And now, he reasoned, he had an opportunity to help build Israel's agricultural strength.

Almost all of the Angora goat and mohair wool business in the

United States is centered on the Edwards Plateau near Uvalde, in South Texas. From his friends in the area, Kallison recruited Texas ranchers who were willing to donate goats to the Israeli project. Next, he sent instructions to the head of the department of animal husbandry in Israel. "Angora goats are very delicate," Perry wrote. "You need to have someone come to Texas A&M for training to care for them."

The Yodfat Kibbutz, the destination for the Texas goats, was a settlement in an area of Galilee without electricity or roads. When the Israeli representatives Yoram Avidor and Yehuda Agmor arrived at the ranch, Perry Kallison sent them to various Texas goat ranches, including one owned by W. S. Orr of Rock Springs. (Years earlier, some Israelis traveling in the Texas Hill Country had spotted Orr's "little white animals which resembled goats but did not actually look like them."[26]) Yoram recalled Perry's kindness: "He put us up in a hotel and paid all of our expenses while we were there," he said. "He had a large store in San Antonio and he told us to choose whatever we wanted—clothes, tools, anything we could use when we got back to Israel. For us, it was like being in 'Wonderland.'"[27]

Determined to help Israel and its people not only to survive but also to prosper in the Promised Land, Perry promoted the Israeli goat mission on the *Trading Post*. And in a widely-disseminated letter dated "August 1964 in the 16th year of the State of Israel," he noted:

When the children of Israel dwelt in the wilderness of Sinai, before they entered into the Promised Land, they used goats for milk, food, clothing, and for covering the tabernacle (Exodus 26:7). Even today, in Galilee, one may still see the young shepherd leading his flock homeward as the sun sets over the western sea.

Modern Israel, however, envisions a new industry: mohair, the lustrous fabric woven from the hair of the Angora goat. The climate and terrain of Israel, in which the goats have been raised successfully since ancient times, is like that of Texas. The farmers and cattle growers know well how fortunate would be their endeavor if only the herds, even a foundation herd, could be theirs. Such herds could well be the lifeline of the hill country of Israel, and the mohair industry could strengthen this young oasis of democracy.

Rancher W. S. Orr has donated a $500 registered sire and all that remains is the purchase of one hundred goats at a cost of $50 each.[28]

Although they fell short of the initial goal, the Israelis, with Perry's help, did raise enough money to acquire seventy-five Angora kids from the Schreiner Y-O Ranch at Mountain Home.[29] Both Jews and non-Jews who were sympathetic to the young country donated goats to Israel. An apple grower in New York heard about the project and contributed the airfare to ship the herd from Texas to New York. El Al, the Israeli national airline, contributed one of its passenger planes to fly the herd home to Israel. When the airplane touched down in Tel Aviv, this first use of the sleek airline to transport farm animals drew photographers to the airport.

A year later, the second Israeli "goat emissary," Yehuda Agmor, returned to San Antonio with his new bride. In a stone cottage Perry and Frances had built near the caretaker's house, the newlyweds spent their honeymoon on the Kallison Ranch. In the Agmors' honor, the Kallisons held a dinner there, entertaining the Israeli couple as though they were visiting heads of state. All of Morris's downtown tenants were invited. Tents were erected. Barbecued beef smoked on grills. Beer, wine, and hard liquor flowed, along with drinks like Big Red and Coke. For entertainment, the ranch manager staged cockfights, three at a time, in arenas the size of large dining room tables, despite the sport's illegal status and the gambling that invariably accompanied the rooster battles. The Israeli visitors joined in—and none of the law enforcement officers in attendance registered any objection.

The goats, however, fared not so well in their new home in Israel. Although the terrain around Yodfat appeared similar to that of Texas Hill Country, the scrub was different. Due to overgrazing and misuse of the land, the Yodfat vegetation had grown low and dense. When the goats were put out to pasture, stunted trees and bushes snagged the Angoras' fine wool coats. With heavy hearts, the residents of Yodfat shipped the Angora goats to other *kibbutzim* scattered throughout Israel.[30] Happily, the delicate animals thrived in their new homes—and Israeli representatives returned to San Antonio a few years later with money from the Ministry of Agriculture to buy more. This time, two hundred and fifty Texas Angora goats were sent from the Uvalde rancher Dolph Briscoe, Perry's longtime friend (who later would serve as governor of Texas from 1973 to 1979). Airlifted on Labor Day, they were grazing in Israel two days later.

In his later years, Perry no longer regularly attended weekly services at Temple Beth-El, but he remained dedicated to Israel. After his and Briscoe's lobbying efforts, support for the Texas effort to help Israelis develop a goat industry came also from the US government, which backed Israel as the United States' strongest ally in the Middle East. In December 1967, Perry briefed President Lyndon Johnson on the status of the Texas Angora goat project just before Johnson was to host Israel's Prime Minister Levi Eshkol at the LBJ Ranch, some sixty miles away. At the same time, Perry sent his old friend the president a gift from Kallison's store with a note: "With all of the heavy burdens that come across your desk, I thought perhaps this little branding iron would help hold them down."[31]

Several years after the goat-lifts, Perry traveled to Israel. It was 1970, when Israel was in a tense standoff with Egypt and other surrounding Arab states after Israel's victory over Egypt, Jordan, and Syria—the main participants in 1967's Six Day War. Perry was a member of a six-man delegation of San Antonio Jewish leaders trying to raise money for Israel through the United Jewish Appeal. They met with Israeli Prime Minister Golda Meir, traveled to the Suez Canal, and dived into a bunker as part of an air raid rehearsal. Then they went to the Negev desert, "which reminded Perry of the Texas Hill Country, and which he also thought might be suitable for raising goats."[32]

For Perry Kallison, his experiences with the Israelis sharpened his awareness of his own heritage. He related the experience of the Jews in Israel to the early lives of Nathan and Anna Kallison. Just as his parents had escaped oppression from the Russian czar in 1890 and had made a new life for themselves in Texas, these Jews of Israel had escaped oppression in Eastern Europe and were trying to carve out a life of freedom in another new and still largely undeveloped land.

Israel's victory in the Six Day War had a powerful and dramatic effect on Jews all across the United States. "The Six Day War was huge," recalled Michael Beldon, a San Antonio businessman who accompanied Perry on the trip to Israel. Tiny Israel's incredibly swift victory over the combined forces of the surrounding Arab nations surprised the world, infusing Jews with a renewed sense of pride. "The [quick and decisive] victory in the war made every Jew in the world stand taller," Beldon explained. "Jews came out of the wood-work—to be Jews," said Morris Spector, a San Antonio physician who also joined them on the trip. Men such as Perry Kallison, Beldon, and Spector had been dedicated to the cause of Israel for decades, but for other Jews in San Antonio, the war aroused feelings of identification with Judaism and Israel which they previously had failed to experience—or had even avoided. The Six Day War victory also signaled the death knell for the American Council on Judaism, an organization with prominent San Antonio members that had opposed for decades any identification between American Jews and the cause of Zionism and of Israel. Rabbi Samuel Stahl, later the rabbi of Temple Beth-El, said the 1967 war signaled a new era in which Jewish religious institutions were strengthened in San Antonio's Jewish community.[33]

Perry's buoyant feelings of pride and satisfaction about Israel's "David over Goliath" victories were tempered, however, by the sobering realization that a Goliath of another sort threatened his family's business.

FOURTEEN

Changing Times

FROM THE GREAT SOCIAL protests that brought civil rights laws for minorities, opened doors for women to rise and break "glass ceilings," and mobilized a generation against the war in faraway Vietnam, the times were—as the song went—"a' changin'." Across America, the 1960s will be remembered as both turbulent and transformational. In Texas, the turmoil was especially painful—and close to home: President John F. Kennedy was assassinated in Dallas on November 22, 1963. A Texas-size native son from a small Hill Country town near San Antonio became the state's first President of the United States. Just five years later, with Texas and the entire country politically polarized by the Vietnam War, Lyndon Baines Johnson chose not to run again. Four days following President Johnson's announcement, civil rights champion Dr. Martin Luther King Jr. was gunned down in Memphis. Two months later, presidential candidate Robert F. Kennedy was shot and killed in Los Angeles. A new reality of anguish and impermanence swept the nation.

The 1960s also brought harsh new realities for the Kallisons. Perry Kallison had first glimpsed the dawn of a new era in 1954, the day he attended the grand opening of Fed-Mart, a different kind of department store. Thousands had gathered for the festive evening event in front of the nearly block-long store at Military Road and Zarzamora Street in San Antonio. As the crowd surged into the store, giant searchlights lit the sky like those at a Hollywood movie premier. In the postwar era, the giant new discounter was promising that its Family Savings Centers would "save you money on just about everything for your family, your home, and your car." Flanked by four of his department managers from Kallison's store, Perry carefully checked the prices on the displays of leading brand names in furniture, appliances, clothing, and sporting goods equipment. He was stunned.

For decades, Kallison's had competed successfully against larger stores and had thrived by employing innovative marketing and merchandising strategies. They had pioneered buying in bulk—purchasing railroad carloads of merchandise directly from manufacturers. They marketed aggressively, taking advantage of new media—first radio, then television. Even during hard times, the store eked out profits by selling at rock-bottom prices and offering generous terms on long-term credit. But in Fed-Mart, Perry Kallison saw a new breed of discounter—one strong enough to dictate the prices it paid manufacturers. Leaving the store, Perry turned to the other Kallison's managers who had accompanied him, and said quietly, "We can't compete with that."[1]

For family-owned retail stores in urban areas across America, downtowns, as well as profits, were shrinking. The arrival of Fed-Mart was one early signal that change was coming to San Antonio—change that would determine which businesses would flourish and which would fade into history. A nationwide revolution in retailing would soon bring to cities wave after wave of new discount stores with which retailers like Kallison's Big Country Store would have to compete. Even in the apparel world, denim and western wear were becoming fashion staples—and no longer the exclusive province of stores like Kallison's, which had dominated the city's western wear retail trade and prided itself as the exclusive distributor of famous brands such as Stetson and Resistol hats.

But the changes that began in the 1950s and accelerated in the 1960s involved more than the arrival of another breed of retailer. An even larger phenomenon was transforming the nation. Despite determined efforts by resourceful businessmen like Morris and Perry Kallison to save and revive them, downtowns in general were dying.

Dramatic and often traumatic change was spurred by the suburban-ization of American cities and the growth of a new middle class. They were part of a powerful dynamic in which automobiles, free-ways, and shopping malls combined to reorganize American lives—and a new consumerism, whetted by the new medium, television, altered perceptions of what constituted "the good life." The federal government hastened the growth of suburbia by guaranteeing home loans at low interest rates and by fostering a new national network of interstate highways and urban freeways.

Surrounded by the new subdivisions, "big box" stores like Wal-mart quickly multiplied along what previously were cornfields and vacant rural highways. And as inner cities across America declined in the 1960s, Kallison's sprawling downtown farm and ranch store, with its 125 employees, was struggling. For nearly seventy years, the Kallison family enterprises had prospered and multiplied. But Kallison's Big Country Store, which Nathan had opened as a one-room harness shop over half a century earlier and, with his sons had built into a thriving and storied institution, was starting to lose money.

Kallison's loyal customer base—several generations of farm and ranch families from all over South Texas—was steadily dwindling. Farmers and ranchers began selling out to larger operators or else to the developers who were bulldozing land for malls and subdivisions. Many dedicated farmers and ranchers near San Antonio, Austin, and other urban centers, experiencing erratic—and often substandard—earnings for their cattle and produce, now faced the reality that their land was worth far more as suburban real estate than as farmland. Indeed, farmers and ranchers found they could even make better money selling deer- and dove-hunting leases on their property than by raising crops and cattle. By the end of the twentieth century, Texas A&M economists estimated that the agricultural value of rural Texas land now represented only 16 percent of its actual market value. Furthermore, as the children and grandchildren of those longtime

Kallison customers grew up, they were already moving from their rural homes to seek greater economic opportunity in the suburbs of San Antonio or other cities.

Stark statistics revealed the transformation of Texas from a rural to an urban state—and to a new suburban economy as well. When Nathan Kallison arrived in San Antonio in 1899, rural residents comprised 82 percent of Texas's three million people. In 1945, a year after Nathan died, the Texas population had doubled to six million, with 50 percent still living in the countryside. By the end of the 1960s, though, barely one-third the number of Texas farms and ranches that had operated in 1930 now remained. Between 1945 and 1990, the farm population in Texas kept falling—from 1.5 million to about 245,000. And the vast majority of cattle and crop production that was left came from a still smaller number of bigger, more efficient enterprises. Indeed, this continuing transformation was a national phenomenon with ramifications for everyone.[2]

Resourceful and determined merchants like the Kallison brothers continued to innovate, trying to keep up with change—or at least to live with it. By the 1950s, Morris's son Jimmy, son-in-law Seymour Dreyfus, and Perry's son Pete all had joined the business. They offered new ideas and fresh energy to keep the store viable. Morris's younger son Jack, by then an Air Force veteran, lawyer, and certified public accountant, had meanwhile joined his father's real estate business.

Kallison's store kept expanding its range of merchandise, still hoping to keep old rural customers and win new buyers from the city and suburbs. In the late 1950s, Kallison's even advertised in *Cattleman* magazine its cut-rate prices for punch bowls and Christmas gifts—a far cry from the staples of a farm and ranch store —to entice customers into the store during the holiday season.[3]

They also dreamed up new promotions to draw people in. During the 1959 San Antonio Livestock Show and Rodeo at the Joe and Harry Freeman Coliseum, Kallison's lured rodeo-goers to the store with a raffle to win a full-grown steer, "transformed into hundreds of pounds of the best beef you ever ate."[4] They ran cooperative ads, sharing the cost with General Electric Company, Westinghouse, and various farm goods manufacturers, for everything from cattle medicines to weed killers. When newspaper advertising became available in color in the late 1950s, Kallison's bought dozens of full-page ads and supplement inserts. Whenever innovations came on the market, Kallison's quickly adopted and promoted them. At the 1960 Livestock Show and Rodeo, Kallison's raffled off one of the hottest new homemaker's conveniences—the "Good Housekeeper" pushbutton sewing machine.[5]

The Kallison family was banking on the store's distinctive identity and character, which they described in a 1962 *San Antonio Express-News* promotional story: "Kallison's has a personality all its own—a unique combination of the old and the new. It is neither completely 'old-fashioned and country,' nor completely 'citified' with fancy and expensive features. It retains the best of both, maintaining the charm of the Old West and the courteous and personal attention of the old-fashioned general store combined with the fast-moving progressive concepts of today's mass merchandising techniques." The piece also noted that a "series of murals depicting authentic scenes of the Old West to enhance the charm of Kallison's décor" was nearing completion.

Right next to that article, a half-page ad dramatized the problem Kallison's faced—one that could not be solved with personality or paint. Wolff & Marx, a venerable fine clothing emporium founded in 1876, announced the closing of its city store. It displayed photographs of the original nineteenth-century Wolff & Marx building, its 1930s replacement, beside pictures of a sleek, very modern white brick structure all the way out in North Star Mall, where the clothier was moving its entire downtown business.[6] Like other major San Antonio retailers, Wolff & Marx had decided to move to the suburbs, San Antonio's new demographic center—far north of downtown. A virtually new city was rising to the north and west along the outer loops of the city's many new expressways. The majority of San Antonio's people now lived there—and the merchants followed them.

When it opened in September 1960, North Star Mall brought to San Antonio its first major suburban shopping center. Built in the city's fastest-growing residential area north of downtown, the mall offered "sixty acres of air conditioned landscaped shopping pleasure." North Star was innovative developer James W. Rouse's first effort at building a shopping center that would become more than just a collection of leading retail stores. With its movie theaters, restaurants, and pleasant meeting places, Rouse envisioned the mall serving as an entertainment and community center. His vision paid off. North Star soon was a fabulous success, a forerunner of the modern malls that soon were sprouting in suburbs around cities throughout America. "Suburbia" had arrived, engendering what later would be called "Edge Cities."[7]

While other major, longtime downtown retailers led by Wolff & Marx, Joske's, Frost Brothers, and Karotkin Furniture decided that they must follow their customers to the suburbs or die, Morris and Perry Kallison hung on, stubbornly and loyally committed to remaining downtown. That's where their hearts were—as well as their investments in downtown real estate. If Morris and Perry suffered a fundamental weakness, it was their unwillingness to take advantage of the new perspectives which their sons might bring to the business, having studied modern management methods in college. But unlike their father Nathan, the brothers refused to share major responsibilities with their sons or listen to their advice.

When Jimmy Kallison, a graduate of the University of Texas at Austin, returned from service in World War II and Korea, he tried to promote change. He urged the introduction of such business practices as cost accounting and inventory control systems. His ideas were ignored. Cooperating with other nearby businessmen, Jimmy Kallison nevertheless worked tirelessly to bring more business into

San Antonio's declining downtown and to Kallison's store. As president of the Downtown Association, he spurred programs to improve traffic flow, provide landscaping along downtown streets—and even to pipe music into the heart of Old San Antonio. A 1964 contract with the Muzak Corporation called for recorded music to be played through ten loudspeakers mounted on South Broadway between Commerce and Houston Streets.[8]

But the efforts of the Downtown Association alone could not solve the problems of inner city merchants like Kallison's, which still depended on the patronage of customers from surrounding rural areas. The burgeoning suburbs were more conveniently located for farmers and ranchers, as well as for the new middle-class majority, than Kallison's downtown store. Worse yet, new farm and ranch stores were now opening in these outlying areas.

Backed by his degree in business administration from Texas A&M, Perry's son Pete Kallison urged his father to spend more time focusing on the store's precarious finances, and to update the antiquated bookkeeping instead of walking the sales floors. Attention to the store's balance sheet was badly needed, but with sharply declining sales, the store was now dependent on Perry as its main draw and top salesman. The Ol' Trader, who knew the location and price of every item, was still greeting old friends and customers while leading them to the cash register.

Of Nathan and Anna's four grandsons, Morris's younger son Jack was perhaps the best qualified to advise, and most frustrated in his efforts to effect change. After earning graduate degrees in both accounting and law, Jack Kallison attempted in various ways to introduce modern management and financial strategies to the operation of Kallison's store. First, he tried to convince Leslie Hunter, the store's longtime bookkeeper, to prepare an income and expense statement so that Perry and Morris could see how the business was really doing. Hunter did not cooperate.

Perry Kallison finally became intrigued, though, and asked Jack to help set up an accounting office in the store, as Jack had done with his father's real estate empire, which he now was helping to manage. "I'd like to do that," Jack replied, "but we'll have to hire some people." To which Perry responded, "We can't do that. We don't have the money." Jack finally convinced his uncle to hire one man to work on financial statements, but he "never could figure out whether Perry ever looked at them."

Jack also urged his uncle to reevaluate the store's many departments, which had grown haphazardly over the years whenever Morris and Perry saw new products come on the market. "They needed to eliminate departments that were losing money, get rid of departments that were no longer needed, and add new ones that might be profitable," Jack recalled. "They didn't realize it was going to be over one of these days."[9] In the meantime, Fed-Mart was touting itself as "an aggressive, fast-growing organization using the newest merchandising methods."[10]

Morris and Perry, now in their sixties, had been enjoying their lives and work, living comfortably with the profits from the "good years" and the notion that their momentum would continue to escalate. Their interests had diverged markedly, though, and the synergy from their joint creativity no longer fueled the family enterprise. Perry the dedicated rancher and Morris the high-flying city developer now had little in common. In the late 1950s and early 1960s, Morris and Perry belatedly tried to modernize the store's buildings with major remodeling; it finally became the last major store in downtown San Antonio to install air conditioning. They borrowed money for the improvements from D. & A. Oppenheimer, their long-time bankers. And on the theory that "if you can't beat 'em, join 'em," the Kallisons invested a million dollars into building their own huge downtown discount store, which spread out over two and a half acres on South Flores, twelve blocks south of the main store. A full page of articles in the *San Antonio Light* heralded the 1963 opening of "Kallison's Warehouse Showrooms."[11]

The modernization and expansion came far too late—and the expenditures just pushed the Kallisons further into debt. The store's strength had always been centered on Perry's and Morris's personalities and personal relationships. They were banking on all those decades of close ties with their customers. But those old customers were even older now, needing less, or moving elsewhere, or dying—and there were not enough newcomers to sustain the business.

Finally, the store's ability to stay afloat rested on Jimmy Kallison's skill and ingenuity in working with the General Electric Company to sell a steady volume of its home appliances and TV sets. GE was willing to share advertising costs, give generous credit to Kallison's, and supply financing for customer purchases from its credit company. But when the day that GE wanted to be paid finally arrived, Kallison's did not have the money. GE cut off Kallison's supply of its merchandise, and the store lost its single largest source of revenue.[12]

As the store's debts mounted, Perry felt tremendous pressure, as he had to decide which of their bills to pay. "It devastated him," Jack Kallison said of his uncle. "He couldn't pay his bills. People would call him and he had no answers."

"The question was how to compete," recalled Perry's youngest child, Frances Rae (Bobbi) Ravicz. "They couldn't compete and they couldn't cope. The whole concept that Kallison's store was built on was from another era. The world had passed them by."[13]

In a familiar story about family-owned enterprises, bitter arguments among the Kallisons also added to the store's crises. The quarrels, accusations, and demands accelerated between brothers and sisters—and then between Morris and Perry and their surviving sister Tibe, who also fiercely guarded her niece Susan Neustadt's interests. A unified Kallison front was always presented to San Antonio, and in Washington Tibe spoke proudly of Perry's prominence as a Texas rancher and cattleman, and of Morris's accomplishments to friends who were real estate developers. But the family unity was shredded, never to be repaired in their lifetimes. Tibe came to San Antonio for

Anna's funeral on May 8, 1959, and stayed to place her parents' home on the market and dispose of its contents at 116 Thelma Drive. She would not return to the city again except to attend family weddings and funerals.

Nathan and Anna Kallison's generosity in gifting all their assets equally among their four children two decades before was now reaping unforeseen consequences. From the beginning, Morris and Perry Kallison had resented sharing ownership and income from the store and family-owned real estate with their sisters, who challenged the brothers' business judgments yet did not contribute to the store's work. Pauline and Tibe had been angry that their brothers kept them in the dark about the store's finances. For years Morris and Perry refused to send their sisters any financial reports. The sisters' only information came at the end of the year when they were told to pay their share of the store's income tax, even though their brothers did not share the income. Fierce arguments then ensued between brothers and sisters, usually without resolution. The sisters suspected, but could not prove, that the brothers were using the store's Builder's Supply Company to furnish construction materials for their own building projects. (Morris was sole owner of most of his real estate ventures, but had shared several of them with his brother Perry.)

Morris and Tibe, who was six years younger, became the principal antagonists, rarely speaking to each other. Perry was conflicted, still feeling affection for his sisters even when they were uncooperative. When Tibe demanded that she and Pauline receive a share of store profits, Perry alone would sometimes write checks for them. After it became obvious that the Kallison's store now was in deep trouble, Tibe and Pauline's daughter Susan had another concern—that the store's growing financial problems threatened the family's other jointly owned assets: the store property itself and three other downtown properties, as well as the Kallison Ranch.

For a number of years, the sisters had agreed to mortgage family-owned real estate to pump desperately needed funds into the beloved store. But the time came in the early 1960s when the now-widowed Tibe, who lived in Washington, DC, and her niece Susan Neustadt Miller, who had inherited Pauline's interests and lived in Baltimore, refused to place further debt on the downtown real estate jointly owned by Nathan and Anna Kallison's four heirs. It came to a standoff, with cruel words flying in all directions. Without more real estate as collateral, Kallison's patient and loyal bankers refused to provide further loans for the store's operating capital.

For years, Morris had not involved himself in running the store, even though he kept an office there to meet friends and clients. As the store hemorrhaged money and downtown real estate was fading in value, Perry and Morris now argued bitterly about the mortgages Morris had assumed as he continued to develop his own new downtown ventures. Perry feared that those mortgages with San Antonio bankers would make it even more difficult for the store to borrow money. Perry's concerns were realistic, because San Antonio's entire downtown was in peril. More and more city stores and offices were moving to the outlying suburbs. In his zeal to restore the downtown, Morris refused to take advice, or even to recognize the deep risk of making new investments in the area. He continued to build new buildings downtown, creating a pyramid of debt. His flamboyant lifestyle continued unaltered, and his sons were horrified by what appeared to be a megalomaniacal pursuit. He was driven: Morris Kallison would win, at all costs.

Then, in the midst of their financial crisis, in February 1966, the Kallison family was jolted by deep personal tragedy: Morris Kallison, at seventy, died unexpectedly after a heart attack. He was buried in the Kallison family plot beside the founders of the family empire, Nathan and Anna. His larger-than-life presence in San Antonio at an end, the city itself felt the impact of the loss.

In addition to his interest in the store, Morris left behind his own fleet of commercial downtown properties, along with his plans and dreams for a renaissance in downtown San Antonio. With one of the last downtown "holdouts" now gone, his death cemented the end of an era. Morris's sons Jimmy and Jack would carry on his real estate business, but Morris's death brought to a head the problems that had been building for years at Kallison's store.

In 1967, with Kallison's store deeply in debt to its bankers and suppliers, and Morris Kallison's estate encumbered with its own debts and taxes, the remaining family members who still jointly owned the downtown store, real estate, and the ranch were forced to close the store and to separate their interests in the real estate. In a giant going-out-of-business sale that started at noon on Sunday, April 23, for both the downtown store on South Flores and the Kallison Warehouse Showrooms, the stores' merchandise—from cattle medicine to cowboy hats, branding irons to boys' blue jeans—was liquidated. The city-block-long building that housed the original "Big Country Store" eventually would be sold to the county for a planned addition to the Bexar County Courthouse.

The hardest, and most heartbreaking, ordeal for sixty-four-year-old Perry Kallison, "the Ol' Trader," was facing the sale of the Kallison Ranch's herd of registered Polled Hereford cattle—the prize-winning cows and bulls recognized for decades as among the best breeding stock in the United States. Valuable as they might be, the cattle had become a luxury when funds were desperately needed to pay the store's debts.

Humberto (Bert) Reyes, the young cattle auctioneer whom Perry had helped to begin an auction business, remembered the night Perry called, asking him to come to his home early the following morning. After Frances Kallison had served the two men a breakfast of ham and eggs, Reyes recalled, Perry haltingly asked him to arrange an auction to sell the family's entire herd. "Perry looked like he had aged twenty years overnight," Reyes said. "He was very sad."[14]

The sale of the four hundred bulls, cows, and calves was conducted by Humberto and Ruben Reyes on May 30, 1967, at the Union Stockyards in San Antonio. Proceeds from the "distress sale" could in no way compensate Perry for his work—thirty-five years of labor building his beloved, prize-winning herd. At the sale, as he had on his radio show, Perry spoke from his heart, expressing yet again a deeply held conviction: "All in all, cattle people are the best people in the world."[15]

For nearly seventy years, Perry Kallison and his father Nathan before him had been in the forefront of progressive efforts to conserve Texas's farmland. They had done pioneer work in developing new grasses and seeds and better breeds of cattle—achieving big advancements over the late nineteenth and early twentieth centuries, when longhorns roamed South Texas. And as Texas continued to evolve from a rural to an urban economy, Perry and other ranchers tried to remain economically viable by dedicating part of their land to recreational uses. But now, the good years were over.

True to his nature, though, Perry refused to quit. In a one-story building on Nogalitas Street, he opened a small store, selling a limited assortment of ranch and farm supplies. A few of his old clients, and some new ones as well, came in to buy barbed wire, cattle medicine, farm gates, and branding irons, and to visit with the Ol' Trader. Gary Schott, the third generation of his family to shop at Kallison's, came with his wife Madelyn to buy a cowbell to use at the annual fundraiser of the Helotes 4-H Club. "You pick out whichever bell you want," Perry told them. They accepted his gift of the biggest bell in the store, and were still ringing it at 4-H events twenty-five years later.[16] Customers seeking the very best in authentic and stylish western clothing shopped at Pete Kallison's western wear store—one shop in the Kallison Block Building, another in a southside shopping center.[17] Princess Grace (actress Grace Kelly) and her husband Prince Rainier III of Monaco stopped in to buy boots and cowboy hats for themselves and their children while in San Antonio for the World's Fair, HemisFair '68.

But the western wear business would soon undergo radical change, as well. For years, Kallison's held a near monopoly in San Antonio on some of the biggest brands—Stetson and Resistol hats, Levi's jeans, and Tony Lama and Larry Mahan boots. When stars like

Gene Autry, Roy Rogers, and actor Cliff Robertson would come to town for the rodeo, they dropped into Kallison's. But in late 1969, a buyer reported back from New York that "denim was the new look." Managers from Joske's, the city's top department store, and from Sears, Roebuck & Company soon dropped in to see what Kallison's was selling. Both retailers opened stores in the malls, as did specialty stores—selling fine cowboy hats, boots, and fashionable jeans. With volume purchases from manufacturers, they soon beat Kallison's best prices.[18]

Just as merchandising and rural Texas had changed, so had the radio business, which consolidated and searched for new ways to appeal to its diverse urban markets. Perry continued to broadcast the *Trading Post* from his home until April 26, 1981, when KMAC radio changed hands. Despite protests from the Ol' Trader's loyal audience, the new owner decided to switch the format to all rock 'n roll and to increase its revenues from advertising. In its forty-six-year history, the *Trading Post* had never charged its listeners for placing notices on the program or taken a promotion fee from an advertiser.

When the San Antonio Chamber of Commerce awarded Perry Kallison the Joe Freeman Award for outstanding community service to agriculture in 1965, advertising executive Jack Pitluck Jr. told the audience, "This morning you heard the 9,346th Kallison's *Trading Post* broadcast, the longest continuous rural radio broadcast in the world." Of Perry's accomplishment with the *Trading Post* program, Pitluck added: "Kallison has built what might have been only another commercial radio program into a South Texas service institution and has used it to help his fellow man."

A year after the Ol' Trader left the air, in the summer of 1982, Perry's sister Tibe, widowed since 1958 but healthy all her life, died in Washington, DC, at age seventy-nine. She had contracted a rare and devastating disease, Creutzfeldt-Jakob syndrome (a version of which was later known as "mad cow disease"). Her sisters-in-law outlived her: Ruth Kallison died in July 1993 at the age of ninety-two, and

Frances Kallison died in December 2004, at the age of ninety-six. Each was memorialized at Temple Beth-El.

After a form of degenerative disease began to afflict his body, Perry finally closed his small farm and ranch store on Nogalitas Street. When he began to lose his ability to walk, he looked down and grinned. "These legs have traveled many miles." As it had for his mother, dementia kept him bedridden in his final years. On February 13, 1999, at the age of ninety-five, the Ol' Trader "went away." He was laid to rest in the soil of Temple Beth-El Cemetery in San Antonio near Nathan and Anna Kallison, surrounded by the many friends he had made from all walks of life. In the eulogy, his longtime friend Rabbi David Jacobson described Perry as an expansive, warm man steeped "in the pride of South Texas," belonging to "a generation who felt obligated and duty bound to serve their communities." The following year, the San Antonio Livestock Exposition inducted Perry Nathan Kallison posthumously into its Hall of Fame. A century of Kallisons had come and gone, adding their own legacy to the astonishing sweep of twentieth-century America.

EPILOGUE

NATHAN AND ANNA KALLISON'S accomplishments were not confined within the bricks and mortar of their store nor the barbed-wire fences of their ranch. Their legacy of hard work, solidarity, faith, love of family and country, respect for the land, and compassion for their fellow human beings has flowed through the five generations of Kallisons who continue the journey Nathan and Anna began as immigrants.

Much of the ranch still looks as it did when Nathan first saw it. Nearly 1,200 acres of Kallison Ranch's most scenic and environmentally sensitive acres have become part of the Government Canyon Wildlife and Natural Area—a state park created in 1993 and operated by the Texas Department of Parks and Wildlife. Underneath the land is Edwards Aquifer, an immense and fragile underground reservoir upon which San Antonio is totally dependent for its supply of fresh water. For decades, the quantity and quality of water from the vital reserve have been threatened by a tidal wave of commercial and residential development on ground above the aquifer. Nathan and Anna's descendants made it possible for Government Canyon—rather than commercial developers—to acquire this significant acreage for the park.[1]

The state park is dedicated solely to land and water conservation, wildlife preservation, nature studies, and outdoor recreation. Although Perry Kallison's award-winning Polled Hereford cattle no longer graze through the Hill Country, generations of visitors will now camp and hike in that preserve, study flora and wildlife, enjoy a quiet escape from city life, and view the natural splendor that captured the heart and the imagination of a young Russian émigré more than one hundred years before.

Nathan and Anna surely would approve of the way their values have been carried forward in the heritage they bequeathed the twenty-first century Kallisons. If the family's first realized dream was freedom and the second, success, then the third must surely be the broad opportunities that have allowed succeeding generations to live the Kallison values. Their twentieth-century grandchildren Jimmy, Jane, Susan, Nathan, Maryann, and Bobbi instilled in their own children a thirst for knowledge and a belief in the importance of faith, family, and service to humankind. The fifteen who grew up in the next generation have all achieved success in their professions. Almost all of them are college graduates, including the family's first three PhDs: a mathematician, an economist, and a psychologist. Most have remained in Texas. Although they grew up in comfort, none of their careers have been focused principally on material success. Many have been involved in service to their neighbors—to the needy at home and those across the globe. Morris Kallison's oldest grandson is a distinguished college professor in Texas. Only one of Nathan's great grandchildren has followed Morris's penchant for commercial real estate development and, with his insurance-broker brother, is a major contributor and fundraiser for medical research. Another is the owner of a bindery; he and his wife have been community leaders and have raised four idealistic and accomplished children. After a productive and satisfying career in social work counseling hospital patients, his sister, married to an eminent neurologist, enjoys a new life in residential real estate. Their two sons, both bar mitzvah, attended college: the older, a recent graduate; the younger, a sophomore. Another great grandchild has served as an officer of the World Bank, arranging loans for humanitarian projects in developing countries. One serves the people of Texas as an expert in environmental and energy policy. Another graduated from law school and became an effective advocate for and writer on women's rights and other causes for social justice. Her brother, who created a court-reporting and conference-recording business, leads an effort to provide instruments to needy musicians. Two are journalists; three are teachers; one is an adoptive mother and facilitator for adoption of orphans by American parents. One great-grandson, who equals Jimmy Kallison in his passion for flight, has been an executive with major aircraft manufacturers and has raised two artist sons. Another great-grandson is an architectural and fine arts photographer and talented musician; still another, a clinical psychologist. Only one of Nathan's descendants (this author) farms and raises cattle, encouraged by his Uncle Perry who advised that "it's in your blood, boy!"

These grandchildren and great-grandchildren are carrying on in the ancient Jewish tradition of educating their children and of caring for those less fortunate, contributing to the wider world because they understand that they are blessed to have benefitted from Nathan Kallison's vision.

The Questions We Never Asked

A T DAYBREAK, my grandfather and I would walk together across the white sand beach and then, hand in hand, wade into the gentle surf of the Gulf of Mexico. Dressed in his scratchy woolen two-piece swimming suit, he would splash the salty water all over his face and body, an exercise he found invigorating. On those annual summer vacations to Corpus Christi or Galveston, other family members slept late, and so we two early risers became special companions during this sunrise ritual. He was old and slowed by a stroke, but still determined in will and clear of mind. I was eight years old and always eager to embrace the adventures of each new day. From those trips, I remember his still-strong grip, how he would squeeze my soft biceps and quietly advise, "You've got to be strong, boy."

Back home in San Antonio, Nathan Kallison and I shared other experiences. On Sundays, Uncle Perry—the youngest of Nathan's four children—would pick us up at his parents' home, where I lived with my divorced mother, Tibe. We would ride the eighteen miles out to the ranch, stopping along the way for Papa Kallison to buy the Sunday newspaper for his ranch foreman and a bag of penny candy for the foreman's children.

Once at the ranch, they allowed me to ride with them, usually in a battered old truck, as they checked on the integrity of the ranch's barbed wire fences. We paused along the way so Nathan and Perry could survey the crops and inspect their fat herd of registered Polled Hereford cattle. Later in the day, the remainder of our large family would join us at the ranch for a barbecue. I still can remember the smoky, pungent aroma of goat roasting on a spit.

Saturday mornings, my mother would drop off Papa Kallison and me at the Uptown Theater to watch the double feature westerns starring the Lone Ranger and his sidekick Tonto, Roy Rogers and his wife Dale and faithful horse Trigger, along with a galaxy of other cowboys in white hats including Tom Mix, Hopalong Cassidy, and Red Ryder. My grandfather loved watching those Hollywood versions of the life he actually had lived as a rancher in the Southwest at the turn of the twentieth century.

Decades passed before I realized fully the important opportunities I had missed during those special times spent with Nathan Kallison. Why hadn't I asked him and my grandmother about the experiences of their early lives? It didn't occur to me to inquire about where they were born and where had they grown up. I had no idea then that Nathan Kallison, only seventeen, had made a hazardous trip across Europe in 1890 to escape horrors in Russia, or that he had been sent to work as a child to help support his widowed mother. I did not know where he and my grandmother came from, nor how they had made their way to America. What were their lives like as Jews living under the reign of an oppressive, cruel czar, for example? How did they escape raids on Jewish villages? Why did they come to Texas? How did they start what became a huge business—the largest farm and ranch supply store in the Southwest? How and why did a Jewish merchant become an important Texas rancher?

I certainly had ample opportunity to ask those questions and many others. My reality was the San Antonio lives of the grandparents whom I loved—Texans. Until I was almost fourteen, I lived with them in their San Antonio home. Yet I knew far more about Sam Houston and his victory in the Texas War of Independence from Mexico than about how my own grandparents had escaped a different revolution in Russia.

To the amusement of grandparents, aunts, and uncles, I also

became the self-appointed family expert on World War II. After reading the daily newspapers, listening to the radio, and watching the newsreels at the movies, I would announce at family gatherings the latest news about how our American soldiers and sailors were faring against their German and Japanese enemies. I learned a lot of history early on—but very little about the remarkable lives of the people with whom I lived. I never realized that they were listening with other ears. They were attuned to the terror inflicted on the Jews in Europe. Would their relatives or childhood friends survive? None did. Nathan and Anna never talked about it in front of us children.

Later, as a young adult, by which time I had become a newspaper reporter and had written several books, I still knew little more than a few fragments about how my mother, her sister, and two brothers had grown up in early twentieth-century Texas. Sadly, my grandparents, my mother, my aunts and uncles are all gone now—as are several members of my own generation—without leaving behind more than the barest outline of our family's early history.

During my teenage years, my great fortune was to become the adopted son of Dr. Jacob Kotz, whom Tibe Kallison married in 1946. My life with them in Washington, DC, was vastly different from that of my Texas roots. My father was exceedingly kind to me, understanding and encouraging, and a man beloved by an entire community. My mother, Tibe, steered us into a social life of dress-up parties (no Texas jeans and boots), theater, symphonies, art exhibitions, travel, private schools, and golf. Like Nathan, Dr. Kotz had no pretensions. He worked night and day, delivering babies, performing life-saving surgeries, entering into research with Dr. George Papanicolaou, pioneering the "Pap Smear" with his patients. He was such a towering figure that Texas and its jingoistic bravado quickly receded as a frame of reference—and from my consciousness in general, except for the four cousins whom I still considered siblings. (After Pauline's death in 1953, my cousin Susan graduated from the University of Texas and came to live with us in Washington until her marriage in 1955.) My visits to Texas were fewer and farther between. Wrapped up in my own life, I seldom reflected upon the remarkable lives of Nathan and Anna Kallison.

For that matter, I never asked, and my stepfather never spoke about, his own immigrant experience—how early in the twentieth century his own father and mother, Abraham and Anna Kotz, emigrated to America and Washington, DC, from Russia, along with the first two of their five children: six-year-old Samuel, and Jacob, age four.

In recent years, I have learned that my lack of knowledge about my immigrant forebears is not that unusual or surprising a phenomenon. Like the Kallisons, the lives of the Kotzes and millions of immigrant American families have been poorly documented and preserved—a loss for the families themselves and for a wiser understanding of our nation's history. It astounds me today to consider the many consequences of the massive migration that brought two million Jews—including my grandparents—to America from Russia and Eastern Europe during the brief span between 1880 and 1920, when anti-immigrant sentiment led Congress to curtail immigration.

There are explanations about why we have lost so much family history. Many new immigrants to America in the late nineteenth and early twentieth centuries did not want to talk about their painful lives in Russia or even about their early struggles as new immigrants in America. They were focused instead on survival, on forging new lives for their families in a promising new land. And many of our first-generation American-born parents—and even we of the second generation—became so preoccupied with achieving success and integrating ourselves fully into mainstream American society that we, too, neglected to learn and ponder the relevance of that immigrant history to our own lives—as well as to the larger story of America.

My hope is that this book will encourage others to pursue a quest that I have found richly rewarding. In studying my own family roots, I have gained deeper understanding about myself and a far greater appreciation of the debt I owe to my immigrant grandparents and to my own parents for the opportunities that have blessed my own family and my generation. As a veteran journalist and historian, I only now have become fully aware that the most important history of our country is not found in the grand events of wars and presidencies, but rather in the everyday lives of our citizens—how they worked hard to support their families; how they coped with hardships, discrimination, and human tragedy; and how they contributed to their own communities and nation. And I now appreciate more fully the critical importance of those immigrants to the vitality and greatness of our country.

There is now a burgeoning new school of family historical research with dozens of new books examining not only the stories of immigrant families that have come to America from every part of the world in the last century, but also those of families that have been in this country for many generations. Much family research was initially spurred by Alex Haley's influential 1976 book *Roots*, in which he traced the history of families from their capture in Africa through their early days as slaves in America and finally to freedom. Today, thousands of Americans comb through archives to learn about their own families' roots. Others also are wondering how to conduct such a search. Perhaps with this book I can point the way for those who want to pursue their family histories but don't know where to start. Most people are unaware, for instance, that the tools of modern research—specifically new computer technology—make it far easier to conduct historical research than it was in the recent past. Millions of vital old records and documents, newspaper articles, and books have already been scanned into computer databases, providing information that can easily be accessed at home by anyone with basic computer skills. And the race to computerize the historical record of human knowledge has just begun.

A series of circumstances prompted me to begin this exploration of my family's past. It began in 2001 when Katherine Armstrong, the chairman of the Texas Parks and Wildlife Commission, suggested that I write a history of the Government Canyon Natural Area, a beautiful twelve-thousand-acre nature preserve outside San Antonio where today visitors can hike, camp, and explore the flora and fauna of the Texas Hill Country. Government Canyon is made up of land from a dozen former historic Texas ranches, including the most beautiful part of our family's Kallison Ranch. I declined to take on the project, but my curiosity was aroused. I had enjoyed visiting the family ranch as a child, but now realized how little I knew of its history. With my interest piqued, I asked Hollace Weiner, a talented author of Texas history, particularly Jewish history, to research and write a short essay on the history of the Kallison Ranch. Soon afterwards, Hollace invited me to participate in a program of the Southern Jewish Historical Society. About the same time, Professor Char Miller, a renowned historian with a strong interest in Texas history, encouraged me to write a book about the Kallisons of Texas. Char was fascinated about how a Jewish immigrant became a Texas rancher. He fully understood the contributions my family had made to the development of South Texas. The ultimate push came from my wife, Mary Lynn Kotz, an author herself. She had been goading me for years to write about my Texas family, which we had discussed since our first date.

But where to begin? I have spent most of my life as a reporter, not unaccustomed to searching for needles in haystacks and piecing together small fragments of seemingly unrelated information, but I quickly realized that this book would represent a new and daunting challenge. Unfortunately, Nathan and Anna Kallison had not kept any diaries that I could find, nor had their children. Old letters, bank account records, almost all of the store and ranch records had long before been consigned to the trash heap. Nathan and Anna had died decades earlier, and their four children also had died without passing on more than a few good anecdotes and fragments of information to their eight children. Most of us felt certain that Nathan and Anna Kallison both were born somewhere in Russia, but one cousin and his father insisted they were from Sweden, as the name Kallison possibly suggested.

The first significant breakthrough in researching this book came from a telephone book. Using the numerous computerized telephone directories available on the Internet, I quickly found the names, addresses, and telephone numbers of thirty-eight Kallisons living in various parts of the country. I wrote to each Kallison asking for their help—and then watched the mailbox, hopefully.

Two weeks later a reply arrived that provided the first key to unlocking the mystery of our family's origins. Lynn Tavia Kallison, an artist and musician in Los Angeles, wrote that her father believed we were related, and recalled his family going from Los Angeles to meet their "Kallison relatives" at their ranch in Texas. With high hopes, my wife and I met Tavia Kallison and her father at a Los Angeles restaurant. At age ninety-six, Marvin Kallison had driven his own car halfway across Los Angeles to join us for dinner. Marvin explained that he was the grandson of Joseph Kallison, a tailor, who emigrated from Russia to Chicago in 1886. Joseph's son Samuel and his family later moved to California, where Marvin grew up. He was almost certain that Joseph and Nathan Kallison were first cousins. And Marvin brought with him an unexpected and surprising gift. It was a copy of his family's genealogical history, dating back to the mid-nineteenth century in Russia. It showed that Joseph Kallison came from a village in the Ukraine called Ladyzhinka.

Later that night, I opened the website Google Search and entered the word "Ladyzhinka." The search produced a single entry: "Waldheim Cemetery," which turned out to be a vast burial ground for more than forty thousand Jews—including a section for immigrants from Ladyzhinka—in the Chicago suburbs. I asked Hilde Cohen, a graduate student at the University of Illinois at Chicago, to visit the Waldheim Cemetery, where a guide directed her to an area containing gravesites of half a dozen people named Kallison. Inserted in a small frame on each headstone was a black and white photograph of the deceased Kallison. With her cell phone, Hilde took pictures of headstone photographs and sent me the results by email. I was ecstatic at what I saw and recognized. The pictures gave me names for people who appeared in my own pile of old unidentified family pictures. One photograph matched the face of a stern-looking old lady sitting with young Nathan and Anna and their first two children. We now knew she was Nathan's mother Dina, and we had the dates of her birth and death. Other gravestone photographs helped solve a baffling mystery. For years we had puzzled over the identity of two handsome men posing in a photograph with a young Nathan Kallison. We now learned they were Nathan Kallison's older brother Jacob and his younger brother Sam.

One computer search after another revealed fragments of information that together began to tell the story of the Kallison family as it came to America. From ancestry.com, with its voluminous records of ship passenger manifests, I learned the details of how Jacob Kallison, Nathan's older brother, arrived in New York in 1890, aboard the *Werra*, a German ship in which Jacob was among the eleven hundred passengers crammed into its third-class compartments.

Other new information came from old city directories, which preceded the advent of the telephone, and listed the home and work addresses of a city's citizens. I found Nathan Kallison listed in the 1894 Chicago city directory as proprietor of his own harness shop located in Chicago's crowded West Side ghetto. Later, the San Antonio city directories showed Nathan's business had expanded into "general merchandise." The family's economic progress was indicated by a succession of addresses, beginning with Nathan's first room rentals for his family, and then, as a homeowner, moving through a progression of ever higher-income neighborhoods.

The computerized records of the Illinois Factory Inspector revealed how Nathan built his harness business on West Twelfth Street in Chicago, increasing his staff from one employee in 1894 to four workers by 1899. Records of the Cook County Clerk in Chicago provided the 1895 date on which Nathan and Anna applied for a marriage license. It also produced the documents confirming the date in 1896 when Nathan and his brother Jacob officially became naturalized citizens of the United States.

Computerized US Census records revealed reams of valuable information about the Kallisons. The 1900 census showed Nathan's country of birth as Russia, the date he came to America as 1890, the address of his rented home in San Antonio, Texas, and his occupation as a self-employed harness maker. The 1910 census showed that Nathan and Anna now owned their own home and were the parents of four children: Morris, age fourteen; Pauline, age eleven; Tibe, age eight; and Perry, the youngest at age seven.

The still little-known website newspaperarchive.com contains millions of pages of American newspapers dating back to the middle of the nineteenth century. From those newspaper stories, I uncovered a closely held family secret: how Nathan and his oldest son Morris were indicted in 1927, charged with violating the Prohibition laws.

The clerk of Bexar County, Texas, has led the nation in computerizing the record of every property transaction made in San Antonio in the last one hundred and fifty years. In those records, I learned the details of how Nathan and Anna bought their first home in 1902, and how they paid for it with a down payment in gold dollars and a loan from a bank. The deed on that first purchase is signed by Nathan in Hebrew script and Anna's signature is marked by an X, indicating their limited knowledge of written English even as they were becoming successful in their harness business.

Today's access to computerized records even includes high school and college yearbooks, where I found the Kallison children's photographs and descriptions of their favorite activities, including youngest child Perry as a champion debater.

I have touched on only a few of the research resources on which I have relied. Other sources will be found in the book's notes and bibliography. New means of high-speed research on the Internet are arriving at a rapid rate. With easier access to research material, I hope that other Americans will pursue and cherish the histories of their own families.

ACKNOWLEDGMENTS

Y GRATITUDE to those who contributed to this book begins with loving appreciation for my wife Mary Lynn Kotz, who has wisely, skillfully, and tirelessly edited every book and magazine article I have written over many decades—as well as scores of newspaper stories. She has taught me that the events of history cannot be told accurately without understanding the lives of individual human beings. In her own career, Mary Lynn has written extraordinary books and articles about remarkable people, ranging from American presidents and their families to path-breaking artists Robert Rauschenberg and Georgia O'Keeffe.

Historians Char Miller of Pomona College in California and Hollace Weiner of Fort Worth first urged me to write about the Kallisons of Texas and generously shared their extraordinary knowledge. Dr. Mary Volcansek, professor of political science at Texas Christian University, kindly brought this book to the TCU Press and to the Center for Texas Studies at TCU, of which she is the executive director. At the TCU Press, the book was edited and produced by director Dan Williams, editor Kathy Walton, associate editor Rileigh Sanders, production manager Melinda Esco, marketing coordinator Rebecca Allen, book designer Barbara Whitehead, and intern Leah Fiorini.

For the last three years, Ellen Braaf, a gifted writer and editor of children's books and stories, and the Mid-Atlantic Regional Advisor for the Society of Children's Book Writers and Illustrators, has been my indispensable researcher. Without Ellen's ingenuity, resourcefulness, and skills, *The Harness Maker's Dream* would lack much of its richest material. Josh Israel, an outstanding reporter in Washington, DC, helped with initial research, as did Kiley Wonn. Our son Jack

Kotz, a fine arts and architectural photographer and author of *Ms. Booth's Garden,* guided picture selection for the book.

Matt DeWaelsche, archivist and assistant director of the Texana Genealogical Department at the San Antonio Public Library, and Tom Shelton, photo archivist at the Institute of Texas Cultures in San Antonio, shared their files and their personal knowledge of the history of San Antonio. Alex Dunai provided genealogical research on the Kallisons in Russia. Lynn Tavia Kallison and her father Marvin Kallison of Los Angeles made available an important family genealogical history. Other researchers who helped include: Hildie Cohen, Diane Claitor, Allen Fisher, and other archivists at the Lyndon Baines Johnson Presidential Library; Martha Utterback of the Daughters of the Texas Republic Library; Barbara Rust in the National Archives-Southwest Region; Beth Standifird at the San Antonio Conservation Society; the staffs of the Government Canyon Natural Area in San Antonio and of the Department of Texas Parks and Wildlife. Professor and author Samuel G. Freedman and Dr. Eleanor Sorrentino were invaluable advisers.

Frances Rosenthal Kallison, who was mentally vibrant until her death in 2004 at age ninety-six, provided a rich source of information, including her master's thesis from Trinity University, *100 Years of Jewry in San Antonio.* All of Nathan's grandchildren of my generation were generous with records, stories, photographs, and memories as were their adult children from the next Texas generation. Those include: Jack, Jimmy, Pete, Kal, and Nancy Kallison; Susan Neustadt Miller, Maryann Kallison Friedman, Jane Kallison Dreyfus, Frances Rae "Bobbi" Ravicz, and her four children: Li Ravicz, Mara Ravicz Hudack, Marisol Ravicz, and Elenita Ravicz; John and Mark Dreyfus, and their father Seymour Dreyfus. Other Kallison and Letwin family members who helped include Joni Barg, Gilda Letwin Cohen, Philip Cohen, Laurie Gerber, Teresa Greenblatt Gerber, Bob and Sam Glast, Teresa Herpts, Diana Kallison, Steven Joel Kallison, Muriel Lash, April Weiner Solomon, Eleanor Kallison Sprowl, and Lenore Kallison Weiner.

Others who provided interviews and resource material include: Richard Alterman, Yoram Avidor, Michael Beldon, Lloyd Benke, Marie Holland Brown, Richard Calvert, Aaron Charles, Iris Fanger, Tom C. Frost, Michael Gillette, Ira A. Glazier, Alice Gold, Richard Goldsmith, Hugh Hemphill, Wayne Hanselka, Florence "Boots" Hoffmann, Marilyn Jorrie, Lenore Karp, Carmen Luna, Joan Lufrano, Edith McAllister, Taddy McAllister, Clarice Arbetter Meer, Janice Meer, Myrtle Nickel, Jesse Oppenheimer, John Oppenheimer, Humberto "Bert" Reyes, Stuart Rockoff, Gary Schott, Neal Scott, Helen Marie Schuhart, Millard Schuhart, William Sinkin, Harry Swearingen, Mary Lee Gussen Sloan, Morris and Rose Spector, Rabbi Samuel Stahl, Bryan Stone, Harold and Esther Vexler, Diana Weil, Rae Weil, and Dorothy Jo Weiss.

In this brief summary, I can only mention a few of the dozens of authors whose valuable work I drew from. (I have tried to cite carefully all my sources of information and to list them in the bibliography.) On the history of Jews in Russia, I benefited especially from: *The Russian Under Tsars and Soviets* by Salo W. Baron; *The Russian Jewish Reader* by Evan R. Chester; *Migration from the Russian Empire* by Ira C. Glazier. On the early history of Jews in the United States, particularly Chicago, I benefited from: *World of Our Fathers* by Irving Howe; *The Russian Jews in the United States* by Charles S. Bernheimer; *The Jews of Chicago* by Irving Cutler. Of the many books about San Antonio and Texas on which I relied, I would mention: Char Miller's *Deep in the Heart of San Antonio* and Char Miller's *On the Border: The San Antonio Story* by T. R. Fehrenbach; *Women of the Depression* by Julia Kirk Blackwelder; *Texas: A Political History* by Light Townsend Cummins; *San Antonio: Then and Now* by Paula Allen; *Crusade for Conformity* by Charles C. Alexander; *The Businesses that Built San Antonio* by Marianne Odom and Gaylon Finklea Young; *San Antonio: A Historical and Picture Guide* by Charles Ramsdell.

Important to my research were books about Jews in Texas and the South, including: *The Quiet Voices: Southern Rabbis and Black Civil*

Rights 1880s to 1990s by Mark K. Bauman and Berkley Kalin; *The Chosen Folks: Jews on the Frontiers of Texas* by Bryan Edward Stone; *Jewish Stars in Texas: Rabbis and Their Work* by Hollace Ava Weiner; *Lone Stars of David: The Jews of Texas* by Hollace Ava Weiner and Kenneth D. Roseman; *Deep in the Heart: The Lives & Legends of Texas Jews* by Ruth Weingarten and Cathy Schechter (edited by Rabbi Jimmy Kessler); *Pioneer Jewish Texans* by Natalie Ornish; *Halff of Texas: Merchant Rancher of the Old West* by Patrick Dearen; *Memories of Two Generations* by Reverend Alexander Gurwitz, translated by Rabbi Abram Prero; *Galveston: Ellis Island of the West* by Bernard Marinbach; *The Provincials: A Personal History of Jews in the South* by Eli Evans; *Being Rapoport* by Bernard Rapoport, as told to Don Carleton.

And finally, I appreciate the help of my cousin Jack B. Kallison, who, with Alex Sharlack, wrote a book about his father Morris Kallison: *He Soared with Eagles: A Visionary Whose Achievements Transformed and Inspired a Dynamic Great City.*

1654   Twenty-three European Jews form first Jewish settlement in the United States in New Amsterdam, later named New York.

1731   Fifty-six Canary Islanders establish the Royal Villa of San Fernando de Béxar, the first regularly organized civil government in Texas.

1773   San Antonio de Béxar becomes the capital of Spanish Texas, grows in five years to 2,060 settlers and mission Indians.

1821   Mexican War of Independence from Spain begins in 1810, ends with the signing of the Treaty of Cordova in 1821, ceding Mexican territory.

1825   Czar Nicholas I of Russia (1825-1855) issues six hundred edicts prescribing restrictions on Jews; sends young Jewish boys, including two children of the Kallison family, to certain death in the army.

1835   Dina Elloff, daughter of Perry and Nettie Elloff, mother of Nathan Kallison, born near Kiev, Russia.

1836   Texas declares independence from Mexico; Alamo falls after thirteen-day siege by Mexican army; Texas wins independence after decisive Battle of San Jacinto.

1844   Empresario Henri Castro, a Frenchman descended from Portuguese Jews, establishes land-grant colony near San Antonio; most of the thirty-five colonists are recruited from France's Alsace region.

1845   Texas enters the United States as the twenty-eighth state of the Union.

1846   Mexican War begins in the wake of border skirmishes when President James K. Polk sends General Zachary Taylor to the Rio Grande.

1848   Mexican War ends with Treaty of Guadalupe Hidalgo. The United States gains California, Arizona, New Mexico, the Rio Grande boundary for Texas, parts of Utah, Nevada, and Colorado.

1854   First Jews settle in San Antonio, most from German states that in 1871 will become part of a united Germany.

1855   Czar Alexander II comes to power in Russia, promising better lives and rights for Jews.

1856   Hebrew Benevolent Association organized by Jews in San Antonio for burial of the dead.

1860   Abraham Lincoln elected the sixteenth US President; Joseph Kallison born in Ladyzhinka, Russia.

1861   The Civil War begins. Southern states secede from the Union. San Antonio Jews are divided in their loyalties: Bankers Daniel and Anton Oppenheimer fight for the Confederacy; Samuel Wolfson for the Union in the First Battle of Manassas.

1873   Nathan Kallison, second son of Dina Elloff and Moshko Kallison, born in Ladyzhinka, Russia.

1874   Temple Beth-El of San Antonio Texas holds opening ceremony, Members raise $12,000 in gold to build temple at Jefferson and Travis Streets.

1875   Anna Letwin (future wife of Nathan Kallison) born near Kiev, Russia.

1880   Population of United States reaches 50,189,209, including 250,000 Jews. The majority are German immigrants and their descendants.

1881   Czar Alexander II assassinated. His son, Alexander III, unleashes repressive laws against Jews. Young widow Dina Kallison hides her sons Jacob (ten), Nathan (eight), and Samuel (six), from marauding Cossacks who are burning villages and killing Jews. James A. Garfield, inaugurated as the twentieth US President in March, is assassinated after serving only 199 days in office. Chester A. Arthur succeeded to the presidency and completed Garfield's term.

1885   Bryan Callaghan II organizes San Antonio's first "Political Machine."

1886   Statue of Liberty dedicated in New York Harbor. Joseph Kallison (twenty) becomes first member of family to escape Russia. Finds work as a tailor in Chicago. Six Jews convicted and hanged, charged with fomenting the Haymarket Riot at 1886 labor rally in Chicago.

1890   Nathan Kallison (seventeen) immigrates to the United States, arrives in New York months after older brother Jacob. Both find work as apprentice harness makers in Chicago. Brother Samuel joins them in 1891, their mother Dina Kallison in 1894.

1890   Anna Letwin (fifteen) immigrates to United States from Russia, works as mother's helper for a relative in Chicago.

1890   Idaho and Wyoming enter the Union as the forty-third and forty-fourth states. Agudas Achim Synagogue organized in San Antonio, Texas.

1894   Nathan Kallison opens his own harness shop in Chicago at 163 West Twelfth Street in the West Side Jewish ghetto. His shop survives despite the depression of 1893-96 and violent labor strife.

1895   Nathan Kallison (twenty-two) marries Anna Letwin (nineteen) in Chicago. They live behind his shop; she works with him as clerk and cashier.

1896   Nathan and Anna Kallison's first child, Morris Kallison, born at home behind Nathan's harness shop in Chicago.

1896   Kallison brothers Nathan, Jacob, and Samuel take oath as United States citizens at Cook County Courthouse, Chicago. William McKinley elected twenty-fifth US President.

1898   Pauline Kallison, second child of Nathan and Anna, born at home in Chicago. Illinois State Factory Inspector reports Kallison harness shop has four employees. Spanish American War begins after sinking of the battleship USS *Maine*. Colonel Theodore Roosevelt trains his Rough Rider regiment in San Antonio.

1899   Nathan and Anna Kallison move to Texas, open harness shop in downtown San Antonio, at 124 South Flores Street.

1900   San Antonio population is 53,321, remains largest city in Texas, where 82 percent of population is rural. Jewish population in the city is approximately five hundred.

1900   Kallison family joins Temple Beth-El, Reform congregation. Temple Beth-El dedicates new building at Travis and Jefferson. Birth of Ruth Brown Dubinski (future wife of Morris Kallison) in San Antonio, Texas.

1901   Nathan Kallison buys a vacant lot; sells the property a year later at profit of $350.

1901   President William McKinley visits San Antonio on May 3, two months after he was sworn in for a second term. McKinley is assassinated four months later on September 6, 1901 in Niagara Falls, New York, and Theodore Roosevelt becomes the twenty-sixth US President.

1901   Spindle Top gusher near Beaumont heralds great oil wealth for Texas. First gasoline powered automobile—a Haynes-Apperson—arrives in San Antonio. City sets auto speed limit at six miles per hour.

1902   Birth of Nathan and Anna Kallison's third child, Bertha (later called Bertie, Birdie, Tibe, Tibby) is born in rented house on Dashiell Street.

1903   Nathan Kallison pays $1,775 to purchase first home at 125 Mission Street in San Antonio.

1903   Perry Kallison, Nathan and Anna's fourth child, is born at home. Morris Kallison enters Bonham Elementary School.

1904   The *San Antonio Daily Light* Society Page reports Nathan and Anna Kallison attending a party hosted by a prominent San Antonio photographer.

1905   Pauline Kallison enrolls in Bonham Elementary School.

1907   The "Galveston Experiment" begins. New York philanthropist Jacob Schiff helps ten thousand Eastern European Jews immigrate to the United States, steering them to Texas and the Midwest, rather than to New York and the East.

1907   Nathan Kallison buys 278 2/3 acres of ranch land west of San Antonio for $5,050; sells it six months later for profit of $2,613.

1908   Nathan Kallison sells harness-making business to L. Frank and Company, adds general merchandise to his ranching supply store.

1908   Rodfei Shalom, an Orthodox Congregation, founded in San Antonio.

1908   Tibe Kallison enters Bonham Elementary School.

1909   Morris Kallison becomes Bar Mitzvah at Temple Beth-El; Perry Kallison enrolls at Bonham Elementary School.

1910   Nathan Kallison establishes Kallison Ranch, buys 2,563 acres of land from heirs of Jacob Hoffmann, an original settler in the 1844 Henri Castro land grant. At ranch entrance, Kallison places a sign: "Established for Development of Better Farming and Ranching."

1910   Morris Kallison leaves school at age fourteen to work full time in Kallison's store; becomes an amateur boxer known as "Kid Morris."

1910   Population of San Antonio is 69,614. Lieutenant Foulois pilots first military flight at Fort Sam Houston. Chamber of Commerce charted. Luxury Saint Anthony Hotel opens.

1911   Nathan Kallison qualifies to vote, obtains poll tax receipt from county tax collector.

1912   Nathan Kallison moves family to large three-story Victorian-style home on San Pedro Avenue.

1913   Pauline Kallison enters Main Avenue High School.

1914   Archduke Franz Ferdinand of Austro-Hungarian Empire is assassinated, triggering World War I.

1914   US Agriculture Department Extension Service created. Nathan Kallison was one of the first ranchers to cooperate with the agency to test new agriculture methods and products.

1915   Jewish factory manager Leo Frank lynched by Georgia mob after his conviction in 1913 for the rape and murder of a thirteen-year-old employee. Later evidence indicates Frank's innocence. Case stirs anti-Semitism and rise of anti-immigrant groups, including the Ku Klux Klan.

1915   Tibe Kallison enters Main Avenue High School at age thirteen.

1916   Pauline Kallison enters the University of Chicago, transfers after one year to the University of Texas in Austin.

1917   United States enters World War I in April 1917 and is soon heavily engaged with the Allies against Germany in murderous trench warfare. In San Antonio, seventy thousand soldiers train at Fort Sam Houston; Kelly and Brooks Fields open to train pilots.

1917   Morris Kallison drafted, becomes first sergeant in field artillery.

1918   Armistice signed, ends World War I. Russian Czar Nicholas II and family killed as revolutionaries overthrow the czarist regime and Communists take control of the government.

1918   World-wide Spanish flu epidemic kills fifty million people. In San Antonio, the mayor orders closure of all schools, churches, public amusement places; military quarantine enforced at area military bases where thousands of soldiers are stricken.

1918   At age fifteen, Tibe Kallison becomes a freshman at the University of Texas in Austin.

1919   US Congress approves the Volstead Act, prohibiting sale or consumption of alcohol in the United States. Widespread bootlegging in San Antonio continues while "wets" and "drys" argue. Temple Beth-El board censures Rabbi Samuel Marks after he writes article criticizing prohibition laws.

1920   Women gain right to vote as Congress approves and the states ratify the Nineteenth Amendment to the Constitution. Anna and Pauline Kallison vote in first election.

1920   Morris Kallison marries Ruth Dubinski, daughter of Mr. and Mrs. Benjamin Dubinski of San Antonio. After service in the US Army, Morris becomes a manager at Kallison's store.

1920   Election returns communicated for the first time by radio when Leo H. Rosenberg of station KDKA in Pittsburg, Pennsylvania, broadcast the news that Republican Warren G. Harding was elected twenty-ninth US President, defeating Democrat James M. Cox.

1921   San Antonio is devastated by a historic flood: downtown businesses including Kallison's store and hundreds of other suffer millions of dollars in damages. Fifty-one Mexican Americans killed as flood sweeps through west side barrio.

1921   Perry Kallison (eighteen) drops out of the University of Texas after freshman year, works full time as bookkeeper at Kallison's and with father at the ranch. James Morris Kallison born to Morris and Ruth Kallison.

1922   Tibe Kallison graduates from the University of Texas at eighteen, enrolls in the University of Chicago graduate school, works at Jane Addams's Hull House with poor pregnant women and children.

1923   Nathan Kallison changes store name to "Kallison's Department Store," expanding merchandise to meet needs of both rural and city customers.

1923   Ku Klux Klan holds statewide initiation rites at San Antonio Speedway. In early 1920s, Klan controls Texas state legislature and city governments; directs hatred against Negroes, immigrants, Catholics, Jews. Rabbi Ephraim Frisch of Temple Beth-El speaks out against Klan.

1925   Tibe Kallison is elected first chairman of Temple League, created by Rabbi Ephraim Frisch and his wife Ruth to engage young adults in cultural and civic activities.

1926   Death of Dina (Dinah) Kallison in Chicago at age eighty.

1926   Kallison's store expands during Roaring Twenties' boom; Nathan Kallison builds the architecturally praised Kallison Block, a large retail and office building on South Flores Street.

1927   Nathan and Morris Kallison are charged in federal court with advertising and selling whiskey-making equipment and utensils, and are indicted for violating prohibition's Volstead Act. Nathan found innocent, Morris found guilty, pays $700 fine.

1927   Kallison Ranch innovates: demonstrates that Durham wheat can be grown successfully in South Texas; invites public to watch new Harvester Thresher—first of its kind in Bexar County. The Kallisons show their neighbors and customers the wisdom of advice from agricultural scientists who tell Texas farmers and ranchers that they should diversify, rather than depend solely on volatile cotton and cattle markets for their income.

1927   Pauline Kallison marries Isadore Neustadt, Chicago clothing manufacturer. Temple Beth-El holds first service in its new building at the corner of West Ashby and Belknap. Perry Kallison is an usher.

1928   Morris and Ruth's daughter Jane Kallison is born at Santa Rosa Hospital.

1928   KABC and KONO, San Antonio's first major radio stations, start broadcasting.

1929   Herbert Hoover takes office as thirty-first US President, the first Republican to carry Texas.

1929-40 New York Stock Exchange crashes on October 29, 1929, which became known as "Black Tuesday." The Great Depression sets in. By 1933, twenty-five million Americans are out of work. Thousands line up in front of the Bexar County Courthouse for $3 per family relief payments and surplus food; San Antonio schoolteachers paid in scrip, not money. The "Dust Bowl" drought and wind destroy one hundred million acres of farmland, including six million acres in Texas with another three million acres abandoned. Thousands of Texas farmers lose their land; twenty displaced families are invited to live in tents on Kallison Ranch.

1929   The Alamo National Bank Building opens and the Nix professional building is completed, ends major downtown construction in San Antonio for almost thirty years.

1930   Despite Great Depression, Kallisons enlarge the store, add automotive supplies to product line, and purchase a foundation herd of registered Polled Hereford cattle to upgrade the Kallison Ranch.

1930-40 Kallison family also expands. 1930: Tibe Kallison marries Benjamin Lasser, salesman for Fairchild Publications; 1931: Perry Kallison marries Frances Rosenthal of Fort Worth. More grandchildren born: Jack Brown Kallison, son of Morris and Ruth in 1931, Suzanna Neustadt and Nathan Kallison Lasser in 1932, Maryann Kallison in 1933, Perry (Pete) Kallison Jr. in 1934, and Frances Rae (Bobbi) Kallison in 1940. Nathan buys homes for himself and Anna and for their children in new Olmos Park suburb of San Antonio. In 1935, Isadore Neustadt dies; Tibe Kallison and Benjamin Lasser divorce.

1933   Prohibition repealed by Twenty-First Amendment to
          Constitution. Trucks laden with beer roll out of Pearl Brewery.

1933-45   Leader of the National Socialist German Workers' (Nazi) Party,
          Adolf Hitler rules as chancellor and—upon President von Hind-
          enburg's death in 1934—supreme leader (Führer) of Germany.

1933-40   Franklin D. Roosevelt defeats incumbent Republican Herbert
          Hoover in 1932 presidential election, rallies the country proclaim-
          ing "We have nothing to fear but fear itself." Roosevelt initiates
          New Deal programs to combat the Great Depression. The Works
          Progress Administration (WPA) and Public Works Administra-
          tion (PWA) pay workers to restore San Antonio's Spanish mis-
          sions and build the San Antonio River Walk. Civilian Conserva-
          tion Corps (CCC) erects twenty-seven camps in Texas, develops
          thirty state recreational parks; seventy other Texas camps house
          men working on forests and soil conservation. Civil Works
          Administration buys cattle from bankrupt farmers, processes
          meat in government-operated canning plant in San Antonio, dis-
          tributes canned meat to the destitute.

1934-45   Nathan and Anna Kallison and their four children all support
          President Roosevelt and his New Deal programs, believing they
          helped the country's efforts to combat the Great Depression.

1934   Kallison's store enjoys its best year: it is the nation's largest partic-
          ipant in a new Federal Housing Administration (FHA) guaran-
          teed loan program, hiring unemployed craftsmen to work on
          home repairs and new houses. Kallison's also prospers by selling
          merchandise at wholesale prices with long-term credit. Perhaps
          most important to their success, the Kallisons rely on their per-
          sonal relationships with two generations of customers, trusting
          they will honor their debts, even though they are presently unem-
          ployed and not considered creditworthy.

1935   Perry Kallison elected president of San Antonio Jewish Social
          Services and also serves as president of Texas Polled Hereford
          Society.

1936   Perry Kallison launches the *Trading Post*, a 7:00 a.m. daily radio
          program. As the "Ol' Trader," he offers free service for listeners to
          list items to buy or sell, developing strong personal bonds with
          rural audiences all over South and Central Texas.

1938   San Antonio police break up sit-down strike by pecan shelling workers; Temple Beth-El Rabbi Frisch defends the workers and criticizes factory owners, including a member of his own congregation. Temple board of directors unsuccessfully tries to silence the rabbi.

1938 Adolph Hitler and his Nazi party take total control of German government. He preaches violent anti-Semitism, claiming Germany would regain its lost power after it purified the German race by eliminating the Jews. Jews were gradually deprived of all rights and deported or taken to concentration camps.

1938 Perry Kallison chairs the Sixteenth Annual Appeal for the Jewish Social Service Federation. Perry and his wife Frances are leaders in efforts by American Jewish organizations to help Jews escape from Germany.

1939 England and France declare war against Nazi Germany.

1939 Perry Kallison is elected as rural chairman for the San Antonio-Bexar County Community Chest.

1940 Franklin D. Roosevelt elected to an unprecedented third term. Eleanor Roosevelt, the first president's wife to hold a news conference in the White House, continues to devote herself to humanitarian causes.

1940 Frances Kallison joins Sister Mary Victoria to establish Guadalupe Community Center, first to bring services to poor in West Side Mexican American neighborhoods. Alamo Stadium completed. San Antonio population is 353,584.

1941 Japan bombs American military bases in Hawaii and the Philippines on December 7. United States declares war on Japan as President Roosevelt call attacks "a day of infamy." San Antonio becomes nation's largest military complex outside Washington, DC, with tens of thousands of soldiers and airmen trained at Fort Sam Houston, Randolph Field, and the new San Antonio Aviation Cadet Center. Kelly Field grows into massive supply and maintenance center with twenty-five thousand employees. Brooke General Hospital treats wounded soldiers and airmen.

1941 Lieutenant James (Jimmy) Kallison enlists in the US Army Air Corps where he serves as a flight instructor. Kallison Ranch entertains hundreds of soldiers and airmen. In 1943, Lieutenant Kallison marries Ruth Friedman of San Antonio.

1944 Nathan Kallison dies of a stroke at age seventy-one.

1945 World War II ends with defeat of Germany in June and of Japan in August after United States drops heretofore secret atomic bombs on Hiroshima and Nagasaki, killing an estimated 150,000 to 246,000 people.

1945 Perry Kallison serves as chairman of the Rural Bexar County Chapter of the American Red Cross.

1946 Pauline Kallison Neustadt marries Lieutenant Colonel Max Blumer, US Medical Corps. Tibe Kallison (Lasser) weds widower Jacob "Jack" Kotz, MD, and moves to Washington, DC. He adopts Nathan (Nick) Kallison.

1946-66 Morris Kallison embarks on expansive real estate career, builds twenty-five new downtown buildings and remodels nearly two hundred older buildings in a twenty-year effort to revitalize downtown San Antonio. In the 1950s, he becomes downtown's largest property owner and taxpayer, winning awards from San Antonio Conservation Society for beautifying his properties and from General Services Administration for providing quality office space at reasonable prices.

1946-82 Perry Kallison, in cooperation with the US Extension Service, Texas A&M, and agricultural products manufacturers, demonstrates on the Kallison Ranch the latest in farm equipment, seeds, feeds, and veterinary supplies to improve farmers' incomes and practices of land conservation. He contributes money and time to help other ranchers and encourage young people to become farmers and ranchers.

1947-48 Perry Kallison serves as president of Temple Beth-El.

1948 British control over Palestine, established by mandate following World War I, ends May 14, 1948. On that day a Jewish homeland—the State of Israel—is born. The United States recognizes the new country that same day.

1948 Congressman Lyndon Johnson appears on *Trading Post* radio program with an endorsement from Perry Kallison on Election Day; wins Senate seat over Governor Coke Stevenson by a much-disputed margin of eighty-seven votes. Despite a banner headline to the contrary claiming "Dewey Defeats Truman," the incumbent president retains his office.

1949 Harry S. Truman's second term swearing-in was the first presidential inauguration in which a rabbi participated and the first to be broadcast on television.

1949 Record seven-year Texas drought begins. In 1953, Perry Kallison heads $50,000 Chamber of Commerce fundraiser to hire rainmaker to produce rain by seeding clouds with silver iodine. Effort fails.

1949 San Antonio municipal airport expands and vehicular traffic flows on the city's first expressway; both are projects for which Morris Kallison is a leading advocate to attract new business and modernize the city.

1949 Kallison's Feed and Seed department moves across Flores to its own space in the Kallison Block, freeing space to sell latest home appliances.

1950 Joe Freeman Coliseum opens in San Antonio after ten-year campaign with Perry Kallison as principal advocate. Stock Show and Rodeo there will draw hundreds of thousands of visitors and add millions to San Antonio economy.

1950 Kallison Ranch partners with E. B. Stull Company in failed early experiment using aerial spray defoliant to kill mesquite and other brush from South Texas ranch pasture.

1950-60 Kallison's store's most prosperous era: the largest farm and ranch supply store in the Southwest, Kallison's is the leading San Antonio merchant in selling the "new" invention—television sets—and consumer home appliances.

1950-53 The "Cold War," an ongoing state of tension between the United States (and its Western Bloc allies) and the Soviet Union (and its Eastern Bloc allies) from the late 1940s through the early 1990s, heats up with an armed conflict in Korea.

1952 Perry Kallison helps found the South Texas Polled Hereford Association.

1952 Kallison Ranch has the Reserve Champion Female "Diamond Domino Gold" at Fort Worth Fat Stock Show, one of dozens of awards won by Kallison Ranch herd of registered Polled Hereford cattle. Kallison ranch breeding stock is sold all over the United States and around the world.

1953 Pauline Kallison Neustadt Blumer, fifty-five, dies after four-year battle with cancer. Five-star General Dwight D. Eisenhower, victorious in World War II European theater, is inaugurated as the thirty-fourth US President.

1953 Administrators at Luther Burbank Vocational High School honor Perry Kallison, noting that "Whenever we've had a problem or needed something, someone would always say, 'Why don't we call Perry Kallison?' And he always came through."

1954   Fed-Mart opens in San Antonio; first new-style discount department store to challenge Kallison's and other traditional retail stores.

1955   San Antonio voters approve council-manager form of government, opposed by "political kingmaker" Morris Kallison and old-style city and county politicians.

1956   Seven-year record drought in South Texas finally ends with flooding and soaking spring rains.

1958   Dr. Jack Kotz, husband of Tibe Kallison Kotz, dies at age sixty-two.

1959   Perry Kallison honored by the San Antonio Market Institute for achievement making San Antonio a great livestock marketing center.

1959   Death of Anna Letwin Kallison.

1960   North Star Mall opens in suburban San Antonio; population shift impacts downtown businesses; many merchants follow customers to suburbs. Morris and Perry Kallison remain determined to keep Kallison's store downtown.

1960   Perry Kallison hosts and endorses vice-presidential candidate Lyndon Baines Johnson on *Trading Post* broadcast the morning of 1960 election, helping him and presidential candidate John F. Kennedy carry Texas and win the election.

1963   Kallison's Warehouse Showroom opens downtown in effort to compete with suburban discount stores. Business continues to decline.

1963   Lyndon B. Johnson becomes the thirty-sixth US President after the assassination of President Kennedy on November 22 in Dallas.

1964   Perry Kallison helps Israeli emissaries acquire Angora goats to found Israel's mohair industry.

1964-65 Congress enacts the Civil Rights Act of 1964, prohibiting racial segregation and outlawing discrimination against racial, ethnic, religious minorities, and women. A year later, Congress passes the Voting Rights Act of 1965, prohibiting states from imposing "voting qualification or prerequisite to voting, or standard, practice, or procedure . . . to deny or abridge the right of any citizen of the United States to vote on account of race or color."

1965   San Antonio Chamber of Commerce honors Perry Kallison with the Joe Freeman Award for outstanding community service to agriculture. Kallison's *Trading Post* broadcast noted as longest continuous rural radio broadcast in the world, and Perry Kallison is credited with turning "what might have been only another commercial radio program into a South Texas service institution and using it to help his fellow man."

1966   Morris Kallison dies unexpectedly from heart failure. The family is in crisis as they try to save Kallison's store, now debt-ridden and losing money. Tibe and Pauline's daughter Susan refuse to mortgage any more family-owned assets to cover growing losses.

1967   Perry Kallison in Texas delegation meets with Prime Minister Golda Meier in Israel, whose victory in Six Day War swells ranks of Jewish supporters in Texas and the country.

1967   Kallison's store closes after sixty-eight years. To pay store debts, Perry Kallison is forced to sell at auction the entire herd of Kallison Ranch's beloved registered Polled Hereford cattle. Kallison family divides remaining assets, including real estate and ranch. Perry Kallison opens small farm and ranch supply store on Nogalitas and rebuilds cattle herd; with son Pete, runs two western wear stores.

1968   Dr. Martin Luther King Jr., leader of the Civil Rights Movement, is assassinated on April 4, precipitating inner-city riots all over the nation, but not in San Antonio. Calm in San Antonio credited to early successful efforts by Rabbi David Jacobson of Temple Beth-El and other ministers to quietly end segregation in restaurants, hotels, and other public facilities. HemisFair '68 opens in San Antonio on April 6, becomes key in reviving downtown San Antonio as tourist and convention center.

1975   Good Government League domination of city politics ends; rise of Mexican American political power.

1981   Perry Kallison's *Trading Post* program ends after forty-six years, nation's longest-running farm radio program.

1982   Tibe Kallison Kotz dies at age seventy-nine.

1993   Ruth Brown Dubinski Kallison dies at age ninety-two.

1999   Perry Kallison dies at age ninety-five.

2003   Perry (Pete) Kallison Jr. dies at age sixty-eight.

2004   Frances Rosenthal Kallison dies at age ninety-five.

2006   James Morris "Jimmy" Kallison dies at age eighty-five.

2012   Suzanna (Susan) Neustadt Miller dies at age eighty.

2013   Alvin Friedman, husband of Maryann Kallison Friedman, dies at age eighty-one.

NOTES

One: To Freedom

1. *Shtetls* were small Jewish towns or villages within the "Pale of Settlement." From the Latin *palus* meaning stake, the "Pale" describes an area in czarist (Imperial) Russia in which Jews were allowed to establish permanent residency. An area of approximately 386,000 square miles (about the size of Texas and New Mexico combined), its boundaries and population of Jews shifted over time. By 1835, the Jews of Russia had been forced to live in the twenty-five provinces of the so-called "Pale of Settlement": Lithuania, Byelorussia, the southwestern provinces (the Ukraine), and parts of Poland—an area extending from the Baltic to the Black Sea. According to Yiddish poet Moishe Glaser, *shtetls* were distinguished by four essential characteristics: "(1) *mestechko*—legal permission to be a community; (2) three *minyans* (literal translation 'count,' is a traditionally mandated quorum of ten Jewish men—thirteen years of age or older—required for public worship) to support a rabbi and a prayer house; (3) a *cheder*—Jewish elementary school; (4) a *merchatz*—public bath." All records were destroyed after Nazis invaded the village in 1942, murdered the remaining Jewish residents, and buried them in a mass grave. (Barry Antler, "Ladyshinka, Ukraine," *The Wandering Jew* [blog], www.mywanderingjew.blogspot.com.)

2. *Revizskaya Skazka* (Revision List), June 26, 1818, Kiev Province, town of Uman, translated by Alex Dunai, 2012.

3. Irving Howe, *World of Our Fathers: The Journey of the Eastern European Jews to America and the Life They Found and Made* (New York: Simon & Schuster, 1976), 10; Chester G. Cohen, *Shtetl Finder Gazetteer: Jewish Communities in the 19th and Early 20th Centuries in the Pale of Settlement of Russia and Poland, and in Lithuania, Latvia, Galicia, and Bukovina, with Names of Residents* (Westminster, MD: Heritage Books, 2007), 37.

4. Khazars were semi-nomadic, culturally distinct Turkic people who established a stronghold in Eurasia from the latter part of the sixth century through the beginning of the eleventh century. Their medieval Khazar Empire occupied portions of present-day Russia, Kazakhstan, Ukraine, Georgia, Crimea, Turkey, and the northern part of the Caucasus Region, which is located between the Black and Caspian Seas. Also known as Khazaria, it was a link to the Silk Road and a major trade route between the Middle East and Northern Europe.

5. Weakened by local feuds and Mongol invasions, Ukraine subsequently was

taken over by the Grand Duchy of Lithuania, and then by the Polish-Lithuanian Commonwealth. In the mid-seventeenth century after an uprising against the Poles, a new Ukrainian state was established.

6. Uman revisions lists from 1818, 1850, and 1858. Places of registration noted in revision lists—official documents which updated Russian tax and military rolls—were often different from place of residence.

7. Leaders in the American South used a similar technique to keep poor whites under control by touting their superiority to African Americans.

8. Howe, *World of our Fathers*, 11.

9. After Czar Ivan IV (Ivan the Terrible) conquered the town of Polotsk in 1563, he was asked what to do with the Polotsk Jews. "Those who consent to baptism are to be baptized," he replied. "Those who refuse are to be drowned in the Polot River." During his seventeenth century invasion of Poland, Czar Alexei ordered the massacre of Polish Jews. A century later, Czarina Elizabeth (1741-1762) expelled all Jews from Russia, allowing them to return in the future only if they adopted the Russian Orthodox religion. Evan R. Chesler, *The Russian Jewry Reader* (New York: Behrman House, 1974), 15-21; Jacob Frumpkin, ed., *Russian Jewry* (New York: Thomas Yoseloff, 1966), 87.

10. Chesler, *The Russian Jewry Reader*, 20.

11. Howe cites *My Past and Thoughts* author Alexander Herzen who further describes the fate of those boys as ". . . one of the most awful sights I have ever seen . . . boys of twelve or thirteen might have survived it, but little fellows of eight and ten . . . were going to their graves." Howe, *World of Our Fathers*, 6-7.

12. Ibid.

13. *Revizskaya Skazka* (Revision List), May 22, 1858, Kiev Province, town of Uman; *Revizskaya Skazka* (Revision List), October 30, 1850, Kiev Province, town of Uman, translated by Alex Dunai, 2012.

14. Howe, *World of Our Fathers*, 7-8.

15. A bomb tossed by Ignacy Hryniewiecki, an impoverished Pole from a privileged class, killed Czar Alexander II. Hryniewiecki, who was killed in the attack, was a member of the Narodnaya Volya (The People's Will)—an ethnically and socially diverse revolutionary group.

16. M. Osherovich, "Russian Jews in the United States," *Russian Jewry*, eds. Jacob Frumkin, Gregor Aronson, and Alexis Goldenweiser (South Brunswick, NJ: Thomas Yoselof, 1966), 435-6.

17. No records of her husband's cause or date of death have been found.

18. Thirteenth Census of the United States—1910 Population. Census Place: Chicago Ward 27, Cook, Illinois; Roll: T624_271; Page: 17B; Enumeration District: 1208; Image: 97; FHL Number: 1374284. Accessed at www.ancestry.com. *The*

Redman Family: A Genealogical Study of the Redman Family, researched and compiled by Doris Redman, family tree of Chaya (Ida) Kallison, 5.

19. After exploring conditions in steerage on ships such as the SS *Werra*, a US congressional investigating committee reported that "filth and stench . . . added to inadequate means of ventilations," creating an atmosphere that was "almost unendurable. . . . In many instances, persons, after recovering from seasickness, continue to lie in their berths in a sort of stupor, due to breathing air whose oxygen has been replaced by foul gases." Howe, *World of our Fathers*, 42.

20. The Barge Office was used to handle immigrants after the nearby processing center at Castle Garden (known today as Castle Clinton National Monument) closed in April 1890.

21. "By the Thousands," *The World*, May 10, 1891.

22. "City and Suburban News," *New York Times*, May 7, 1890.

23. "Windom at the Barge Office," *New York Times*, May 9, 1890, 8.

24. Castle Garden, (Castle Clinton National Monument), located on the waterfront in the Battery at the southern tip of Manhattan, served as the first official US immigration center from 1855 to 1890. The Barge Office, authorized by an act of congress in 1878, took over for Castle Garden, serving as the Port of New York immigrant processing center from May 1890 until Ellis Island—a federally operated immigration center—opened on January 1, 1892. In June 1897 a fire destroyed the wooden building complex on Ellis Island. Once again, the Barge Office served as a temporary immigration processing center until Ellis Island reopened in December 1900. Ellis Island operated as an immigrant processing center until late 1924.

25. Clifton Daniel, John W. Kirshon, and Ralph Berens, eds., *Chronicle of America* (Mount Kisco, NY: Chronicle Publications, 1990), 484-489.

Two: Chicago

1. Shifts in the wind spread flames north and east—sparing the O'Learys' residence and the Holy Family Church, a Roman Catholic congregation where they worshipped.

2. "The Loop" refers to Chicago's historic central business district bounded by the city's elevated railway. It derives its name from the turnaround on State Street in front of Marshall Field & Company where cable car lines first converged in 1882. Donald L. Miller, *City of the Century: The Epic of Chicago and the Making of America* (New York: Simon & Schuster, 1996), 265-266.

3. Jane Addams, *Twenty Years at Hull House with Autobiographical Notes* (New York: MacMillan, 1910), 99-101.

4. Irving Cutler, *The Jews of Chicago: From Shtetl to Suburb* (Urbana: University

of Illinois Press, 2009), 62.

5. Ibid.

6. Sephardic Jews are descendants of Jews from Spain, Portugal, North Africa, and the Middle East. Ashkenazi Jews are descendants of Jews from France, Germany, and Eastern Europe.

7. Eli A. Faber, *Time for Planting: The First Migration, 1654-1820* (Baltimore: Johns Hopkins University Press, 1992), 4.

8. Gerald Sorin, *A Time for Building: The Third Migration, 1880-1920* (Baltimore: Johns Hopkins University Press, 1992), 7.

9. A majority of the Jews immigrating to the United States from the German states in the nineteenth century between 1820 and 1880 came from Prussia—including Poznan and Silesia and other parts of Poland annexed by Prussia, as well as from Alsace, Bavaria, Baden, and Swabia. In that period, Jews also came to the US from Lithuania, Slovakia, Romania, and czarist Russia. Hasia R Diner, *A Time for Gathering: The Second Migration, 1820-1880* (Baltimore: Johns Hopkins University Press, 1992), 35.

10. Sorin, *A Time for Building*, 7.

11. Irving Cutler, "Jews," in *Encyclopedia of Chicago*, edited by Janice L. Reiff, Ann Durkin Keating, and James R. Grossman (Chicago Historical Society, 2005), www.encyclopedia.chicagohistory.org/pages/671.html.

12. Sorin, *A Time for Building*, xv.

13. Ibid.

14. As older groups achieved economic mobility and moved to other parts of the city, they sold to newcomers the institutions they had built. In that fashion, the home of Sacred Heart Academy, established by the Irish in 1860, became the site of the Chicago Hebrew Institute in 1903. Myriam Pauillac, "Near West Side," in *Encyclopedia of Chicago*, www.encyclopedia.chicagohistory.org/pages/878.html.

15. Charles S. Bernheimer, *The Russian Jew in the United States: Studies of Social Conditions in New York, Philadelphia, and Chicago, with a Description of Rural Settlements* (Philadelphia: John C. Winston, Co., 1905). Jane Addams, *Twenty Years at Hull House*.

16. Bernard Horwich quoted by Cutler, *The Jews of Chicago*, 60.

17. *Matzo (matzah or matzoh)* is the unleavened bread traditionally eaten by Jews during the eight-day festival of Passover, which commemorates the ancient Israelites' freedom from slavery in Egypt.

18. Cutler, *The Jews of Chicago*, 58, 60.

19. Ibid., 61.

20. Ibid., quoted from *Chicago Tribune*, July 19, 1891.

21. *The Sentinel Presents 100 Years of Chicago Jewry* (Chicago: Sentinel Publishing Co., 1948).

22. Translation from German to English: *landsmanshaften*: country teams; *vereinen:* unite.

23. Cutler, *The Jews of Chicago,* 88.

24. Although many harness makers feared blacklisting from company owners, they nevertheless established a union. In 1890, just as Nathan was arriving in Chicago, one hundred and fifty harness makers left work because manufacturers ignored their demands for higher wages.

25. Bernheimer, *The Russian Jew in the United States,* 135.

26. William N. Fitz-Gerald, *The Harness Makers' Illustrated Manual* (New York, 1875), 19.

27. For Orthodox Jews, *shuls* (Yiddish word for places of worship) had to be within walking distance of their homes.

28. Cutler, *The Jews of Chicago,* 74.

29. Bernheimer, *The Russian Jew in the United States,* 135.

30. *100 Years of Chicago Jewry,* 7.

31. John Patrick Barrett, *Electricity at the Columbian Exposition* (Chicago: R. R. Donnelly & Sons, 1894), 6.

32. Nineteenth century American journalist, editor, and author Murat Halsted wrote, "Look from a distance at night, upon the broad spaces it fills, and the majestic sweep of the searching lights, and it is as if the earth and sky were transformed by the immeasurable wands of colossal magicians; and the superb dome of the structure that is the central glory of the display, is glowing as if bound with a wreath of stars. It is electricity! When the whole casket is illuminated, the cornices of the palaces of the White City are defined with celestial fire. The waters that are at play leap and flash with it. There are borders of lamps around the lagoon. The spectacle is more resplendent than the capitals of Europe ever saw when ablaze with festivals to celebrate triumphant peace or victorious war."

33. Certificate of Death (#21443) for Dina Kallison, July 24, 1926, issued in Cook County/Chicago, IL.

34. As her sons had done before her, Dina moved in with family—most likely with Jacob and Ida and their sons, two-year-old Perry, named after Dina's father, and infant Abe. Five years later, on May 9, 1899, the widow Dina remarried. Her second husband was the widower Judel Stuhlman, a fifty-eight-year-old carpenter who immigrated from Russia in 1890. They lived just two doors down from Jacob and Ida on North Ashland Avenue. Dina continued to give her daughter-in-law a helping hand. Ida Abidor Kallison birthed seven sons—Perry P., Abraham (Abe), David

(Daniel), Samuel, Isaac (Isadore), Maurice (Morris), and Victor—in nineteen years, before passing away in 1919. Jacob Kallison remarried within a year of Ida's death. His second wife, Bertha, was a forty-five-year-old émigré from Russia. Twelfth Census of the United States. Illinois, Cook County, City of Chicago, 14th Ward, 39th Precinct (NARA T623).

35. Paul N. Hasluck, ed., *Harness Making* (London: Cassell and Company, Limited, 1904), 9-29, 111-126. Nathan Kallison listings in 1894 Chicago City Directory, 893. Harness: 163 W 12th Street; Home: 175 Newberry Avenue. (Library of Congress.)

36. Cutler, *The Jews of Chicago*, 67-69.

37. C. C. Martin, *The Harness Maker's Complete Guide* (Chicago: Jefferson Jackson, 1891).

38. Anna Kallison Americanized her name—changing "Hannah" to "Anna" in social situations. However, on some legal documents, her name appears as "Hannah Kallison."

39. Mary Lynn Kotz interview, August 1982, Fort Worth, Texas.

40. Cook County (Chicago, IL) Marriage License Application, Document #228282, January 12, 1895.

41. *1895 Chicago City Directory*, 922.

42. Stephen Thernstrom, Ann Orlov, and Oscar Handlin, eds. *Harvard Encyclopedia of American Ethnic Groups* (Cambridge, MA: Belknap Press, 1980), 734-748.

43. US Department of Labor, Immigration, and Naturalization Service Card, Certificate #2224, October 12, 1896.

44. Annual Reports of the Chief State Factory Inspector of Illinois: Fifth Annual Report of the Factory Inspectors of Illinois for the Year ending December 15, 1897 (Springfield, IL: Phillips Bros., State Printers, 1898), 49, 181. Sixth Annual Report of the Factory Inspectors of Illinois.

45. Jane Addams, *Twenty Years at Hull House*.

46. Tenement lots were usually developed in stages. Many contained back buildings or rear tenements—old, single family homes converted into or replaced by apartment houses, which were surrounded on three sides by five- to six-story buildings. Access to rear tenements (the dirtiest and dingiest of substandard housing) was through the adjacent buildings that fronted the street.

47. In fact, Jews had twice the incidence of pneumonia and rheumatism as their non-Jewish counterparts (Bernheimer, 328).

48. Physicians Certificate of Death (#9939) for Frael Kallison. Issued by State Board of Health State of Illinois Cook County City of Chicago Board of Health, October 20, 1893.

49. New Mexico was granted statehood on January 6, 1912; Arizona was granted statehood on February 14, 1912. They became the forty-seventh and forty-eighth states, respectively.

50. Author's interview with Frances Kallison.

Three: Deep in the Heart

1. Protests from local medical doctors about the spread of disease had finally forced reluctant city officials to start building a sewer system and clean water supply. To the Kallisons' relief, the city's downtown finally was starting to get a safe, reliable water supply to replace the ancient *acequias*—irrigation ditches in which water and sewage intermixed, threatening the city with rampant dysentery, cholera, and other diseases. Nathan and Anna also were early beneficiaries of the water system built by George Washington Brackenridge, who had started his own Water Works Company, from which he pumped and piped water to city residents, first from springs near the source of the San Antonio River, and then from artesian wells he drilled on his own property. *San Antonio Daily Light*, November 10, 1899.

2. Willis R. Woolrich and Charles T. Clark, "Refrigeration," *Handbook of Texas Online*, www.tshaonline.org/handbook/online/articles/dqr01.

3. *San Antonio Daily Express*, August 11, 1899, 9.

4. "The Floods Ravages," *San Antonio Daily Express*, July 1, 1899, 1.

5. "Climate Records for San Antonio," NOAA online. National Weather Service Weather Forecast Office, www.srh.noaa.gov/ewx/?n=satclidata.htm.

6. "Daily Report of Business," *San Antonio Daily Express*, August 16, 1899, 9.

7. Fehrenbach, T. R. *The San Antonio Story*, 111.

8. "For Three Generations: The Mercantile Center of South Texas," *San Antonio Express-News*, September 19, 1965.

9. Author's interview with James Kallison, July 2006.

10. Char Miller, *Deep in the Heart of San Antonio*, 4-6.

11. *Handbook of Texas Online*, "Jews," 1; "Bexar County," 5.

12. *San Antonio Light*, November 1, 1959, 28.

13. *San Antonio Light*, December 22, 1949, 8C.

14. "Kallison Builds Big Business by Holding Friends," *San Antonio Express*, December 31, 1933, 37.

15. Frances Kallison citation in Kallison Block history compiled by Kathy Cruse, San Antonio Conservation Society, September 1984.

16. Early breweries included the City Brewery, founded in 1884 and located north of town on the banks of the San Antonio River. It went bankrupt in 1887 but was succeeded by the San Antonio Brewing Association (SABA), later known as the

Pearl Brewing Company. Char Miller, "'What, No Beer?': Pearl Brewery and the Building of San Antonio," *South Texas Studies* 2005, 28-47.

17. The Menger Hotel bar was later renamed the Roosevelt Bar "in memory of (the Rough Riders') sojourn there." The army continued to station and train cavalry in San Antonio long after mechanized warfare displaced the principal role of horses in combat. Thomas W. Cutrer, "First United States Volunteer Cavalry," *Handbook of Texas Online*, www.tshaonline.org/handbook/online/articles/qlf01; Fehrenbach, *San Antonio Story*, 147.

18. *San Antonio Gazette*, January 27, 1905, 8.

19. When Sam Kallison returned to Chicago, he went back into the harness business there, as well as starting a dry goods business with his wife Celia. Sam Kallison died in 1933.

20. When Sam Letwin arrived in Chicago, he got a job sweeping out a small grocery store where he slept on the floor. There was a high school next door. When he saw the boys his age come outside, he would go over and give them a nickel to show him how to read the newspaper. After leaving the Kallisons in San Antonio, Sam Letwin hopped a freight train and went to look for work in the oil fields. He picked up metal debris on the road and salvaged equipment from the oil fields, eventually becoming a successful entrepreneur and developer of new oil wells. Mary Lynn Kotz interview with Sam Letwin, August 1982.

21. Tibe Kallison's first name evolved from her given name of Bertha to Tibe (Tybe, Tybbe) over the course of decades. Not a problem for her family who first nicknamed her "little bird," legally the unofficial name changes caused some confusion. In 1975, her nephew Jack B. Kallison, an attorney and her brother Morris's younger son, signed an affidavit in a Bexar County court, testifying that Bertha Kallison, Bertie Kallison, and Birdie Kallison were indeed the same person. Records of Bexar County, Texas, Deed of Records/Affidavit, Document #549185, Book 07573, Page 0870, filed May 2, 1975, www.gov.propertyinfo.com/tx-bexar.

22. Fehrenbach, *San Antonio Story*, 122-23.

23. Records of Bexar County, Texas. Deed Records: Book 00195, Page 0236, filed September 20, 1903, www.gov.propertyinfo.com/tx-bexar.

24. On the deed filed October 22, 1902, Nathan Kallison signed his name in Hebrew. The letters of his first name spelled out Moishe (Moses/Morris), not Nathan; Anna—known at that time as Hannah—affixed hers with the mark of an "X." Records of Bexar County, Texas. Deed Records: Book 00189, Page 0364, filed April 4, 1901, www.gov.propertyinfo.com/tx-bexar. Records of Bexar County, Texas. Deed Records: Book 00212, Page 0145, filed October 22, 1902, www.gov.propertyinfo. com/tx-bexar.

25. "Surprise Party to Venerable Lady," *San Antonio Sunday Light*, December 18, 1904, 18.

26. US Census for Isaac Raffee. Year: 1900; Census Place: San Antonio Ward 7, Bexar, Texas; Roll: 1612; Page: 4A; Enumeration District: 107; FHL microfilm: 1241612. *San Antonio Sunday Light*, December 18, 1904, 18. That same evening, halfway around the world in the Kallison's native Russia, workers struck the Putilov manufacturing plant in St. Petersburg. Protests against autocracy spawned other strikes throughout the city. The number of demonstrators swelled to eighty thousand, and mobs clashed with police—the night's violence a prelude to the Russian Revolution, which fourteen years later would overthrow Czar Nicholas II and bring Lenin, Stalin, and the Communists to power.

27. San Antonio City Directory 1905, 551.

28. Texas Transportation Museum website, www.txtransportationmuseum.org/history.htm.

29. Nathan Kallison's saddle and harness manufacturing company was sold to one of his principal competitors, L. Frank and Company Harness and Saddlery—a wholesale manufacturer located at 212 West Commerce Street. Established in 1870 by Lazarus Frank—a German Jew and one of the founders of Temple Beth-El, one of San Antonio's oldest Jewish congregations—the saddlery was a family-run business. When the 1908-1909 San Antonio City Directory was published, Nathan's business was described for the first time as "mdse" (merchandise).

30. *San Antonio Light*, February 4, 1909, 7, 9; *San Antonio Light and Gazette*, January 9, 1910, 13; *San Antonio Light*, January 26, 1909, 10.

Four: The Land

1. The six-pointed Jewish Star of David is formed by six crossed lines.

2. Natalie Ornish, *Pioneer Jewish Texans* (Dallas: Texas Heritage Press, 1989), 73-84.

3. Tom Fulton, United States Senate Committee on Agriculture, Nutrition, and Forestry 1825-1998; S. Doc. 105-24. Chapter 3: *From Golden Age to the Great Depression: 1900-1929*, www.access.gpo.gov/congress/senate/sen_agriculture/ch3.html.

4. In 1908, male wage-workers seldom earned more than $600 per year. Female wage workers earned even less—often below $400 per year. *The Leather Workers' Journal* (Official Publication of the International United Brotherhood of Leather Workers on Horse Goods) Volume XII-No.1 Kansas City, MO, September 1909, 272; Scott Nearing, "Wages in the United States, 1908-1910," (New York: The MacMillan Company, 1911), 137, 144-46.

5. *San Antonio Express Magazine,* June 12, 1949, 6-7.

6. The family's name was originally Huffmann; it was changed to Hoffmann after their arrival in the United States. Texas land records and author's interview with Florence Hoffmann.

7. A. J. Sowell, *Texas Indian Fighters of Southwest Texas* (Abilene: State House Press, 1986), 828-834. (Facsimile Reproduction of the Original published in1900.)

8. Martha Doty Freeman, *A History of Government Canyon State Property, Bexar County, Texas* (Austin: Texas Parks and Wildlife Dept., 1994), 42-48.

9. The sale excluded the 30 x 30 gravesite of Jacob Hoffmann, with provision for his widow Caroline to be buried there as well. Their graves later were moved to the Zion Lutheran Community Cemetery in Helotes. Mary Lee Gussen Sloan, *And the Snake Slept: Culebra, The Story* (San Antonio: Government Canyon Edition, self-published by Hoffmann descendants, 2003).

10. Bexar County land records. Deed of Records: Book #348, Page 289, Grantors: Hoffmann, F. and Hoffmann, J.; Grantee: Kallison, Nathan, Instrument date: December 27, 1910, www.gov.propertyinfo.com/tx-bexar.

11. The Texas state legislature renamed the college Texas A&M University in 1963, reflecting its expanded offerings and diversified student body.

12. *San Antonio Express Magazine,* June 12, 1944.

13. US Department of Agriculture, States Relations Service, Office of Experiment Stations, Experiment Station Record, Volume 34, January-June, 1916, Washington, UNT Digital Library, www.digital.library.unt.edu/ark:/67531/metadc 5020.

14. *Handbook of Texas Online,* "Texas in the 1920s," 2.

15. *San Antonio Jewish Record,* July 1, 1927, Vol. 4.

16. In the eighteenth century, flax had been grown at Mission San Antonio de Valero and other early Spanish missions. However in the early twentieth century, it was not a large cash crop for South Texas ranchers. Christopher Long, "Bexar County," *Handbook of Texas Online,* www.tshaonline.org/handbook/online/articles/hcb07.

17. Nathan thought Herefords were beautiful. He affectionately called his petite younger daughter Tibe "my little white-faced heifer."

18. *San Antonio Light,* June 12, 1967, sec. 7, 2.

Five: Tradition!

1. *Yarmulke* (Yiddish)—also *kippah* (Hebrew): head covering worn by Jews during prayer services. Some Jews wear these skull caps at all times. *Shul:* a Yiddish word for Jewish house of worship used most often by Orthodox Jews. Agudas Achim held

its first services at the Hebrew Institute and in private homes until 1893, when congregants were able to buy land at Guilbeau and Aubrey Streets on the west bank of the San Antonio River. In 1896, Rabbi Moses Sadovsky consecrated the first synagogue building at that site. The synagogue's first president, Max Karotkin, who came to the United States from Russia in 1881 and founded Karotkin Furniture on Main Avenue between Commerce and Houston Streets, became a "mover and shaker in Jewish causes." After the congregation built a new synagogue in 1923 at Main and Quincy, Rabbi Gerson Feigenbaum led the Agudas Achim congregation from its Orthodox roots to its present Conservative ideology, seeking a middle ground between the Reform and Orthodox practices of Judaism. It became the largest synagogue in San Antonio. Rodfei Sholom, a synagogue serving Orthodox Jews in San Antonio today, had not yet opened its doors when the Kallisons moved to San Antonio in 1899. Its first building, in 1908, was an old adobe house located on Wyoming Street. In 2012 it had a membership of over three hundred families. Members are from Reform, Conservative, secular, and Orthodox backgrounds coming not only from the United States but from Israel, Mexico, South Africa, South America, and Europe. In the 1920s when Agudas Achim transitioned to a conservative synagogue, some of its more traditionally observant members joined Rodfei Sholom. "History of Rodfei Sholom," www.rodfeisholom.com/history.html; (also noted in an interview with William Sinkin); *Congregation Rodfei Sholom*, "About Us," www.rodfeisholom.com/about.html.

2. Reform's leader in the United States was Rabbi Isaac Mayer Wise, an 1846 immigrant from Bohemia, who eventually settled in Cincinnati, where in 1873 he founded the Union of American Hebrew Congregations. In 1889, the organization of Reform congregations became an arm of the Central Conference of American Rabbis. The Kallisons' Temple Beth-El in San Antonio was an early member of the Central Conference, which offered guidance to congregations and leadership and training for Reform rabbis at its Hebrew Union College in Cincinnati. At its convention in Pennsylvania in 1885, the Central Conference had adopted the so-called "Pittsburgh Platform," which dismissed "such Mosaic and rabbinical laws to regulate diet, priestly purity, and dress." The platform stressed that Reform Jews should follow laws that they believe "elevate and sanctify our lives" and must reject those customs and laws that are "not adapted to the views and habits of modern civilization." In boldly asserting their independence from the strictures of Jewish orthodoxy, the rabbis at that first meeting of the Central Conference went so far as to feature both pork and shellfish on the banquet menu—foods strictly banned by kosher dietary laws set forth in Leviticus, the third book of the Five Books of Moses (the Torah), where the kinds of kosher and non-kosher animals are listed. By 1935, many Reform rabbis and congregations decided that the Americanization of religious observance

had gone too far. The Columbus Platform of the Central Conference called for reinstituting more Hebrew into services, the use of a cantor, and restoration of the bar mitzvah for boys—with bat mitzvah added for girls.

3. *Kashrut* (Jewish dietary laws); contrary to a popularly held belief, these laws were not instituted for health reasons. Rather, they are mandatory statutes to be observed without question. According to Maimonides, a twelfth century Jewish philosopher and Torah scholar, the laws of *kashrut* "train us to master our appetites; to accustom us to restrain our desires; and to avoid considering the pleasure of eating and drinking as the goal of man's existence." (Alfred J. Kolatch, *The Jewish Book of Why*, [Middle Village, New York: Jonathan David Publishers, 1981], 84-85.)

4. As with congregations in the north and east, the formation of Temple Beth-El grew directly out of the new European Reform movement, which first stirred during the French Revolution as Jews were released, albeit briefly, from social ostracism and ghetto confinement. Reform took firm root in Germany between 1810 and 1820, spread throughout Western Europe in the 1840s, then was transplanted to the United States by the first wave of German Jewish immigrants, who formed a temple in Charleston, South Carolina. The movement's broad goal was to permit religious Jews to take full advantage of new freedoms and opportunities available to them for the first time within the larger communities in which they lived, in a country in which freedom to worship was a founding principle. American Jewish Committee Archives online American Jewish Yearbook, Vol. 5 (1903–1904), 472-473, www.ajcarchives.org/main.php?GroupingId=10032; American Jewish Committee Archives online American Jewish Yearbook, Vol. 2 (1900-1901), 472.

5. William Sajowitz, *History of Reform Judaism in San Antonio, Texas, 1874-1945.* Thesis (Rabbinic)—H.U.C.-J.I.R., 47.

6. Elsewhere in the state, a chain of dry goods stores founded by the Sanger brothers in McKinney in 1857 expanded from the original outpost, with Decatur, Weatherford, Dallas, Waco, and other cities. Other retailers were E. M. Kahn & Company in Dallas, founded by Emanuel Meyer Kahn in 1872; E. S. Levy & Company in Galveston, founded in 1877 by Abraham Levy and L. Weis; Levy Brothers Dry Goods Company, in Houston, founded in 1887; Sakowitz Brothers in Galveston, Houston, and other cities, founded by Samuel and Simon Sakowitz; Kruger Brothers Jewelry Company (forerunner of Zale Jewelry Corporation) founded by Sam and Julius Kruger in Fort Worth (circa 1907); the Neiman Marcus Company, founded in Dallas in 1907 by Herbert Marcus, his sister Carrie M. Neiman, and Carrie's husband, Abraham L. (Al) Neiman. Natalie Ornish, *Pioneer Jewish Texans* (Dallas: Texas Heritage Press, 1989), 132-160.

7. They were fulfilling one important aspect of the Jewish concept of

Tzedakah—the greatest act of charity is to bury the dead, because one can expect nothing in return. Less than a year later, Mrs. Lorch became the first person buried there. Frances R. Kallison, *100 Years of Jewry in San Antonio.* Thesis (M. A.), Trinity University, San Antonio, 1977, 19-20.

8. Samuel Marks, "Early History of the Jews in San Antonio," the *Reform Advocate,* 1913, 9; Kallison, *100 Years of Jewry in San Antonio,* 40-41.

9. Independent Order of Odd Fellows, founded in Baltimore, Maryland in 1819, is a benevolent society (also known as Three Link Fraternity, standing for friendship, love, and truth) dedicated to "improve and elevate the character of man" (www.ioof.org). Congregation Beth-El By-laws (Preamble).

10. The forty-four charter members of Temple Beth-El were Louis Zork, B. Oppenheimer, Samuel Mayer, A. Michel, Daniel Marx, A. B. Frank, E. Moke, A. Halff, L. Mandelbaum, Sol Deutsch, T. H. Philipson, A. A. Wolff, A. Kern, Simon Frank, A. Sulnon, M. Koenigheim, Louis S. Berg, Henry L. Berg, S. M. Koenigheim, Max Goldfrank, H. Frank, B. Schwarz, Moses Oppenheimer, Daniel Oppenheimer, Solomon Halff, Samuel Moritz, Ferdinand Mayer, L. Veith, A. Kahn, Lazarus Frank, Josef Treuer, S. Frank, L. M. Michael, A. Sichel, B. Moke, A. M. Koenigheim, M. Haas, Adam Joseph, M. Morrison, Henry Michel, Philip Sulzbacher, A. Zork, A. Morris, and Max Mayer.

11. Sajowitz, *History of Reform Judaism in San Antonio,* 1-2.

12. Fehrenbach, *San Antonio Story,* 128.

13. Kallison, *100 Years,* 15-16.

14. Ibid., 20-22.

15. Ibid., 31-32.

16. Ibid., 24.

17. *San Antonio Daily Light,* December 15, 1899, 8.

18. *San Antonio Daily Light,* October 13, 1899, 4; *San Antonio Daily Light,* October 6, 1899, 5; *San Antonio Daily Light,* September 17, 1899, 5.

19. Sajowitz, *History of Reform Judaism in San Antonio,* Thesis (Rabbinic)— H.U.C.-J.I.R., 24.

20. Bar mitzvah translated from the Hebrew/Aramaic is "son of the command-ment."

21. *San Antonio Sunday Light,* May 5, 1901, 7.

22. *The Book of Gold* was to be preserved in the archives of the temple and a counterpart enclosed in the cornerstone of the new building.

23. Leon Czolgosz—born in Michigan in 1873, the son of Roman Catholic immigrants from Poland/Russia—was employed as a wire mill worker in Cleveland, Ohio, until he suffered a breakdown in 1898 that forced him to return to his family's

farm. Influenced by anarchist speakers, he committed himself to the cause even though the anarchist groups he approached rebuffed him. When captured by authorities after shooting President McKinley, Czolgosz identified himself as "Fred Nieman" or "Fred Nobody," later saying, "I didn't believe one man should have so much service, and another man have none." Found guilty after a brief trial, he was put to death in the electric chair on October 29, 1901.

24. Temple Beth-El Archives: "Past Confirmants and Bar Mitzvahs: Record of Boys and Girls Who Have Been Bar Mitzvah and Confirmed in Temple Beth-El, San Antonio, Texas, by Rabbi Samuel Marks 1897-1918." Confirmation Service program, May 18, 1918.

25. Tom McGowan, "Man of Word, Says Son: Morris Kallison's Dad Laid Groundwork for 'Empire,'" *San Antonio Express,* December 10, 1962, 11; Arthur L. Coleman, "For Land's Sake," *San Antonio Express* and *San Antonio News,* September 9, 1956, 10G.

26. West End Lake was later renamed Woodlawn Lake. *San Antonio Light,* August 15, 1917, 6.

27. Mary Lynn Kotz interview with Susan Neustadt Miller, February 2012.

28. "Bonham School Overcrowded," *San Antonio Express,* October 8, 1905, 19.

29. *San Antonio Light,* May 17, 1914.

30. Char Miller, *On the Border,* 73.

31. Fehrenbach, *San Antonio,* 77-79, 159.

32. Bernard Marinbach, *Galveston, Ellis Island of the West* (Albany: State University of New York Press, 1983).

33. Between 1921 and 1923, Agudas Achim, founded in 1899 as an Orthodox synagogue, transitioned to a Conservative congregation.

34. Z. Gurwitz, *History of Orthodox Jews and their Synagogues,* Gurwitz/Galveston (Gurwitz Vol 2, 277); Memories of Two Generations. S.l: s.n. (translated from the Yiddish by Amram Prero), 1900.

35. Gurwitz, *History of Orthodox Jews and their Synagogues,* 276.

36. Ibid., 213-14.

37. It was not long before the sons and grandsons of these shop owners in Little Jerusalem gained success in the wider society, becoming lawyers, doctors, public officials, and corporate scions. Sam Rosenman, the son of a West Commerce Street shop owner, became a member of President Franklin Roosevelt's so-called "brain trust." Bernard Rapoport founded the American Income Life Insurance Company and became an important philanthropist for liberal causes. Morris Spector's grandson and namesake became a distinguished San Antonio physician.

38. Bryan Edward Stone, *The Chosen Folks: Jews on the Frontiers of Texas* (Austin: University of Texas Press, 2010), 136.

39. *San Antonio Light,* August 18, 1915, 4.

40. Charles C. Alexander, *Crusade for Conformity: The Ku Klux Klan in Texas, 1920-1930* (Texas Gulf Coast Historical Association, 1962), 36.

41. Bernard Rapoport (as told to Don Carleton), *Being Rapoport: Capitalist with a Conscience* (Austin: University of Texas Press, 2002), 7.

42. Ibid., 7-8.

43. *San Antonio Gazette,* October 22, 1906, 3.

44. "Mass Meeting of Jews is Planned," *San Antonio Light,* January 27, 1916, 5.

45. Hollace Ava Weiner and Kenneth D. Roseman, *Lone Stars of David: The Jews of Texas* (Waltham, MA: Brandeis University Press, 2007), 3.

46. Samuel M. Stahl, *Making the Timeless Timely: Thoughts and Reflections of a Contemporary Reform Rabbi* (Austin: Nortex Press, 1993).

47. Norman D. Brown, *Hood, Bonnet, and Little Brown Jug: Texas Politics, 1921-1928* (College Station: Texas A&M University Press, 1984).

48. Author's telephone interview with Marilyn Jorrie, May 29, 2012.

49. *San Antonio Jewish Record,* August 22, 1924, 4; *Texas Jewish Press,* July 25, 1941, 3.

50. Frances R. Kallison, *100 Years of Jewry in San Antonio,* M. A. Thesis (San Antonio: Trinity University, 1977), 92.

Six: War, Peace, and Prosperity

1. Kelly Field was dubbed the place "Where Uncle Sam's Eagles Hatch."

2. Endorsing the US entry into World War I, the *San Antonio Light* asserted: "Our good intentions have been misconstrued, our patience has been abused, our forbearance has been outraged." Even before war was declared, San Antonio benefited economically from the 1916 Mexican Expedition, in which one hundred fifty thousand members of the National Guard were dispatched to Mexico in an unsuccessful effort to stop Pancho Villa and his guerillas from raiding the Texas border. Many members of the Guard trained at Camp Wilson (part of Fort Sam Houston), practiced gunnery at Leon Springs Military Reservation, and learned tactical maneuvers at Camp Bullis. During World War I, Camp Wilson, renamed Camp Travis, provided the training site for one hundred thousand soldiers. Kelly Field served as the training site for two hundred fifty thousand men being trained as pilots and flight crews; Gosport (later Brooks) Field was created to train pilots for balloons and airships. (Char Miller, "Battle-Ready City: San Antonio in the Great War," in *Winds and Words of War: Political Propaganda Posters from World War I* [Seattle: Marquand Books, 2008], 12-18.) The military growth would continue after the war ended, triggering the new prosperity that transformed San Antonio during the Roaring Twenties.

3. Jack B. Kallison, with Alex Scharlack, *He Soared with Eagles: Morris Kallison,*

a Visionary Whose Achievements Transformed and Inspired a Dynamic Great City (San Antonio: privately printed, 2011).

4. Morris recalled that as a youth, he would lie down on the ground at the ranch and gaze up at the sky, vowing that one day he would "soar like an eagle." (Author's interview with Morris's son Jack B. Kallison.) *San Antonio Light,* "Around the Plaza," March 22, 1977, 9; Author's interview with James Kallison, August 2006.

5. In 1941, the Jewish Welfare Board along with the Salvation Army, Young Men's Christian Association (YMCA), Young Women's Christian Association (YWCA), National Catholic Community Services, and National Travelers Aid Association formed the USO—a private, nonprofit, civilian organization dedicated to "enhance the quality of life of the US Armed Forces personnel and their families" ("History of the USO," www.uso.org/About-Us/The-Organization/History /History.aspx). Harry David Kroll, ed. of "Kelly Field in the Great War," (San Antonio: Press of San Antonio Printing Company, 1919).

6. A Jewish social club associated with Temple Beth-El.

7. The well-planned effort may have been spurred by a sermon several months earlier in which Temple Beth-El's Rabbi Samuel Marks chastised his congregation for their failure to extend hospitality to the troops stationed in San Antonio during the previous year's High Holy Day observances.

8. The Texas State Board of Health made the following suggestions on how to prevent flu outbreaks in schools: "Every day . . . disinfectant should be scattered over the floor and swept. All woodwork, desks, chairs, tables, and doors should be wiped off with a cloth wet with linseed, kerosene, and turpentine. Every pupil must have at all times a clean handkerchief and it must not be laid on top of the desk. Spitting on the floor, sneezing, or coughing, except behind a handkerchief, should be sufficient grounds for suspension of a pupil. A pupil should not be allowed to sit in a draft. A pupil with wet feet or wet clothing should not be permitted to stay at school."

9. The United States Department of Health and Human Services, "The Great Pandemic: The United States in 1918-1919," www.1918.pandemicflu.gov/your_ state/texas.htm.

10. Ralph W. Steen, "World War I," *Handbook of Texas Online,* www.tshaonline. org/handbook/online/articles/qdw01. Published by the Texas State Historical Association.

11. Fehrenbach, *San Antonio Story,* 167.

12. While these armistices ended the fighting, a series of treaties the following year officially ended the war, but November 11 was always celebrated as "Armistice Day" (now Veterans' Day) in the United States.

13. When Tibe arrived on the University of Texas campus in 1918, the school

was only thirty-seven years old, and far from becoming the great institution of learning that it is recognized as today. In the years she was there, 1918 through 1922, only a few substantial buildings existed. The university was only just beginning its change from "a sleepy small town college housed in a hodgepodge of mismatched buildings" into becoming a powerful, sophisticated institution. In Tibe's day, the salaries for most of her professors were so meager that some made ends meet by keeping a cow in their yards for milk and chickens for eggs. Richard Holland, ed., *The Texas Book: Profiles, History, and Reminiscences of the University* (Austin: University of Texas Press, 2006).

14. Mary Lynn Kotz interview with Tibe Kallison, Broad Run, Virginia, June, 1981.

15. Pauline graduated from Main High School in 1916. During her three years there, she was a member of the High School Photographic Art Club, which evolved into the High School Scientific Society. It exposed students to emerging technologies and encouraged them to explore the natural world. In April 1916, Pauline played the role of "Louise Parker"—an elegant thirty-year-old single woman—in Hubert Henry Davies's four-act comedy "A Single Man" staged by the Powers School of Expression and Dramatic Art. Like her older sister, Tibe excelled in the performing arts. She studied piano with J. M. Steinfeldt, mastering works by Bach and Haydn for one of her recitals. Even before she reached Main Avenue High School, Tibe was involved with the B Minor Music Club for students five to fifteen years old and helped to organize programs when she was just eleven years old. In 1915, under the direction of Mrs. C. C. Denison, the music club staged an operetta, "The Fairies Reunion," in the Grand Opera House. Then twelve and in her last year of grade school, Tibe—along with Melvin Wolff—performed as "Pink" in the "Rain-beau" Dance. At fourteen, Tibe served as recording secretary for the Junior Music Department of the Council of Jewish Women, which was organized in the home of Mrs. Eli Hertzberg in May of 1917.

16. During World War I years, Nathan and Anna's youngest child Perry spent his extracurricular hours with the debate club, from grade school onward. At age fourteen, Perry was a member of the Patrick Henry Debating Society—an auxiliary of the debating group at Main Avenue High School. In January 1917, while legendary Mexican revolutionary leader Pancho Villa was terrorizing American communities near the US border, outwitting the American army sent to capture him, young Perry and his group debated: "Resolved that the United States should intervene and establish a strong government in Mexico." Arguing against intervention, Perry and his partner Robert Garcia won the debate. The judges "declared Mr. Kallison the best speaker of the afternoon."

17. Official records, University of Texas, 1920-21.

18. Peggy Whitley, "1920-1929," *American Cultural History*, Lone Star College-Kingwood Library website, wwwappskc.lonestar.edu/ popculture/decade20.html.

19. In the 1930s, "Department Store" was dropped and the store name reverted to "Kallison's."

20. *San Antonio Express*, Silent Rich advertisement, May 7, 1922, 21.

21. *San Antonio Light*, August 2, 1925.

22. *San Antonio Light*, October 4, 1925.

23. *San Antonio Light*, July 7, 1925.

24. San Antonio Library, Texana Collection, Frances Kallison papers, oral history interview with Ruth Kallison.

25. The sudden destructive power of a flash flood had almost claimed Morris's life six years earlier. He had hired a jitney and driver to take him out to the Kallison Ranch early Sunday morning, April 19, 1915. Fifteen miles out on Culebra Road, heavy rains had caused nearby Leon Creek to overflow its banks. Rushing water surged over the road, rising at an alarming rate of about three feet per minute. Morris and the jitney's driver abandoned the car and scurried up the nearest telephone poles where they spent the day and night. People in the vicinity seeing the submerged car reported that its occupants had drowned, but fortunately, that news never reached Anna and Nathan. When the waters receded, the jitney company sent out a search party and brought Morris and the driver back to town.

26. In 1923, Agudas Achim dedicated their new synagogue. Between 1921 and 1923, they transitioned from an Orthodox to a less-restrictive Conservative synagogue. *San Antonio Light*, September 10, 1921; Texas Jewish Historical Society website, www.tjhs.org/SanAntonio/AgudasAchimHistory.html.

27. *San Antonio Light*, August 31, 1924, Real Estate and Business section.

28. *American Builder*, March, 1926, 157.

29. "Kallison Block History," City of San Antonio, Office of Historic Preservation.

30. The prohibition case was neither the first nor the last time Nathan Kallison would find himself in court to defend his actions or petition for his rights. In 1914, he had been sued for misrepresenting the efficacy of a well on a tract of land he sold to I. W. Poland. Expecting the water level to average between ten and twelve feet with sufficient water for seventy-five head of cattle—but finding the well "practically dry and of no use or benefit"—Poland stopped payment on the $700 and $4,600 loans at 10 percent interest that he had arranged with Nathan to finance the balance of the $6,100 sale. The jury found for Poland and awarded damages but allowed Nathan to rescind the sale. Both Kallison and Poland appealed the judgment, but their appeal was denied.

31. *San Antonio Light,* June 22, 1927.

32. *Kerrville Times,* June 30, 1927; *Weimer Mercury,* July 1, 1927.

33. Daniel Okrent, *Last Call: The Rise and Fall of Prohibition* (New York: Scribner, 2010); Reefer Madness Teaching Museum website, www.reefermadnessteachingmuseum.org; Norman D. Brown, *Hood, Bonnet, and Little Brown Jug: Texas Politics, 1921-1928* (College Station: Texas A&M Press, 1984); Light Townsend Cummins, *Texas: A Political History* (Boston: American Press, 1990), 441-442.

34. Gurwitz, 64.

35. Char Miller, "'What, No Beer?': Pearl Brewery and the Building of San Antonio," *South Texas Studies* 2005, 28-47.

36. Rabbi Jill Jacobs, executive director of Rabbis for Human Rights-North America, suggests that the term *tikkun olam,* not found in the Bible, may have originated as early as the second century CE in the text of the *Aleynu.* This prayer extolls God and speaks of the relationship between God and the Jewish people. In modern times, it concludes every Jewish prayer service. Though *tikkun olam* has always been connected with the human responsibility for fixing what is wrong with the world, what that means and what it entails has evolved and changed over the centuries. Today, many see it as the motivation behind their involvement in social justice causes. While the term may not have been as popular as it was beginning in the 1950s, the duty to fix what's wrong in the world coupled with charitable giving *(tzedakah)* and acts of loving kindness *(gemilut hasadim)* were obligations of faith the Kallisons as a family and as individuals embraced all their lives.

37. National Council of Jewish Women website, www.ncjw.org/About us/History.

38. "A Faith in the Future, A Belief in Action" is the motto of the NCJW.

39. Tibe Kallison never earned a graduate degree from the University of Chicago. Pauline Kallison, who attended the University of Chicago for two years, did not complete her undergraduate studies at any university.

40. Hollace Ava Weiner, *Jewish Stars in Texas: Rabbis and their Works* (College Station: Texas A&M University Press, 1999), 157.

41. "Temple League to Meet Again," *San Antonio Light,* February 8, 1925, Part 3, 7.

42. Weiner, *Jewish Stars in Texas,* 170.

43. New York Stock Exchange website, www.nyse.com/about/history/timeline _trading.html; The Dow bottomed out in July 1932—down 89 percent from its peak in 1929; Money-Zine.com website, www.money-zine.com/ Investing/Stocks/Stock-Market-Crash-of-1929.

Seven: The Great Depression

1. Ben H. Procter, "Great Depression," *Handbook of Texas Online*, www.tshaon-line.org/handbook/online/articles/npg01.

2. Julia Kirk Blackwelder, *Women of the Depression: Caste and Culture in San Antonio, 1929-1939* (College Station: Texas A&M University Press, 1984).

3. Procter, "Great Depression."

4. *San Antonio Express*, "County Speeds Relief Program," July 15, 1934.

5. Abraham Hoffman, *Unwanted Mexican Americans in the Great Depression: Repatriation Pressures* (Tucson: University of Arizona Press, 1974).

6. 10.2 deaths per population of 100,000 in 1920 and 18.9 deaths per 100,000 in 1929 were attributed to suicide (*Historical Statistics of the United States: Bicentennial Edition, Colonial Times to 1970*, Vol. 1 [Washington, DC: 1975], 58, www2.census.gov/prod2/statcomp/documents/CT1970p1-03.pdf).

7. S. Mintz, "Children and the Depression," Digital History, www.digitalhisto-ry.uh.edu/learning_history/children_depression/depression_children_menu.cfm.

8. "According to the federal Soil Conservation Service, the bowl covered one hundred million acres in 1935." Donald Worster, "Dust Bowl," *Handbook of Texas Online*, www.tshaonline.org/handbook/online/articles/ydd01.

9. Author's interview with Florence Hoffmann, July, 2008.

10. Ibid.

11. *San Antonio Light*, October 17, 1935, A-10.

12. Ibid.

13. *San Antonio Light*, November 29, 1931, 7.

14. *San Antonio Express*, November 26, 1933, 11.

15. *San Antonio Express*, October 23, 1938, E-15.

16. *San Antonio Light*, January 21, 1940, A-8.

17. *San Antonio Light*, October 15, 1930, A-11.

18. *San Antonio Express*, December 31, 1933, 37.

19. *San Antonio Light*, January 1, 1934, 15.

20. The WPA's Federal Writer's Project gave jobs to thousands of unemployed writers, photographers, and artists who produced a stunning history of the Depression era. Some of their still-useful books include a comprehensive guide to Texas and the other forty-seven states. Great artists emerged from Texas, including photographer Russell Lee and folklorist Alan Lomax, who served as Assistant in Charge of the Archive of Folk Song of the Library of Congress and collected the great folk music and blues of the times. After a meeting in Marshall, Texas, in 1934, Lomax hired Huddie "Lead Belly" Ledbetter as a driver and assistant to accompany him on

a recording trip through the South. Their travels included several prison facilities. Nine years earlier, Lead Belly had secured his own early release from the Texas penitentiary at Sugar Land (where he was serving a seven- to thirty-year term for murder), by honoring and appealing to Texas Governor Pat M. Neff in song. Lomax had previously recorded the hot-tempered Lead Belly when the musician and songwriter had been a guest of the Louisiana state prison system. Over the course of his career, Alan Lomax added thousands of field recordings to the library's holdings including songs sung by Augustus "Track Horse" Haggerty, Jesse Bradley, and Tommie Randolph—all of whom served time in Texas prisons. Ben H. Procter, "Great Depression," *Handbook of Texas Online*.

21. Because of the excellent cooling system in that modern structure (built a few years before by Rathman's, a once-prosperous meat producer) and the strict adherence to the sanitary codes, plant administrators boasted that the losses from contamination and spoilage were minimal.

22. "City, County Officials Thankful: Aid Clients Happy," *San Antonio Light*, November 29, 1934, 9; "Drouth Increases Relief Subjects," *San Antonio Express*, July 18, 1934, 16.

23. "National Industrial Recovery Act (1933)," US National Archives & Records Administration website, www.ourdocuments.gov/doc.php?doc=66.

24. "NRA Program Adopted by Kallison's Boosts Business," *San Antonio Light*, August 27, 1933.

25. *San Antonio Express*, July 15, 1935, 12.

26. *San Antonio Light*, March 6, 1935, 1.

27. *San Antonio Express*, March 11, 1935, 14.

28. *San Antonio Light*, February 28, 1932, 9.

29. *San Antonio Express*, August 11, 1935, 9.

30. *San Antonio Express*, May 24, 1936.

31. *San Antonio Express*, May 3, 1936.

32. Author's interviews with Kallison family members and former employees.

33. Author's telephone interview with William Sinkin, May 22, 2010.

34. Right after Perry said "I do" on March 1931, he received a special "endowment"—the proceeds from a unique "First to Fall" marriage pact filed for record in the County Clerk's Office seven years before. Calling themselves "The San Antonio Musketeers," Leon A. Tobias, Leo Dubinski, and Perry Kallison "agreed to pay a considerable sum of money on the first of each month to a trust fund. . . ." According to the pact, "the first of contracting party to marry is to receive in cash two-thirds of the accumulated funds to be presented in check form at a formal dinner . . . immediately after the ceremony, or as soon thereafter as conveniently possible." After the first

marriage, the two remaining bachelors continue the monthly payments until one of them weds. The three considered all contingencies: elopement—without the full knowledge and consent of the other two—resulted in an immediate forfeit; the death of any contracting party cancelled the agreement. Perry was the second San Antonio Musketeer to do the "altar glide." When they checked into the hotel on the first night of their honeymoon—reflective of a time in which modestly prevailed—Frances Kallison was very concerned that she and Perry would be detected as newlyweds. So Perry slipped to the side, gave the porter a nice tip, and instructed him not to tell anyone that they were newlyweds. The next morning when they came down to the lobby, "everyone stared in a laughing manner at them." Perry went up to the porter and said, "Didn't I tell you not say we were newlyweds?" "Yes. And I didn't," responded the porter, "I told them that you were just close friends." (Erwin "E. E." Voigt speaking at the Joe Freeman Awards. San Antonio Public Library, Texana collection, January 1, 1965.) "Miss Rosenthal is Perry Kallison's Bride," *San Antonio Jewish Record,* March 13, 1931, Vol. 7, P.2, Col.4.

35. How little the lives of children from prosperous San Antonio families were touched by the Depression is illustrated by the diary kept by Ruth Friedman as she chronicled her own social activities and those of her teenage friends at Thomas Jefferson High School in the 1930s. Her five-year diary entries, which conclude with high school graduation in 1938, describe a continual parade of parties, dances, dating, and summer vacation trips to Corpus Christi. The girls were "boy crazy" and the company of her boyfriend, classmate, and future husband Jimmy Kallison was highly sought.

36. Despite his 1930s tuberculosis diagnosis, Ben Lasser died of cancer at age ninety-four, having survived his third wife.

37. Anna's instincts were correct. Shoplifting was a growing problem for San Antonio merchants during the Depression and throughout World War II. A San Antonio policewoman in the detective bureau's store protection division—known as "Madam X" to keep her identity secret—said that the majority of offenders were "from the so-called better class." Mexicans did not make up most of the shoplifters, as some believed. She identified a "group of serious offenders" during one Christmas shopping season—army wives who stole articles from various stores because "they had made bets with their husbands or friends that they could steal and get away with it." ("Madam X," *San Antonio Express,* December 24, 1945.) Although Kallison's store was in plain view of the sheriff's office in the Bexar County courthouse, it was victimized by burglars on more than one occasion. In December 1930, a robber cut through an iron bar over a skylight with a hack saw, lowered himself into the store, and broke the back door lock to let in his companion. The two burglars made a systematic search of the building, rifling papers on desks and searching through the

hardware stock. They took tools including several chisels, a revolver, and $1,400 from an unlocked safe. Perry Kallison told the *San Antonio Express* reporter that the safe was unlocked "because he would rather lose the money in the safe than have yeggs wreck the building blasting open the safe and taking the money anyway." (*San Antonio Express*, December 9, 1930, 20.)

38. Weiner, *Jewish Stars in Texas*, 176.

39. Ibid., 175.

Eight: The Ol' Trader

1. Tom Lewis, "Communication in History: The Key to Understanding," *OAH Magazine of History*, Vol. 6, No. 4, (Spring 1992), 26-33.

2. Steve Craig, "The More They Listen, the More They Buy: Radio and the Modernizing of Rural America, 1930-1939," *Agricultural History*, Vol. 80, No. 1 (Winter 2006), 1-16.

3. Hollace Weiner's interview with Frances Kallison, 2005.

4. Alice Goldfarb Marquis, "Written on the Wind: The Impact of Radio During the 1930s," *Journal of Contemporary History*, Vol. 19, No. 3 (July 1984), 388.

5. San Antonio Public Library, Texana Collection, *Trading Post* broadcast, February 4, 1956.

6. Long underwear, also known as Long Johns. San Antonio Public Library, Texana Collection, *Trading Post* broadcast, February 4, 1956.

7. Ibid.

8. *Cattleman*, Vol. LXI, No. 5, Oct., 1974, 58, 186.

9. Bob Boyd, "Perry Kallison Has Many Neighbors," *San Antonio Magazine*, July 1974, 52.

10. Author's interview with Bobbi Kallison Ravicz, August 2012.

11. San Antonio Public Library, Texana collection, *Trading Post* broadcast, December 31, 1955.

12. "Meeting and Greeting at Kallison's," *Cattleman*, Vol. LXI (61), No 5., October 1974.

13. San Antonio Public Library, Texana collection, *Trading Post* broadcast, October 25, 1947.

14. San Antonio Public Library, Texana collection, *Trading Post* broadcast, December 31, 1955.

15. Ibid.

16. Ibid.

17. San Antonio Public Library, Texana collection, *Trading Post* broadcast, October 25, 1947.

18. San Antonio Public Library, Texana collection, *Trading Post* broadcast, December 25, 1947.

19. San Antonio Public Library, Texana collection, *Trading Post* broadcast, July 23, 1955.

Nine: World War II: The Texas Home Front

1. *Frontier Times,* Vol. 20, No. 12, September 1943.

2. The German army invaded Poland in September 1939.

3. "Jewish Group Elects S. A. Man," *San Antonio Light,* January 27, 1946, 5-B.

4. "The Voyage of the *St. Louis,*" American Jewish Joint Distribution Committee Report, June 15, 1939.

5. Only after World War II did the Kallisons learn that the remaining Jews in Ladyzhinka, Nathan's village in the Ukraine, had been slaughtered by German troops in 1941 as they drove eastward towards Moscow and Leningrad.

6. The San Antonio Aviation Cadet Center was renamed Lackland Army Air Field in 1946, but was then changed to Lackland Air Force Base after the air force separated from the army in 1948. Art Leatherwood, "Lackland Air Force Base," *Handbook of Texas Online,* www.tshaonline.org/handbook/online/articles/qbl01.

7. Between March 1943 and April 1945, the Central Instructors School at Randolph Field trained 15,396 pilots as instructors. Timothy M. Brown, "Randolph Air Force Base," *Handbook of Texas Online,* www.tshaonline.org/handbook/online/articles/qbr01.

8. Ray Dery, "Brooke Army Medical Center," *Handbook of Texas Online,* www.tshaonline.org/handbook/online/articles/qnb01.

9. Fehrenbach, *San Antonio Story,* 175-178.

10. Ibid.

11. After World War II, Audie Murphy appeared in forty-four movies, including *To Hell and Back* (1955), in which he portrayed his own life story. He died in a plane crash in 1971.

12. Ralph A. Wooster, "World War II, Texans In," *Handbook of Texas Online,* www.tshaonline.org/handbook/online/articles/qdw02.

13. *Cattleman,* September 1944, 148.

14. Ibid.

15. Wooster, "World War II, Texans In," *Handbook of Texas Online.*

16. More than 50,000 prisoners, mainly Germans, but also about 3,000 Italians and 1,000 Japanese, were housed in makeshift barracks in twenty-one prisoner base camps and in more than twenty ranch camps located throughout the state of Texas. Gradually, security was relaxed. Prisoners were used as agriculture workers and put

to work at military bases as clerks, bakers, waiters, carpenters, electricians, groundskeepers, machinists, and mechanics. Wooster, "World War II, Texans In," *Handbook of Texas Online.*

17. Author attended this dinner.

18. Emily Brosveen, "World War II Internment Camps," *Handbook of Texas Online,* www.tshaonline.org/handbook/online/articles/quwby.

19. None were identified.

20. Author's interview with Ruth Friedman Kallison; Author's telephone interview with Marie Holland Brown, May 19, 2011.

21. USO (United Service Organization) poster, published by the National Jewish Welfare Board Operating Agency, Texas area office, 1943.

22. Author's interview with Susan Neustadt Miller, January 29, 2012.

23. Author's recollection.

24. "If the farmer sold any meat products, even to neighbors, he must obtain ration points for it, and on April 1 and after, the farmer must obtain a permit to slaughter from his County War Board if he expects to slaughter for other purposes than obtaining food for his family." ("Consumers Need Not Declare Food On Hand," *San Antonio Express,* March 14, 1943, 17.)

25. Procter, "World War II," *Handbook of Texas Online,* www.tshaonline.org/handbook/online/articles/npwnj.

26. City of San Antonio Office of Historic Preservation website, www.sanantonio.gov/historic/Surveys/Uptown.aspx.

27. Author's recollection.

28. Perry Kallison's notes for the December 4, 1944 and December 4, 1947, San Antonio Public Library, Texana collection, *Trading Post* broadcasts.

29. *Cattleman,* May 1946, 84.

Ten: The Best Years

1. The Roegelein Company, founded in 1905 as the Packing House Market, was a full-line meat packaging operation—from luncheon meat to fresh pork and beef. Steves Lumber Company, a family-owned business founded in 1866, manufactured wooden components for merchant ships and lumber products for Quartermaster Corps. In 1943, it received a five-star "M" award for meritorious service. (Odom, Mary and Gaylon Finklea Young, *The Businesses that Built San Antonio* [San Antonio: Living Legacies, 1985].)

2. William "Billy" Mitchell (1879-1936) was a pioneer aviator, one of the first to recognize the potential of air power.

3. *San Antonio Express,* August 20, 1953, 1B.

4. San Antonio Public Library, Texana collection, *Trading Post* broadcast, February 4, 1956.

5. *San Antonio Light,* March 14, 1957, 20.

6. In an example of government-media cooperation, the kitchen was demonstrated at the exposition by Anne Anderson, then kitchen-equipment editor of *Better Homes and Gardens* magazine.

7. *San Antonio Express,* August 8, 1948, 5C.

8. Author's telephone interview with Gary Schott, 2009.

9. Ringtail cats *(Bassariscus astutu),* indigenous to the Texas Hill Country, are not really cats but smaller, less known "cousins" of the raccoon (Procyon lotor). J. Knox Jones, Jr., "Mammals," *Handbook of Texas Online,* www.tshaonline.org/handbook/online/articles/tcm03.

10. Author's interviews with Perry Kallison's daughters Maryann Friedman and Bobbi Ravicz, August, 2012.

11. Author's interview and correspondence with Seymour Dreyfus, August 2009.

12. Seymour Dreyfus, former husband of Jane Kallison (Morris and Ruth Kallison's daughter), left work at Kallison's store in 1959. He became successful in real estate and as a community leader before he and Jane divorced in 1984. Author's interview and correspondence with Seymour Dreyfus, August 2009.

13. Ibid.; Author's interview with Seymour Dreyfus's son, John Dreyfus, 2009.

14. Author's interview with Seymour Dreyfus, August 2009.

15. San Antonio Public Library, Texana Collection, *Trading Post* broadcast, December 3, 1960.

Eleven: The Brothers Kallison

1. Author's interview with Jack B. Kallison, April 14, 2010; Jack B. Kallison with Alex Scharlack, *He Soared with Eagles* (privately published by author with Taylor Specialty Books, Dallas, 2011).

2. Kallison, *He Soared with Eagles,* 47-50.

3. Ibid.

4. "San Antonio, Texas (City of Contrasts) Welcomes NATO Delegation, Program, and Calendar," June 5-9, 1956, 4-8. Event sponsored by United States Department of State and the Governmental Affairs Institute, Washington, DC; Citizen's Committee of Greater San Antonio.

5. Jon Ford, "To Yield or Not Yield: Council Undecided on Annexation," *San Antonio Express,* March 23, 1952, 58.

6. "Don Politico Overlooks 1952," *San Antonio Light,* January 1, 1953, 8.

7. *San Antonio Light,* April 6, 1953, 7; *San Antonio Express,* May 11, 1963, 5; *San Antonio Express,* December 27, 1953, 8.

8. The San Antonio City Public Service, now called CPS Energy of San Antonio, is today the nation's largest city-owned utility company serving 707,000 electric and 322,000 natural gas customers in its 1,566-square mile service area, which includes Bexar County and portions of seven surrounding counties. Fourteen percent of all utility revenues are returned to the city of San Antonio, paying more than 20 percent of the city's annual budget. (CPS Energy website, www.cpsenergy.com/About_CPS_Energy/Who_We_Are.)

9. *San Antonio Express,* November 27, 1955.

10. James McCrory, "Kallison Shows Genuine Affection for His City," *San Antonio Express-News,* May 11, 1963, 13-A

11. Author's interview with Jesse Oppenheimer, 2008.

12. Tom McGowan, "He Wears Many Hats: Morris Kallison Calls Self Progressive Conservative," *San Antonio Light,* December 9, 1962, 24-A; Tom McGowan, "Man of His Word: Morris Kallison's Dad Laid Groundwork for 'Empire,'" *San Antonio Light,* December 10, 1962, 11.

13. *San Antonio Light,* June 3, 1963, 35.

14. Lyndon Baines Johnson Presidential Library, letters file, December 31, 1964.

15. Lyndon Baines Johnson Presidential Library, letters file, January 1964.

16. A Texas colloquial expression referring to cattle going together to a salt-lick (log), meaning "getting down to business."

17. Author's interview with Seymour Dreyfus, August, 2009.

18. Author's interview with James M. (Kal) Kallison Jr., 2009.

19. Robert Caro, *The Years of Lyndon Johnson: Means of Ascent* (New York: Alfred A. Knopf, 1982), 303-309.

20. Eldon S. Branda, "Stevenson, Coke Robert," *Handbook of Texas Online,* www.tshaonline.org/handbook/online/articles/fst48.

21. Author's interviews with Perry Kallison's daughters.

22. San Antonio Public Library, Texana Collection, *Trading Post* broadcast, November 8, 1960.

23. San Antonio Public Library, Texana Collection, *Trading Post* broadcast, November 5, 1960.

24. In 2000 Perry Kallison was inducted into the San Antonio Livestock Exposition's Hall of Fame.

25. Miller, *On the Border,* 58.

26. Author's interview with Maryann Friedman, 2009.

27. *San Antonio Sunday Express-News,* May 12, 1985.

Twelve: All in the Family

1. Author's interview with Kal Kallison, 2009.
2. Author's interview with Bobbi Kallison Ravicz, 2010.
3. Author's interview with Jack Kallison, April 14, 2010.
4. Kallison, *He Soared with Eagles,* 12-13.
5. Author's interviews with Bobbi Ravicz, Jane Kallison Dreyfus, T. R. Fehrenbach, and Maryann Friedman, 2009.
6. Author's correspondence with Li Ravicz, August 3, 2008.
7. Author's interview with Carmen Luna, 2009.
8. Author's correspondence with Elenita Ravicz, August 3, 2008.
9. *Cattleman,* November 1946, 124.
10. Author's interview with Kal Kallison, 2009.
11. Ibid.
12. Recounted by Susan N. Miller, January 2012, Scottsdale, Arizona.
13. At the time vaginal smears (later called Pap Smears) were developed by Dr. George Papanicolaou in the 1940s to screen for cervical cancer, the disease was the leading cause of death among women. (Elizabeth M. Shepard, "George Papanicolaou: Development of the Pap Smear," *News from the Medical Center Archives of New York-Presbyterian/Weill Cornell.*) Jacob Kotz also was involved in other research projects including "The Effects of Obstetric Analgesia on the Newborn Infant," as reported in *Journal of the American Medical Association* (JAMA,1939; 113[23]:2035-2038).
14. In the nation's capital, where much of the population is transient, the term "Cave Dwellers" refers to affluent residents, born and raised in the city, who are "invisible" to "official" Washington.
15. In Washington, DC, Tibe Kallison Lasser Kotz "reinvented" herself. In 1943, at a reception she hosted for Jimmy Kallison and Ruthie Friedman's wedding, she signed her name "Bertie." She was known, however, as "Tybe" by most of her social group. Somehow, as a modern woman, she felt that her given name of "Bertha" didn't suit her. After she married in 1946, her new husband called her "Tibby" and that name stuck. In Washington, she created a more sophisticated persona. With this new beginning, she also subtracted six years from her age—and later twelve years, creating birth certificates for 1908 and 1912.
16. Recounted by Frances Kallison, August 1982.

Thirteen: No Business for Sissies

1. R. G. Jordan, "Perry Kallison Receives Plaque for Livestock Industry Service," *San Antonio Express-News,* February 6, 1959.

2. San Antonio Public Library, Texana Collection, *Trading Post* broadcast, November 15, 1947.

3. Wayne D. Rasmussen, "Impact of Change on American Agriculture, 1862-1962," *The Journal of Economic History,* Vol. 22, No. 4 (December 1962), Cambridge University Press (on behalf of the Economic History Association), 588-589. Article Stable URL: www.jstor.org/stable/2116117.

4. "Kallison Ranch Becomes Laboratory for Better Farm and Ranch Methods," *San Antonio Express,* February 16, 1950; R. G. Jordan, "A Dream Comes True," *San Antonio Express-Magazine,* June 12, 1949, 7.

5. *Cattleman,* April, 1953, 108.

6. R. G. Jordan, "'Old Trader' Honored for Soil-Saving Work," *San Antonio Express,* January 10, 1961, 12A.

7. *San Antonio Express,* November 19, 1948, 12.

8. Sixty years later, Helen Marie Schuchart Nickel still treasured the note, remembering Perry Kallison's role in her life. (Author's correspondence with Helen Marie Schuchart Nickel, 2009.)

9. Author's telephone interview with Millard Schuchart, 2009.

10. Author's telephone interviews with Dinah, Ray, and Jon Weil, December 4, 2008.

11. HK Cattle website, www.hkcattle.com.

12. Letter, Terrell F. Gates, Principal, and David L. Rusmisel, Vocational Agriculture Instructor, at Luther Burbank Vocational High School to Perry Kallison, March 10, 1953.

13. *San Antonio Light,* August 6, 1950, 11-B.

14. By the 1960s scientists and environmentalists were challenging the safety of these products both for the farmers using them and consumers who ate food or drank water that contained residue from the chemicals. There was a similar controversy about the efficacy of the army spraying Agent Orange to defoliate the underbrush concealing our enemies in Vietnam.

15. T. C. Richardson and Harwood P. Hinton, "Ranching," *Handbook of Texas Online,* www.tshaonline.org/handbook/online/articles/azr02.

16. Frank Reeves, Livestock Editor, *Texas Ranch and Farm,* August 9, 1959.

17. Hollace Weiner interview with Frances Kallison, May 1, 2004. "Meeting and Greeting at Kallison's," *Cattleman,* Vol. LXI (61), No. 5, October 1974.

18. Author's telephone interview with Humberto "Bert" Reyes, December 20, 2008.

19. Hereford/Polled Hereford breed standards, www.hereford.co.za/why-herefords/breed-standards.

20. Roy Sylvan Dunn, "Droughts," *Handbook of Texas Online,* www.tshaonline.org/handbook/online/articles/ybd01.

21. Ibid.

22. Perry Kallison oral history, San Antonio Public Library, Texana Collection.

23. Author's interview with Seymour Dreyfus, August 2009.

24. San Antonio Public Library, Texana collection. *Trading Post* broadcast, January 1, 1955.

25. Author's email communication with Jim Armistead, Archives Specialist, Harry S. Truman Library & Museum.

26. Ida M. Barkan, "Israel Helped by Texan in New Goat Industry," the *National Jewish Post and Opinion,* Friday, January 8, 1965.

27. Author's interview with Yoram Avidor, December 4, 2008. Letter from Yoram & Ruti Avidor to author, December 14, 2008.

28. Letter from Perry Kallison to Friends and Neighbors, August 1964.

29. Letter, Perry Kallison to President Lyndon Baines Johnson, December 29, 1967, Ex GI 2-11/A-Z, WHCF, LBJ Library.

30. *Kibbutzim:* agricultural communes in Israel. (Plural of *Kibbutz*—from the Hebrew meaning "gathering" or "clustering.")

31. Letter, Perry Kallison to President Lyndon Baines Johnson, December 29, 1967, Ex GI 2-11/A-Z, WHCF, LBJ Library.

32. Author's telephone interviews with Michael Beldon (May 27, 2010) and Dr. Morris Spector (April 16, 2009), San Antonians on the Israel trip with Perry Kallison.

33. Author's interview with Rabbi Samuel Stahl, 2009.

Fourteen: Changing Times

1. *San Antonio Light,* October 21, 1970, 30; Author's interview with Seymour Dreyfus, August 2009.

2. Matt Wagner, *Texas Parks and Wildlife,* publication PWDLFW7000-1155.

3. *Cattleman,* December 1951.

4. *San Antonio Light,* February 15, 1959, 24A.

5. *San Antonio Light,* May 6, 1960, 12A.

6. *San Antonio Express-News,* February 11, 1962, 7-H.

7. Joel Garreau, *Edge City: Life on the New Frontier* (New York: Doubleday, 1991).

8. *San Antonio Light,* November 1, 1964, 36A.

9. Author's interview with Jack B. Kallison, April 14, 2010.

10. *San Antonio Express,* April 7, 1959, 30.

11. "New Merchandising Plan: Kallison's Continues to Set Trends," *San Antonio Light,* March 3, 1963.

12. Author's interview with Seymour Dreyfus, August 2009.

13. Frances Rae "Bobbi" Kallison Ravicz was the owner of the Yarn Barn, a leading seller of materials for knitting, weaving, and other crafts. For many years she spun a neighborly atmosphere in her unique handcraft store which occupied a triangular island of land at 4300 McCullough Avenue in San Antonio. She sold her store in 2008.

14. Author's telephone interview with Humberto "Bert" Reyes, December 20, 2008.

15. *San Antonio Express-News,* April 30, 1967, 4D.

16. Author's telephone interview with Gary Schott, July 23, 2009.

17. The iconic Kallison Cowboy stood atop the roof of Pete Kallison's Western Wear Shop, which he ran until his death in 2003.

18. Author's interview Bobbi Kallison Ravicz, August 2012.

Epilogue

1. After the store was closed in 1967, the Kallison family divided the jointly-owned family assets that remained after payment of debts. In that division, Tibe Kallison Kotz and Pauline's daughter Suzanna Neustadt Miller became owners of the Kallison Ranch, but the property division allowed Perry to continue operating the ranch until he decided to retire. In 2002, Suzanna and Nathan, Tibe's son, deeded 1,170 acres to Texas Parks and Wildlife in a transaction that was a combination of gift and sale to become part of the Government Canyon Wildlife and Natural Area. Later, they sold 1,500 of the remaining ranch acres to Lennar Company, a home builder.

SELECTED BIBLIOGRAPHY

Addams, Jane. *Twenty Years at Hull House with Autobiographical Notes.* New York: MacMillan Company, 1910.

Alexander, Charles C. *Crusade for Conformity: The Ku Klux Klan in Texas, 1920-1930.* Beaumont: Texas Gulf Coast Historical Association, 1962.

Allen, Paula. *San Antonio: Then and Now.* San Diego: Thunder Bay Press, 2005.

Baron, Salo W. *The Russian Jew Under Tsars and Soviets.* New York: MacMillan Company, 1964.

Bauman, Mark K., and Berkley Kalin. *The Quiet Voices: Southern Rabbis and Black Civil Rights, 1880s to 1990s.* Tuscaloosa: University of Alabama Press, 1997.

Berman, Robert Lewis. *A House of David in the Land of Jesus.* USA: Robert Lewis Berman, 2007.

Bernheimer, Charles S. *The Russian Jew in the United States: Studies of Social Conditions in New York, Philadelphia, and Chicago, with a Description of Rural Settlements.* Philadelphia: John C. Winston Co., 1905.

Blackwelder, Julia Kirk. *Women of the Depression: Caste and Culture in San Antonio, 1929-1939.* College Station: Texas A&M University Press, 1984.

Brawley E. A. "When the Jews came to Galveston." *Commentary.* 127 (4): 31-36, 2009.

Bregstone, Philip P. *Chicago and Its Jews.* USA: Philip P. Bregstone, 1933.

Briscoe, Dolph. *Dolph Briscoe: My Life in Texas Ranching and Politics.* Austin: Center for American History, University of Texas, 2008.

Caro, Robert A. *The Years of Lyndon Johnson.* New York: Alfred A. Knopf, 1982.

Chesler, Evan R. *The Russian Jewry Reader.* New York: Behrman House, 1974.

Cannato, Vincent J. *American Passage: The History of Ellis Island.* New York: HarperCollins, 2009.

Cohen, Chester G. *Shtetl Finder: Jewish Communities in the 19th and Early 20th Centuries in the Pale of Settlement of Russia and Poland, and in Lithuania, Latvia, Galicia, and Bukovina, with Names of Residents.* Bowie, Maryland: Heritage Books, 1989.

Cummins, Light Townsend. *Texas: A Political History.* Boston: American Press,

1990.

Cummins, Light Townsend, and Alvin R. Bailey, Jr., eds. *A Guide to the History of Texas.* New York: Greenwood Press, 1998.

Cutler, Irving. *The Jews of Chicago: From Shtetl to Suburb.* Chicago: University of Illinois Press, 2009.

Cutler, Irving. *Images of America: Jewish Chicago: A Pictorial History.* Charleston, South Carolina: Arcadia Publishing, 2000.

Dearen, Patrick. *Halff of Texas: Merchant Rancher of the Old West.* Austin: Eakin Press, 2000.

Diner, Hasia R. *A Time for Gathering: The Second Migration, 1820-1880.* Baltimore: Johns Hopkins University Press, 1992.

Douglas, Susan J. *Listening In: Radio and the American Imagination.* New York: Times Books, 1999.

Evans, Eli N. *The Provincials: A Personal History of Jews in the South.* Chapel Hill: University of North Carolina Press, 2005.

Faber, Eli. *A Time for Planting: The First Migration, 1654-1820.* Baltimore: Johns Hopkins University Press, 1992.

Fehrenbach, T. R. *Lone Star: A History of Texas and the Texans.* New York: Collier Books, 1968.

Fehrenbach, T. R. *Seven Keys to Texas.* El Paso: Texas Western Press, 1983.

Fehrenbach, T. R., and Tom Avellone. *The San Antonio Story: A Pictorial and Entertaining Commentary on the Growth and Development of San Antonio, Texas.* Tulsa, Oklahoma: Continental Heritage, 1978.

Feingold, Henry L. *A Time for Searching: Entering the Mainstream, 1920-1945.* Baltimore: Johns Hopkins University Press, 1992.

Glazier, Ira A., ed. *Migration from the Russian Empire: Lists of Passengers Arriving at U.S. Ports.* Baltimore: Genealogical Publishing Co., Inc., 1998.

Gurwitz, Reverend Alexander (n.d.). *Memories of Two Generations,* trans. Rabbi Amram Prero.

Hanson, Victor Davis. *The Land Was Everything: Letters from an American Farmer.* New York: The Free Press, 2000.

Hasluck, Paul N., ed. *Harness Making.* London: Cassell and Company, Limited, 1904.

Hemphill, Hugh. *San Antonio on Wheels: The Alamo City Learns to Drive.* San Antonio: Maverick Pub. Co., 2009.

Henderson, Richard B. *Maury Maverick: A Political Biography.* Austin: University of Texas Press, 1970.

Herzen, Alexander. *My Past and Thoughts,* trans. Constance Garnett. Berkeley: University of California Press, 1973.

Holland, Richard A., ed. *The Texas Book: Profiles, History, and Reminiscences of the University.* Austin: University of Texas Press, 2006.

Howe, Irving. *World of Our Fathers: The Journey of the East European Jews to America and the Life They Found and Made.* New York: Simon and Schuster, 1976.

Johnson, David R., John A. Booth, Richard J. Harris, ed. *The Politics of San Antonio: Community, Progress, & Power.* Lincoln: University of Nebraska Press, 1983.

Jordan, Terry G. *German Seed in Texas Soil: Immigrant Farmers in Nineteenth-Century Texas.* Austin: University of Texas Press, 1996.

Kallison, Frances. *100 Years of Jewry in San Antonio.* San Antonio: Trinity University masters thesis, 1977.

Kallison, Jack B. with Alex Scharlack, *He Soared with Eagles: Morris Kallison, a Visionary Whose Achievements Transformed and Inspired a Dynamic Great City.* Dallas: Privately published by author with Taylor Specialty Books, 2011.

Kolatch, Alfred J. *The Jewish Book of Why.* Middle Village, New York: Jonathan David Publishers, 1981.

Kelton, Elmer. *The Time It Never Rained.* New York: Forge, 1973.

Lanzone, John A. *Horse, Next to Woman, God's Greatest Gift to Man: A History of the Straus-Frank Company.* San Antonio: Straus-Frank Co., 1970.

Lissak, Rivka Shpak. *Pluralism & Progressives: Hull House and the New Immigrants, 1890-1919.* Chicago: University of Chicago Press, 1989.

Livingston, Mary E. *Voices of America: San Antonio in the 1920s and 1930s.* Charleston, South Carolina: Arcadia Publishing, 2000.

Malouf, Dian Leatherberry. *Cattle Kings of Texas.* Hillsboro, Oregon: Beyond Words Publishing, Inc., 1991.

Marinbach, Bernard. *Galveston: Ellis Island of the West.* Albany: State University of New York Press, 1983.

Marks, M. L. *Jews Among the Indians: Tales of Adventure and Conflict in the Old West.* Chicago: Benison Books, 1992.

Massey, Cynthia Leal. *Helotes: Where the Texas Hill Country Begins.* Houston: Old American Publishing, 2008.

Miller, Char. *Deep in the Heart of San Antonio: Land and Life in South Texas.* San Antonio: Trinity University Press, 2004.

Miller, Char, ed. *On the Border.* San Antonio: Trinity University Press, 2001.

Miller, Char, and Heywood T. Sanders. *Urban Texas: Politics and Development.* College Station: Texas A&M University Press, 1990.

Miller, Char. *Battle-Ready City: San Antonio in the Great War* in *Winds and Words of War: Political Propaganda Posters from World War I.* Seattle: Marquand Books, 2008.

Miller, Donald L. *City of the Century: The Epic of Chicago and the Making of America.* New York: Simon & Schuster, 1996.

Odom, Marianne, and Gaylon Finklea Young. *The Businesses that Built San Antonio.* San Antonio, Texas: Living Legacies, 1985.

Ornish, Natalie. *Pioneer Jewish Texans.* Dallas: Texas Heritage Press, 1989.

Pritzker, Renee Walker. *Texas Rangeland.* Austin: University of Texas Press, 2002.

Rapoport, Bernard. *Being Rapoport: Capitalist with a Conscience.* Austin: University of Texas Press, 2002

Ramsdell, Charles. *San Antonio: A Historical and Pictorial Guide.* Austin: University of Texas Press, 1959.

Reynolds, Richard. *Texas: Then and Now.* Englewood, Colorado: Westcliffe Publishers, Inc., 2005.

Sajowitz, William. *History of Reform Judaism in San Antonio, Texas, 1874-1945.* San Antonio: Thesis (Rabbinic)—H.U.C.-J.I.R. 1945.

Shapiro, Edward S. *A Time for Healing: American Jewry since World War II.* Baltimore: Johns Hopkins University Press, 1992.

Sloan, Mary Lee Gussen. *And the Snake Slept: Culebra: The Hoffmann Story.* Meeker, Colorado: Mary Lee Gussen Sloan, 2003.

Sorin, Gerald. *A Time for Building: The Third Migration, 1880-1920.* Baltimore: Johns Hopkins University Press, 1992.

Sowell, A. J. *Texas Indian Fighters.* Abilene, Texas: State House Press, 1986.

Spulber, Nicolas. *Russia's Economic Transition from Late Tsarism to the New Millennium.* New York: Cambridge University Press, 2003, www.assets.cambridge.org/97805218/16991/sample/9780521816991ws.pdf

Statman, Jan. *Raisins & Almonds . . . and Texas Oil!: Jewish Life in the Great East Texas Oil Field.* Austin: Sunbelt Eakin Press, 2004.

Stone, Bryan Edward. *The Chosen Folks: Jews on the Frontiers of Texas*. Austin: University of Texas Press, 2010.

Tijerina, Andres. *Tejano Empire: Life on the South Texas Ranchos*. College Station: Texas A&M University Press, 1998.

University of Texas Institute of Texan Cultures at San Antonio. *The Jewish Texans*. San Antonio: University of Texas Institute of Texan Cultures, 1992.

Vida, Nina. *The Texicans*. New York: Soho Press, Inc., 2006.

Viskochil, Larry A. *Chicago At the Turn of the Century in Photographs: 122 Historic Views from the Collections of the Chicago Historical Society*. Mineola, New York: Dover Publications, Inc., 1984.

Weiner, Hollace Ava. *Jewish Stars in Texas: Rabbis and Their Work*. College Station: Texas A&M University Press, 1999.

Weiner, Hollace Ava, and Kenneth D. Roseman, ed. *Lone Stars of David: The Texas Jews*. Waltham, Massachusetts: Brandeis University Press, 2007.

Wilson, James A. *Hide & Horn in Texas: The Spread of Cattle Ranching 1836-1900*. Boston: American Press, 1983.

Winegarten, Ruth, and Cathy Schechter. *Deep in the Heart: The Lives & Legends of Texas Jews: A Photographic History* (edited by Rabbi Jimmy Kessler). Austin: Eakin Press, 1990.

Wolff, Nelson W. *Transforming San Antonio*. San Antonio: Trinity University Press, 2008.

Workers of the Writers' Program of the Work Projects Administration in the State of Texas. *Texas: A Guide to the Lone Star State*. New York: Hastings House Publishers, 1940.

INDEX

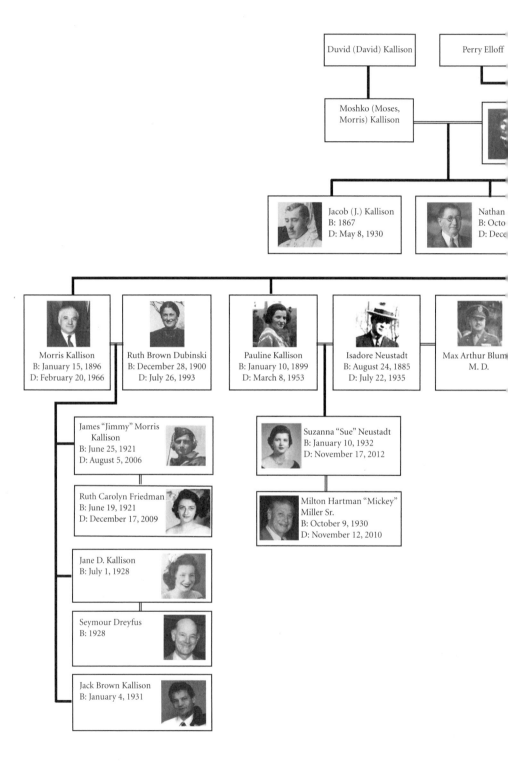

Duvid (David) Kallison

Perry Elloff

Moshko (Moses, Morris) Kallison

Jacob (J.) Kallison
B: 1867
D: May 8, 1930

Nathan
B: Octo
D: Dece

Morris Kallison
B: January 15, 1896
D: February 20, 1966

Ruth Brown Dubinski
B: December 28, 1900
D: July 26, 1993

Pauline Kallison
B: January 10, 1899
D: March 8, 1953

Isadore Neustadt
B: August 24, 1885
D: July 22, 1935

Max Arthur Blum
M. D.

James "Jimmy" Morris Kallison
B: June 25, 1921
D: August 5, 2006

Ruth Carolyn Friedman
B: June 19, 1921
D: December 17, 2009

Jane D. Kallison
B: July 1, 1928

Seymour Dreyfus
B: 1928

Jack Brown Kallison
B: January 4, 1931

Suzanna "Sue" Neustadt
B: January 10, 1932
D: November 17, 2012

Milton Hartman "Mickey" Miller Sr.
B: October 9, 1930
D: November 12, 2010